# THE BERLIN BLITZ
## BY THOSE WHO WERE THERE

# THE BERLIN BLITZ
## BY THOSE WHO WERE THERE

25/26 August 1940-September 1943

Martin W. Bowman

AIR WORLD

**AIR WORLD**

# THE BERLIN BLITZ BY THOSE WHO WERE THERE

First published in Great Britain in 2022 by
Air World
*An imprint of*
Pen & Sword Books Ltd
Yorkshire – Philadelphia

ISBN 978 1 52670 552 5

Typeset by SJmagic DESIGN SERVICES, India.

Printed and bound in the UK by CPI Group (UK) Ltd, Croydon, CRO 4YY

**MIX**
Paper | Supporting
responsible forestry
FSC
www.fsc.org   FSC® C013604

Pen & Sword Books Limited incorporates the imprints of Atlas, Archaeology, Aviation, Discovery, Family History, Fiction, History, Maritime, Military, Military Classics, Politics, Select, Transport, True Crime, Air World, Frontline Publishing, Leo Cooper, Remember When, Seaforth Publishing, The Praetorian Press, Wharncliffe Local History, Wharncliffe Transport, Wharncliffe True Crime and White Owl.

For a complete list of Pen & Sword titles please contact

PEN & SWORD BOOKS LIMITED
47 Church Street, Barnsley, South Yorkshire, S70 2AS, England
E-mail: enquiries@pen-and-sword.co.uk
Website: www.pen-and-sword.co.uk

Or

PEN AND SWORD BOOKS
1950 Lawrence Rd, Havertown, PA 19083, USA
E-mail: Uspen-and-sword@casematepublishers.com
Website: www.penandswordbooks.com

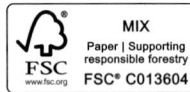

# Contents

On Monday, 3rd June 1940 a German force of 300 bombers attacked Paris causing several hundred casualties. The French decided to retaliate. Farman 223.4 Jules Verne, a former postal aircraft that had been requisitioned by the Aéronautique Navale, slightly larger than a Lancaster or a Boeing B-17, assigned to Lieutenant Commander (Capitaine de Corvette) Henri 'the Pasha' Daillière and crewed by experienced naval aviators: Flight Engineer Corneillet, Navigator Comet (who had crossed the Atlantic before the war), Pilot Yonnet, Radioman Scour and Bombardier Deschamps. Daillière was given the mission to be the first aviator to attack Berlin with ordnance. The Jules Verne took off from the Merignac airfield near Bordeaux on 7th June. The crew proceeded over Normandy, the English Channel, the North Sea and over Denmark and over the Baltic before turning south and heading straight for Berlin at high altitude.

On board the Jules Verne, the crew became increasingly tense. The pilot, Yonnet, wrote that 'like former corsairs, we are facing the enemy alone...like Robert Surcouf, we must strike first, very hard if possible, to have a chance to escape before the enemy could regain his mind.' The Jules Verne reached Berlin just around midnight. Daillière described the approach to Berlin: 'I got ready to release the bombs and realized that someone had failed to install our bombsight, so I pressed my nose to the glass of the cockpit.' The Berlin area was covered by clouds and therefore difficult to find, but all of a sudden Daillière spotted the lights of the Tempelhof airfield and he ordered an approach before accelerating away at low altitude from the airfield. Daillière flew on over Berlin, still at low altitude and unsynching the engines to vary the engine noise for some time in an attempt to create the impression of a proper formation of bomber aircraft. Eventually eight 75 kg bombs were dropped in two runs over what he assumed was a factory complex in the northern parts of the city as flak began firing and searchlights were turned on. A further eighty incendiaries were dropped by *hand by Deschamps and Corneillet and two or three clips of machine gun ammunition were spent in an attempt to hit the searchlights. Flight engineer Corneillet finished the raid by throwing out his shoes at the capital of the Third Reich.*

*The Jules Verne continued its career against Italy once Mussolini declared war on France on 10th June. The aircraft attacked the Marghera industrial centre near Venice and it dropped thousands of propaganda leaflets over Rome. The Jules Verne completed seventeen raids on German and Italian targets before the armistice. Following the fall of France, the Jules Verne was hidden in a hangar, where it was purposefully set on fire in 1942 to avoid having the Germans find the aircraft.*

**This was the first of 363 Luftangriffe der Alliierten Auf Berlin (Allied air raids on Berlin), which was bombed by the RAF Bomber Command between 1940 and 1945, by the USAAF Eighth Air Force between 1943 and 1945 and the French Air Force between 1944 and 1945 as part of the Allied campaign of strategic bombing of Germany and by aircraft of the Red Air Force. On 8th August 1941 the Soviet Union started a bombing campaign on Berlin that extended into early September. Navy bombers, operating from the Moonzund Archipelago mounted eight raids on Berlin with 3-12 aircraft in each raid. Army bombers, operating from near Leningrad made several small raids to the city. In total, thirty-three Soviet aircraft dropped 79,000lbs of bombs on the Reich capital in 1941. The Russians lost seventeen aircraft destroyed and seventy crewmen killed. British bombers dropped 45,517 tons of bombs; the Americans dropped 23,000 tons. By May 1945 1.7 million people (40% of the population) had fled. According to estimates, by April 1945 up to 50,000 people, mostly civilians, died in Berlin.**

# Chapter 1

# 'It's Berlin We Want'

*'When I joined the RAF I did not smoke at all and only rarely had the odd half pint of bitter. On joining the crew at Desborough I found that they were drinking four or five pints a night and smoking about forty cigarettes per day, as these were very cheap and often sent as presents from home. After a few weeks of going out with them, I found I could also drink and smoke without having a hangover. Generally speaking, I found the relationship between local people and servicemen in the pub was good. One night however, there was an incident in Kettering that could have been nasty. An argument developed in the corner of the pub between an RAF man and some locals. Normally, we would have avoided getting involved, but because we'd had a few drinks we felt we should join in on the side of the RAF man. Quite a few other RAF boys did the same. Quite understandingly, the landlord of the pub became alarmed and called the police, who threw everyone out into the street where the argument continued and the situation became ugly. Suddenly, one of the policemen shouted "Come on lads - its Hitler we're fighting and its Berlin we want!"*

*'His comment broke the tension and soon the RAF, the locals and the police were singing patriotic songs together in the middle of Kettering. Eventually, everyone dispersed peacefully.'*

**Leslie Parsons, who trained as a navigator and became a member of a Lancaster crew on 622 Squadron operating from RAF Mildenhall, completing thirty-one operations before starting a second tour on 99 Squadron from Dhubulia, Northern India to attack targets in Burma.[1]**

---

1  *Over Hell & High Water: My Flying Experiences with Bomber Command & SE Asia Command during WW2* by Leslie Parsons (Woodfield Publishing (2001).

# THE BERLIN BLITZ BY THOSE WHO WERE THERE

In April 1939 Ronald Albert Read was working in the road surfacing section at the Road Research Laboratory at Harmondsworth but flying was in his blood. There was that never-to-be-forgotten day that a tiny biplane buzzed into sight in the light evening sky of West London, catching the attention of the 4-year-old boy idly watching. It was 1924 and aeroplanes were a novelty not to be ignored in those post First World War days. All too soon, war clouds would be gathering over Europe again.

On the quiet, sunny Sunday morning of 3rd September 1939, the day of the declaration of war, 'Ron' was visiting a friend when they heard the radio announce the British Prime Minister. 'We listened to the tired, uninspiring tones of Neville Chamberlain, telling us that "a state of war existed between Great Britain and Germany". As soon as the broadcast finished I drove home carefully, with eyes and ears open for the hoards of German aeroplanes we had been led to believe would inevitably bomb us immediately war was declared.' The air raid sirens sounded but there were no enemy aircraft in the sky and no bombs. Everyone expected a devastating attack on London, just as Warsaw had suffered just two days earlier. But it was a false alarm and for the next nine months, the so-called 'phoney war' period, enemy air activity over Britain was negligible. Meanwhile, Read decided that he wanted to join the RAF as a fighter pilot, but he would have a long wait. In February 1940 he went for his conscription interview but there was no recruiting for the RAF. In June this would change and anyone over the age of eighteen was eligible to apply for aircrew. Finally, in October he would be successful and was told to report to Uxbridge RAF Depot where he was recommended for pilot training.

In April 1940 Air Marshal Carless 'Peter' Portal CB DSO DFC took over from Air Chief Marshal Sir Edgar Ludlow-Hewitt as C-in-C Bomber Command. When the decision was taken in May to start strategic bombing of Germany by night, there was little the Luftwaffe could do to counter these early raids. The subject of night fighting was raised at a conference of German service chiefs just before the war. According to Kommodore Josef Kammhuber, the first general of night-fighters in the Luftwaffe, who was present at the conference, it was dismissed out of hand with the words, 'Night fighting! It will never come to that!' But it would and it did.

At the outbreak of war the overall strength of Bomber Command stood at fifty-five squadrons. On paper this sounds a respectable figure but by the end of September it was down to twenty-three home-based first-line squadrons. These consisted of six squadrons of Wellington Is and IAs of 3 Group (with two in reserve) stationed in East Anglia; five squadrons of Whitleys in 4 Group in Yorkshire and six squadrons of Handley Page Hampdens of 5 Group in Lincolnshire.[2] But after high losses of 'Wimpys' (as the Wellington was affectionately known after the cartoon character 'J. Wellington Wimpy' in 'Popeye') and Blenheims in daylight, the Whitley squadrons in 4 Group in north and east Yorkshire were immediately employed in night leaflet dropping, or 'Nickeling' operations, over the Ruhr and North-Western Germany and made no appearance in daylight at all. Seven such raids took place on the first seven nights of the war. After a hiatus, 'Nickeling' resumed on the night of 24th/25th September 1939. The Whitleys carried their bundles further afield and on 1st/2nd October when three Whitleys on 10 Squadron at Dishforth, just over four miles east of Ripon, North Yorkshire, were the first British aircraft of the war to fly over Berlin. Twenty-five-year-old Australian Flight Lieutenant John William Allsop and crew were lost without trace. Allsop left a widow, Eva Constance Allsop of Briar Hill, Victoria.

Weather conditions that night were particularly severe. One aircraft arrived over the German capital at 22,500 feet. The oxygen supply momentarily failed; two of the crew collapsed and part of the mechanism of the rear turret froze so that the air gunner could not open his door. The pilot carried on and the navigator went back to assist the two unconscious members of the crew. He dragged one twelve feet along the fuselage into the cabin and connected him with the oxygen supply. He then threw overboard two-thirds of the leaflets before collapsing in his turn. The pilot brought the aircraft down to 9,000 feet and at this height it became possible to open the door of the rear turret. The air gunner climbed through to the assistance of the navigator, who, however, had already recovered and returned to duty. Besides this raid on Berlin, leaflets were dropped on eight more occasions in the month of October by aircraft operating mostly from an advanced refuelling base at Villeneuve-les-Vertus near Paris. Leaflet raids were continued in January 1940. Owing to very bad weather the raids were only on a small scale in January and up to 25th February. On that date and for five successive nights leaflets were dropped in the Berlin area and in the Hamburg, Bremen, Kiel, Lübeck, Cologne and Rhineland areas. In the first few days of March leaflet raids were flown as far as the Posen area and to Czechoslovakia.

After Chamberlain had resigned the premiership on 10th May 1940 and Winston Churchill had become prime minister, Hitler realized there would

---

2 And six squadrons of Bristol Blenheim IV light bombers in 2 Group.

be no peace deal with Britain and the Battle of Britain began in mid-July. Often outnumbered and nearing exhaustion, RAF fighter pilots did not win the conflict, but they prevented the Luftwaffe from winning it. Without air superiority, Hitler tried a different tack, one which he no doubt came to rue. In July Winston Churchill had addressed the Chief of Air Staff in these words: 'In case there is an attack on the centre of Government in London, it seems very important to return the compliment the next day upon Berlin. I understand you will have by the end of this month a respectable party of Stirlings ready. Perhaps the nights are not yet long enough. Pray let me know.' On the night of Friday, 23rd/Saturday, 24th August, the Luftwaffe rained bombs on London, the first to fall on the capital since 1918. Little damage was done but Londoners were as one with Churchill and American foreign correspondent John Negley Farson summed up the prevailing mood. 'I have never thought of the English as a revengeful nation - a conquering race seldom is - yet one of the most menacing things for Hitler was the way that everyone dispassionately discussed the urgent need for the immediate bombing of Berlin. There was no false sentiment; it was just that no one there believed there was any other answer to the indiscriminate German night-bombing than to bomb Berlin off the map.'[3]

Bomber Command, which up to now had confined its bombing to enemy naval targets on its Baltic coast, retaliated as per Churchill's wishes - though no Stirlings were yet ready - and on the night of Sunday, 25th/Monday, 26th August, 103 Wellingtons, Hampdens and Whitleys were dispatched to bomb Bremen, Cologne, Hamm and Berlin. The flight to the German capital involved a round trip of eight hours and 1,200 miles. Guy Gibson on 83 Squadron at Scampton, recalled: 'Great excitement was caused when the target was announced. We had been waiting for this for a long time. Now we were going to get our chance. Many pilots who had been given an off night immediately began to plead to have themselves put down on the list of the first crews to bomb the German capital. Even "Downwind" Gillan[4] took an aeroplane over from one of his youngest pilots in order to be one of the first over the "Big City". But whoever chose August 25th/26th chose a night when as good a headwind as any faced our medium-range bombers.'[5]

---

3 *Bomber's Moon* published by Victor Gollancz Ltd, 1941.
4 In 1938 John Woodburn Gillan as CO of 111 Squadron flew a Hurricane from Turnhouse in Scotland to RAF Northolt at an average speed of 408 mph which earned him his enduring nickname. He was KIA on 29 August 1941 flying a Spitfire.
5 *Enemy Coast Ahead* by Guy Gibson.

# 'IT'S BERLIN WE WANT'

New Zealand Pilot Officer 'Sammy' Hall (later Group Captain 'Sammy' Hall OBE DFC who achieved a distinguished record as a Pathfinder later in the war) was the first commissioned navigator to be posted to 9 Squadron flying Wellingtons at Honington. He recalled: 'When our Squadron Commander announced Berlin was the destination at briefing it caused no more than normal apprehension - rather a feeling of excitement...an eagerness at having the opportunity of hitting the heart of Germany - in the face of bombastic boastings by Hitler and Goering. At this early stage of the war our main fears during operational flying concerned poor navigation due to lack of aids and sudden deterioration of the weather. We relied on a carefully prepared flight plan plus map-reading. Even astro-navigation had yet to be included in the training curriculum and the sparse radio aids were confined to getting us home. It was possible to raise a QDM (magnetic course home to base) and with greater effort now and again a "fix" - usually second class.

'We took off and crossed the Dutch coast on time which indicated the forecast Met winds were reasonably accurate and on ETA we were in an area of much hostile activity. Timings varied and aircraft were loosely spread. The sky was clear on this occasion - I convinced myself I could identify the Siemens-Schuckert works with the aid of the target map - started the bombing run and released our load; the rear gunner announced he could see the explosions, but to the success of the operation we had no means of telling save that of waiting for the Intelligence report published some months later. There were no fighters seen but flak was heavy. A strong headwind caused some anxiety on the return and there were frequent examinations of the petrol gauges, but we got back to Honington safely - with seventy gallons remaining - not much in the way of a margin for coping with an emergency. Since the weather and particularly the winds at height were much as forecast this was taken as confirmation that we had bombed the designated target!'

Squadron Leader Patrick Foss, a Wellington pilot on 115 Squadron at Marham in Norfolk wrote, 'This was the longest trip we had ever attempted in the Wellington, close to our maximum range with full tanks and minimum bomb load. We set off for Berlin with half a gale blowing from the west, low and middle cloud and murk on the ground. We were given strict instructions to turn back after three and three-quarter hours flying, wherever we were, to be sure of returning to Britain against the gale. As I reached three and three-quarter hours we thought we might be in the Berlin area. We had failed to get any fixes on the route and the weather was heavy cloud and total blackness. We glimpsed below us lakes and forests, but never a light or other indication of a city. There was nothing worth bombing and no time for a search. We turned for home and began to plug back against the gale. After an hour or so we saw lights on the ground, which we identified as an airfield working night-fighters. We made to bomb them but our bomb releases failed to work. We plugged on and finally, over the North Sea, succeeded in losing our bomb load, saving us some petrol. We landed at Marham with less than thirty minutes of fuel remaining after eight and a half hours in the air. Our other crews returned with similar stories. No one was sure he had hit Berlin. We hoped other stations had had more luck.'[6]

They hadn't. Bombing results were unimpressive but the RAF had scored a great victory for morale, one which the BBC was keen to exploit. First, an anonymous RAF bombing leader who had made six operational trips as navigator and bomb aimer broadcast his experiences of his first trip to Berlin. 'I had been over France a few times when the "Jerries" were walking through and I had made the trip to the Ruhr and to Milan. Berlin was a job I really wanted. Of course, I had no real say in the matter at all: it was just luck. The choice lies with the commanding officer. Anyway, I struck lucky because I am not a regular member of any particular crew. So far I haven't flown in the same crew twice. That happens, as I am the squadron bombing leader and change about a great deal.'

A second speaker, a flying officer on a 'heavy bomber squadron' broadcast his account of the raid. 'The wing commander who commands the squadron called in during the afternoon in the usual way for "briefing" - that's to say, to give us all the details of the operation. Half the squadron, he said, would be on Berlin, the remainder on other targets in Germany. He asked if there were any captains and crews who had any particular preference for Berlin. Every man operating that night wanted to go, though the wing commander decided that the fairest way to arrange things was to work it out in order of seniority. Some of the chaps started shooting a line about their seniority - trying to pull a bit of a fast one, in fact, but that didn't cut any ice and the whole thing was properly worked out by the two flight commanders. We have an "A" Flight and a "B" Flight. In the end, however, everybody went, because later in the afternoon, we were taken off the other targets and all put on to Berlin. I think that most pilots, if they were asked for their opinion on the Berlin raid, would say that given moderately decent weather they were quite normal trips. They take longer, of course, than some of the other

---

6  *Climbing Turns: A Pilot's story in war and peace* (Linden Hall 1990).

raids, but distance alone doesn't really make much difference so long as the aircraft can stand up to it as easily as ours do and as long as you have got well-trained captains and crews. In fact, it's precisely the sort of job that we've been trained to do.

'That afternoon, we were given our targets and general instructions and between the briefing and the time of take-off we worked out the details. Soon after dinner we took off, just as day was giving way to night. The light was failing fast as we started on our 650 mile outward journey and by the time we had crossed the odd 200 miles of sea and reached the enemy coast it was dark. We had a favourable wind and saw nothing for the hour and three-quarters that we spent crossing the sea. There was a lot of cloud below us, which began to clear as we approached the Dutch coast. There we ran into intense anti-aircraft fire. Heavy bursts in the distance at about 12,000 feet with continual flashes, which looked like lightning. It wasn't reaching us and we wondered who was getting the benefit of it. Other aircraft were ahead and it looked as though the gunners were concentrating on them. From then on there was nothing at all until we were over Emden when searchlights began to show and to hunt about in the sky. They failed to locate us and we went round them, dodging trouble.

'The captain took over from the second pilot. It is not a difficult operation, changing over, although some people seem to believe that it is like rocking a canoe. All that happens is that the second pilot gets the aircraft dead straight, flying level, slips out of his seat and the captain moves in. The rest of the run to Berlin was uneventful. We were there about twenty minutes before midnight. Searchlights came on, quite a lot of them and flak. There seemed to be a solid rectangle of brilliant light in the sky. It wasn't coming our way then but was making things as difficult as possible for the others who had left a quarter of an hour earlier and were already over the target.

'When our estimated time of arrival suggested that we should have arrived, we headed for the searchlights and dropped a flare to see what was below us. We spotted a river and I had a look at the map to see if it was the one we wanted: there are several stretches of water there. While we were trying to identify it, we were picked up by searchlights at 7,000 feet. They held us and we moved pretty rapidly, taking very violent avoiding action to get away. We got away and again dropped flares to pinpoint our position. In fact we repeated that operation several times and were again caught by searchlights and heavy anti-aircraft fire. Some of the bursts came too close to us to be comfortable, but we thought we had escaped. I know that we flew through big black balls of smoke that looked like balloons. They were only smoke.

'Cloud made it hard to identify the target and gave us a jolt once. We thought a squadron of aircraft was flying over us. There were silhouettes in the light, very clear and very sharp. They were our own shadows thrown onto the clouds by the searchlights. A very strange sight and a very strange feeling, that. For an hour and a half we flew around trying to make sure. Of course, we could have unloaded on Berlin at any time we liked: but - as you know, we don't do indiscriminate bombings. The exact spot still eluded us and the captain decided to come round the searchlights and make a low-level attack. So we descended to one thousand feet - over London that would be a few hundred feet above St. Paul's. We saw fires to the east, caused by other aircraft and followed the river towards them to come over the target area again and into a curtain of flak of all colours and descriptions. We reached the fire, which was now blazing well and easily recognised the Siemens-Schuckert Works with railway sidings alongside. We dropped a long stick of high explosives and incendiaries at a little over 1,000 feet. The searchlights were nearly horizontal by now and the anti-aircraft fire really hot. We could imagine the gunners frantically turning the handles, trying to get their guns to bear on us. Streams of green tracer shells were hose-piping over us as we took evasive action to get away from the target. The captain put the nose down and we came well below that 1,000 feet. The rear-gunner had meanwhile reported the bursts of our bombs with fires and explosions in the works as a result. There was a good fire going in the centre and we had bombed alongside it. Some of our heavy stuff must have landed on the railway. We couldn't miss from that height. All we could do was done, so we climbed through the clouds to 12,000 feet and turned for home with the engines running smoothly.

'Coming home there was not much opposition and the crew had a time for a little relaxation - with hot coffee and biscuits - and perhaps forty winks for some. The wireless operator was exploring the fuselage and came forward again with a wide grin and his hands full of pieces of aluminium to tell us tales of a large series of holes we had collected over Berlin. Against the wind we made the North Sea and flew into the dawn. The wireless operator grew excited again, pointing out quite a large hole in the wing. Reaching home, the captain spoke to the ground and wished them good morning. We touched down after ten and a quarter hours in the air, had a look at the machine and found enough holes to give the riggers a spot of work for a while. Nothing had struck a vital part: but another six inches and they would have got the petrol tanks and then we might have come down somewhere else. That was that. Then we had our interrogation on the trip; after which we were ready for breakfast and bed. It was a good twenty-four hours since we had been there, but we had had an enjoyable trip between times.

'Well, how about those gasworks in Berlin. If one's to judge from results actually seen, I suppose it's my most successful trip so far. As a matter of fact, it was the first time I've been to Berlin, though I have visited a good many other places in Germany. We got a certain amount of AA fire on the way out - but nothing remarkable. By the time we arrived there were already a lot of our aircraft buzzing about and flares were dropping all over the place. One could pick out streets and railways, small parks and places like that. Over the city, the guns were letting off at us pretty heavily, but we were not hit. We found our targets without any difficulty. It was a gas-generating plant only a few miles from the centre of Berlin. Someone else had started two fires in the NE corner of it and we ran up from west to east. My second pilot was flying the aircraft and I was doing the bomb aiming. By this time we were down to 8,000 feet and I could clearly see the outside of the works.

'Perhaps I ought just to explain here, very briefly, how the bombing is done. The bomb aimer is lying flat on his face in the nose of the aircraft looking down through a large glass panel which takes the place of the floor. Allowances have to be made on the bombsight for the speed and direction of the wind, the height and speed of the aircraft and so on; then, when the target comes in line with the pointers on the fore and back sight, the bomb aimer presses the firing switch - and down they go. On this occasion, when the bombs burst, there were four huge explosions across the works. I think that the first one must have hit a gasometer. As far as I can see, there was no other explanation for what happened. There was a violent eruption upwards and outwards. It reminded me of a scene on the films. The first four large explosions were followed by a series of smaller explosions. Two huge fires started and great tongues of flame leaped up - I estimated that they must have been rising to 1,500 feet - then dense clouds of smoke began to pour out. It was the most terrific sight I have ever seen. The bombs had fallen about fifty yards apart. Almost immediately the fires and explosions seemed to link up and for a distance of 200 yards through the works there was this great mass of flames. Next I saw our incendiaries fall on the western edge of the plant. They take longer to get down than the heavy bombs. What part of the works they hit, I don't know, but I could see large clusters of brilliant coloured flashes on the ground. We circled round and watched the fires blazing up. The rear gunner shouted: "Oh boy, it's terrific." The whole of Berlin must have seen them lighting up the sky. In the light of the explosions I had seen, momentarily, two long buildings and a tower. Then the aircraft

9

passed over and I could not see any more from the front, but the rear-gunner said he saw one of the buildings collapse in flames.

'By the time we had circled round twice the guns were getting a little too close and I gave orders to set course for base. From the beginning of the run-up the whole thing took only five or six minutes. About a quarter of an hour after we had left we could still see the reflection of the fire in the sky and about this time we made out another terrific explosion. We were not quite certain whether that was somebody else bombing or whether it was the result of our attacks. Well, that's the story of one aircraft on one raid on Berlin. One is not always so successful, of course, but it may give you some idea of the sort of work the RAF is doing over there.'

Seven aircraft aborted and of the remaining force, twenty-nine bombers claimed to have bombed the city and a further twenty-seven overflew the German capital but were unable to pinpoint their targets because of thick cloud. Only one Wellington was able to bomb the Siemens factory and just ten Hampdens out of forty-six dispatched claimed to have hit the Klingenberg Electric power station. Of the twenty-two Whitleys detailed to attack the Siemens works only two were successful. The Hampden, skippered by 21-year-old Pilot Officer Nicoll Brian Fawcett of Feilding, New Zealand - on 49 Squadron at Scampton - was lost without trace. On 50 Squadron at Lindholme, Pilot Officer G.A.C. Potts put his Hampden down on the sea off Scarborough Pier where the crew was rescued by a passing trawler, and Australian Pilot Officer Robert David Wawn and crew failed to return. Wawn was originally from Waverley, New South Wales and had been granted a short-service commission in the RAF in 1938. A German radio broadcast picked up on 26th August and translated revealed a 'slight error' in the navigation on the part of Sergeant J. Scholfield, describing how the inhabitants of Osthofen and Worms heard the drone of an aircraft flying low, with anti-aircraft batteries firing. Shortly afterwards the Hampden landed at Lautersheim. To the astonishment of the local people who surrounded the aircraft, the aircrew calmly alighted and Wawn addressed the crowd in Oxbridge English. Several German officers immediately arrived on the scene. Wawn announced that he thought they'd landed in Scotland and the people were speaking a Celtic dialect! When asked if they were not surprised at being shot at by AA guns, he replied, 'Oh, no. We're used to that sort of thing in England.' The Hampden's carrier pigeons were still in their baskets: 'Well if we'd released them they'd have had a long flight home!' replied Scholfield.[7]

---

7   via Andy Bird.

'The raid was in fact lousy,' wrote Guy Gibson. 'There was thick cloud over the target itself and I don't suppose more than ten bombs actually landed in Berlin. On the way home the Germans, in their methodical way, had laid a line of flak which stretched in a straight line from Berlin to London and the going was very heavy. Many aircraft landed in the sea on the way home.'[8] Flying Officer N.H. Svendsen, a New Zealander on Gibson's squadron, ditched in the mouth of the Wash where the crew was rescued.[9] Pilot Officer Anthony John George Mills ran out of petrol off Flamborough Head and took to his dinghy with his crew, who were all violently seasick. They were rescued off Grimsby after spending seven hours in the dinghy. Pilot Officer Richard Henry 'Dickie' Bunker DFC crashed, out of petrol at West Boldon in Durham trying to land at RAF Usworth. The skipper and Sergeant G.T. Thomas were seriously injured. The two other crew members were unharmed.[10] Flying Officer Arthur Chamberlain Pitt-Clayton, a Canadian, pulled off a dead-stick landing in the middle of an East Coast minefield and had to sit in his Hampden for a long time, not daring to walk across the sand dunes himself in case he trod on one, while those on land watched him not daring to walk out until a coastguard, who knew a channel, drove up and rescued them. 'This was the second time Pitt had done something like this,' wrote Guy Gibson. 'The last time he had chosen a large country house in Scotland with a very small field nearby and had to wait for two weeks before he could fly his aeroplane out. Perhaps it was something to do with the very pretty girl in the house nearby.' As soon as Gibson landed he got his Hampden refuelled and took off to look for 'Tony' Mills. 'We were in the air six hours, but never saw a thing. When we finally landed back at Scampton I was annoyed to hear that he had been picked up a long time ago, having seen me pass over him twice, and was at the moment having a party with the boys in Grimsby.'[11]

At Honington the returned Wellington crews on 9 Squadron had a visit from the Commander-in-Chief, Air Marshal Sir Carless Portal. 'Sammy'

---

8 *Enemy Coast Ahead* by Guy Gibson.

9 Svendsen was shot down on Düsseldorf on 30 June/1 July 1941 and taken prisoner. Pilot Officer Mills DFC was killed on 24/25 August 1941 when he and a Hampden on 49 Squadron collided over England on return from Düsseldorf.

10 See *The Other Few* by Larry Donnelly. Wing Commander Bunker DSO DFC* (25) who had served with distinction on 620 Squadron during the Arnhem operation was killed on 20 April 1945 when his Stirling took off from Odiham with a flat tyre which caught fire and the rear turret dropped off. He swerved away to prevent crashing into Windlesham village and crashed out of control in a field killing all seven crew.

11 *Enemy Coast Ahead* by Guy Gibson.

Hall was included in the group of officers assembled to meet the 'great man' as he recalls. 'The conversation with the Air Officer Commander in Chief went something like this:

> Wing Commander: 'This is Pilot Officer Hall, Sir.'
>
> AOC-in-C: 'Ah, when did you last operate, Hall?'
>
> Myself (rather eagerly): 'Last night Sir.'
>
> AOC-in-C: 'Good, good. Where did you go?' (I think, 'Doesn't he know? He sent me there.')
>
> Myself: 'Berlin, Sir.'
>
> AOC-in-C: 'Good. What did you think of it?'
>
> Myself (realising this was no time to say that I had been frightened stiff): 'Very interesting, Sir.'
>
> AOC-in-C: 'Good, good and how many trips have you done?'
>
> Myself (proudly): 'Three, Sir.'
>
> AOC-in-C turns on his heel to the squadron commander and says crisply, 'And now I'd like to talk to someone with experience.'

William L. Shirer, the American war correspondent in Berlin, made the following broadcast from the Rundfunk[12] after the raid: 'We had our first big air-raid of the war last night. The sirens sounded at 12.20 am and the all-clear came at 3.23 am. For the first time British bombers came directly over the city and they dropped bombs. The concentration of anti-aircraft fire was the greatest I've ever witnessed. It provided a magnificent, and terrible sight. And it was strangely ineffective. Not a plane was brought down; not one was even picked up by the searchlights, which flashed back and forth frantically across the skies throughout the night.

'The Berliners are stunned. They did not think it could happen. When this war began, Goering assured them it couldn't. He boasted that no enemy planes could ever break through the outer and inner rings of the capital's anti-

---

12  The Reichs-Rundfunk-Gesellschaft (RRG) (Reich Broadcasting Corporation) was a national network of German regional public broadcasting companies active from 1925 until 1945. RRG's broadcasts were receivable in all parts of the country and were used extensively for Nazi propaganda after 1933.

aircraft defence. The Berliners are a naive and simple people. They believed him. Their disillusionment today therefore is all the greater. You have to see their faces to measure it. Goering made matters worse by informing the population only three days ago that they need not go to their cellars when the sirens sounded, but only when they heard the flak going off nearby. The implication was that it would never go off. That made people sure that the British bombers, though they might penetrate to the suburbs, would never be able to get over the city proper. And then last night the guns all over the city suddenly began pounding and you could hear the British motors humming directly overhead, and from all reports there was a pell-mell, frightened rush to the cellars by the five million people who live in this town.

'I was at the Rundfunk writing my broadcast when the sirens sounded and almost immediately the bark of the flak began. Oddly enough, a few minutes before, I had had an argument with the censor from the Propaganda Ministry as to whether it was possible to bomb Berlin. London had just been bombed. It was natural I said that the British should try to retaliate. He laughed. It was impossible, he said. There were too many anti-aircraft guns around Berlin.

'I found it hard to concentrate on my script. The gunfire near the Rundfunk was particularly heavy and the window of my room rattled each time a battery fired or a bomb exploded. To add to the confusion, the air-wardens, in their fire-fighting overalls, kept racing through the building ordering everyone to the shelters. The wardens at the German radio are mostly porters and office boys and it was soon evident that they were making the most of their temporary authority. Most of the Germans on duty, however, appeared to lose little time in getting to the cellar.

'I was scheduled to speak at 1 am. To get to the studio to broadcast we have to leave the building where we write our scripts and have them censored and dash two hundred yards through a blacked-out vacant lot to the sheds where the microphones are. As I stepped out of the building at five minutes to one the light guns protecting the radio station began to fire away wildly. At this moment I heard a softer but much more ominous sound. It was like hail falling on a tin roof. You could hear it dropping through the trees and on the roofs of the sheds. It was shrapnel from the anti-aircraft guns. For the first time in my life I wished I had a steel helmet. There had always been something repellent to me about a German helmet, something symbolic of brute Germanic force. At the front I had refused to put one on. Now I rather thought I could overcome my prejudice.'

Berlin was visited again on the night of Wednesday, 28th/Thursday, 29th August when seventy-nine Blenheims, Hampdens, Wellingtons and Whitleys took part in raids on the German capital and six other targets in

Germany and to French airfields. Flight Lieutenant Jamie Anderson Pitcairn-Hill DSO DFC, on 83 Squadron at Scampton, ditched his Hampden opposite a trawler off Skegness returning from Berlin, all four crew being rescued unharmed. 'Pit', who was described by Guy Gibson 'as straight-laced and true a Scotsman as any… who was always doing things wrong but was always getting his bombs on target' was shot down and killed on 18th September and was buried in the churchyard at Luc-sur-Mer. Twenty Wellingtons claimed 'good' results on Berlin and other targets. Pilot Officer Barr, flying a 115 Squadron Wellington, was one of seven 'Wimpys' that attacked the Klingenberg Electric power station.

His navigator, George Bury, recalled: 'Having been warned that the area was very heavily defended, we decided to fly at 15,000 feet. That was 5,000 feet higher than our normal height. At this height it was essential to use oxygen all the time but after a few hours the masks became wet and uncomfortable to use. But, if taken off, frequent movement was very tiring. As it turned out, the flight as far as we were concerned turned out to be fairly uneventful. Searchlights were very active. Although one did pick us up, he failed to keep us within his beam long enough for the others in the group to join in. When just ahead we saw a Wellington caught by two at the same time and quick as a flash many others concentrated on the same target and he was caught in a cone of at least ten searchlights. The whole area around the aircraft was as bright as day and no matter which way he turned and twisted, they easily held on to him. The last we saw of him he was in a steep dive with shells bursting all around. This was our eighth flight and the first time that we had seen another aircraft. We were beginning to think that we were fighting the whole war on our own.'[13] Another five Wellingtons claimed hits on an adjacent marshalling yard and fires were started at Tempelhof aerodrome by three more. Berlin was the primary target of the Hampdens, the Siemens and Halske factory being attacked by fourteen aircraft, the majority of crews reporting fires and explosions. An oil reservoir at Nordenham and also railway sidings north of Berlin were also attacked but results were unobserved.[14]

On the last night of the month, 31st August/1st September, seventy-seven Blenheims, Hampdens, Wellingtons and Whitleys attacked Berlin, Cologne and airfields in Holland and Belgium. One Hampden was lost. The bombing directive on 21st September released the Whitley Group from anti-invasion duties and gave priority to electric power plants in Berlin.

---

13  *RAF Marham* by Ken Delve. (PSL 1995). One Blenheim and one Hampden were lost.
14  *The Other Few* by Larry Donnelly.

First documented in the thirteenth century and situated at the crossing of two important historic trade routes, by the Second World War Berlin had a population of four million, was the second largest city in Europe and the third largest municipality in the world; one that had been fought over for centuries. It suffered badly during the Napoleonic Wars when the French army occupied Berlin from 1806 to 1809. It had been the capital of the Kingdom of Prussia in 1701 and from 1871 to the end of the First World War it was the capital of the German Empire; then the Weimar Republic, and finally, in 1933, capital of the Third Reich when politically, it was seen as a left wing stronghold. In 1920 Berlin had acquired several previously independent towns and rural communities, creating an enormous metropolitan area encompassing more than 300 square miles; more than 800 square miles if the sprawling suburban area was included. It was no wonder bomber crews called it the 'Big City'. It was 'big' in the length of the flight, which meant flying 1,200 miles there and back, mostly over hostile territory and in the strength of its defences, in spectacle, in significance in the war and in the imagination of those who learnt that it was their target.[15]

Crews would come to know Berlin's overwhelming defences well; too well. When aircrew finally arrived over Berlin, they were stunned by the magnitude of the city itself and resistance offered by her defenders. One pilot described the sight as 'awesome', struck most of all by the 'immensity of the city' and his 'excruciatingly slow progress across it.' Another airman described flying through the formidable flak like a 'giant hand taking hold of the aircraft and shaking it, like a huge dog shaking a rat'. Its air defences stretched across more than thirty-seven miles of searchlights, anti-aircraft guns, decoy fires, decoy marker flares and target indicators. Outside the range of the more reliable 'Oboe' radar network crews relied on onboard $H_2S$ (airborne ground scanning radar system) when this became available.[16] Berlin's location, lying deep inside the Third Reich not far from the Polish border and with no coastline, islands, or lakes, made it almost invisible to RAF airborne radar devices. (The lakes were not visible to $H_2S$ screens because the Germans covered them with large wooden screens to confuse the bomber crews.) The confusion of woodlands, lakes and smaller satellite towns around added to the difficulty of discerning the target areas. $H_2S$ would give good results on targets where distinctive land and sea features could

---

15  *Chased By The Sun; The Australians in Bomber Command in WWII* by Hank Nelson (ABC Books 2002).

16  $H_2S$ was a British 10cm experimental airborne radar navigational and target location aid.

be observed, for example, on a coastal city where the set operator could distinguish water, showing as a dark area from the lighter land mass and the built-up areas showing bright on the cathode ray tube. But on a large city like Berlin the display on the tube was uniformly bright with little of the contrast which would make for easy identification of a particular part of the target. Consequently, Berlin attacks, while the bombs were usually all dropped on the city, tended to yield scattered results. Singularly isolated; a bomber stream heading for Berlin was unlikely to be headed anywhere else. Not enough hours of darkness in the spring and summer nights for the bombers to take off, fly to Berlin and back and land before daylight, made it an autumn and winter target.

Hitler, incensed by the bombing of his capital, ordered the Luftwaffe to switch from day bombings of British fighter airfields in Southern England to night bombing of its industrial cities, beginning with London. What came to be known as the 'Blitz' began on 7th September 1940. London was systematically bombed by the Luftwaffe for fifty-six out of the following fifty-seven days and nights. The Luftwaffe gradually decreased daylight operations in favour of night attacks to evade attack by the RAF and the 'Blitz' became a night bombing campaign after October 1940. 'The "Blitz" soon became easy to handle,' wrote 'Ron' Read. 'The bombs were impersonal and random. It was soon obvious that survival was a matter of pure chance. Our lifestyle accepted that and we enjoyed ourselves, even during the worst times.' The 'Blitz' took the lives of about 43,000 citizens throughout Britain before it petered out in May 1941 when Hitler turned his attention to Russia. He moved the bulk of his military forces east but left enough aircraft on the French coast to mount sporadic sharp attacks on Britain, to remind them that the Luftwaffe was only twenty minutes flying time from London.

Though little damage was done to Berlin on these early raids by Bomber Command, Pandora's Box had been opened. On Monday, 23rd/Tuesday, 24th September the German capital was selected for a special retaliatory effort, the first time that all available Whitleys and Hampdens and Wellingtons would attack targets in one German city. In total, 129 aircraft were given eighteen separate targets, which included three gasworks and six power stations and subsidiary targets such as seven railway yards and the Tempelhof airfield. Weather and icing conditions proved unexpectedly severe, but eighty-four of the bombers managed to reach Berlin. Most of the bombs probably fell in the Moabit area of the city where a power-station was one of the selected targets. The only significant success was at Charlottenburg where incendiaries set fire to a gasometer. Many of the bombs failed to explode, including one that dropped in the garden of the Chancellery. Several houses were damaged in the Tiergarten district and 781 Germans lost their homes. Twenty-two Germans were killed. A Hampden, Wellington and a Whitley failed to return. The Hampden, piloted by Squadron leader 'Tony' Bridgeman DFC on 83 Squadron, was brought down by flak en route to Berlin. Bridgeman bailed out over Bremen and was the only survivor on his aircraft. He was held captive in Stalag Luft III for the rest of the war. Guy Gibson, who always referred to him as 'Oscar' (Bridgeman's middle name) wrote: 'We waited all night; we waited till the grey darkness of the early hours became purple, then blue as the sun rose in the west over Lincoln Wolds and it became daylight. But Oscar never came back.' He recorded the reading of Bridgeman's will in the mess at Scampton and concluded, 'I was the last one left... all my friends had gone now.'[17]

The Wellington that was lost was skippered by Flight Lieutenant Karel Trojáček and his all-Czech crew on 311 Squadron which made an emergency landing at Leidschendam in the Den Haag area of Holland owing to engine trouble. The crew initially went on the run but they were soon captured. Sergeant Karel Kuňka the wireless operator shot himself with a Very pistol because he feared his capture might endanger his family in Czechoslovakia. He died of his wounds a day later in hospital in The Hague.

The Whitley that was lost was flown by Pilot Officer Andrew Woodrow Dunn DFC on 77 Squadron who had taken off from Linton-on-Ouse at 2000 hours with the intention of bombing the large aircraft factory at Spandau on the outskirts of Berlin. Dunn, who was from County Londonderry, had been involved in a number of flying accidents during his first weeks of operational flying, including being forced to ditch off Hastings Pier returning from the raid on Wanne-Eickel. On 10th/11th September Dunn's Whitley was hit by flak on the Berlin operation, when he was again able to bring his aircraft home safely. This time his luck was out. Dropping their flares as they roared over Spandau, the Whitley crew had no difficulty in locating the aircraft factory, but as they turned and made their run over the target, the guns put up a fierce barrage and shrapnel holed one of the petrol tanks. They had been flying for seven hours and fifty minutes when Dunn had to ditch, out of fuel 100 miles east of Hartlepool. They took to their dinghy but Dunn, Dudley Brooking Allen the 19-year-old wireless operator, Sergeant Derek Albert Gibbons the second pilot and Sergeant Savill DFM

---

17  *Enemy Coast Ahead* by Guy Gibson.

had perished before rescue finally came. Only Sergeant G.H. Riley the rear gunner, who drifted for eighty-four hours, survived the ordeal.

On Tuesday, 24th/Wednesday, 25th September twenty bombers were detailed to bomb a power station in Berlin but the Whitley piloted by 20-year-old Sergeant Herbert Cornish crashed on take-off from Linton-on-Ouse killing Cornish and two of his crew when the bomb load exploded. His observer, Sergeant Leslie Hambleton Taylor was just 19 years of age. The wireless operator and the rear gunner were injured.

Pilot Officer David Penman had been flying Blenheims and then Hampdens since October 1938 on 44 'Rhodesia' Squadron at Waddington four miles south of Lincoln. The squadron had been renamed in 1941 in honour of that colony's contribution to Britain's war effort and also to recognise that up to 25 per cent of the ground and aircrew were from Southern Rhodesia. The son of a First World War army officer, David Jackson Penman was born on 14th October 1919 in Edinburgh and educated at the Royal High School. On leaving school in 1937 he had been granted a short service commission in the RAF to train as a pilot. Weather forecasts were far from accurate and one of them was on this, his first trip to Berlin. 'We got there more quickly than expected and our four 500lb bombs were dropped on B56, an area of the city. Apart from heavy gunfire and searchlights we had little opposition. However, on heading home we found we were not making good progress and then realized that a very strong tailwind had helped us reach Berlin and now as a headwind was cutting our ground speed for home.

I did my best to control the fuel consumption and when well out over the North Sea we threw out everything we could, including the machine guns and ammunition. Reducing height to get below the strongest winds saved us from landing in the sea. We were unable to make radio contact, but our selected course heading was good and with the dawn breaking we crossed the English coast at Cromer with engines spluttering from lack of fuel. We crept over the Norfolk coast only to find all possible landing areas spiked with long poles against the threat of invasion. After nine hours twenty minutes in the air I had no option but to do my best with a small, unspiked area. We touched down alright but with brakes locking the wheels skidded into a mound at the end of the area and bounced over it breaking one leg of the undercarriage before coming to rest a bit lopsided but otherwise intact. The aircraft was not badly damaged and was soon flying again.'[18]

---

18  One Blenheim and one Whitley were lost this night.

On 5th October, Air Chief Marshal Sir Carless Portal became the new Chief of Air Staff. Air Marshal Sir Richard Edmund Charles Peirse KCB DSO AFC, who as Vice-Chief of Air Staff had already been closely concerned with the British bombing policy, was appointed the new Air Officer Commander-in-Chief. Born the son of an admiral and educated at Monkton Combe School and at King's College London, Peirse became a midshipman in the Royal Navy Volunteer Reserve and was commissioned in 1912. He was awarded the Distinguished Service Order for his contribution to the aerial attack on Dunkirk on 23rd January 1915.

On the night of 7th/8th October when 140 Blenheims, Hampdens, Wellingtons and Whitleys set out for a number of targets, the main raid was by forty-two Wellingtons and Whitleys on a dozen individual targets in Berlin. One Wellington from the Berlin force was lost. Two nights' later, on 9th/10th October, when seventy aircraft visited many targets, one Wellington was lost and a Whitley on 51 Squadron at Dishforth was forced to ditch in the North Sea 120 miles east of the Firth of Forth at 0715 hours returning from Berlin. A few days later the pilot of the Whitley, Pilot Officer A.W. Millson with his rear gunner, Pilot Officer D. Carless, provided further snippets and regaled listeners to the BBC Home Service in London with the tale of the crew's eleven and a half hours ordeal in a dinghy until rescue came. Millson recalled:[19] 'We were detailed to attack the Neukölln gasworks in Berlin. There was a fair amount of cloud on the way out, but we reached Berlin on time, with the cloud tops at 8,000 feet. This cleared at 4,000 feet and when our dead reckoning indicated that we were over the targets, actually we were about forty miles north of it. Circling round we picked up a landmark that gave us our position and we flew towards the target. The gasworks were already on fire. We were not the only people on the target. So we made a direct run for it, climbing a little. The Germans, however, had a few fighters up in the air and three of them came at us, so we went into the cloud, changed our direction and later came over the target again. So that we could be sure of our bombing, we came down to 3,500 feet and were met by all kinds of anti-aircraft fire. There was heavy and light stuff and machine-gun fire as overweight. We tried to dodge that, came down to about 2,700 feet and bombed Neukölln all in one stick. Our bombs hit the target fair and square. There was a terrific bang, followed by blinding flames. Part of the gasworks certainly went up.'

---

19   With the need for anonymity the men were referred to as 'first' and 'second Speakers'.

Pilot Officer Carless added, 'I saw the fire. The captain had begun to climb as soon as the "bombs gone" [three 500 pounders and five 250 pounders plus one container of incendiaries, at 0030 hours] was given and we got to about 9,000 feet. That fire, from the height we were at, seemed to me to be about half a mile square, with flames three or four hundred feet high. Gas gives a very good blaze. There, those flames were a very angry red. I have never seen a fire so big in my life.'

'Then we came right into nearly everything the Germans could give us,' continued Millson. 'Their anti-aircraft put a hole three and a half feet square into the port wing and there were between three and four hundred holes in the fuselage. When daylight came it was not necessary to put on the lights. Our aircraft are normally blacked out and we use interior lighting. The holes made that quite unnecessary.

'A high explosive shell went straight through the starboard tailplane. Luckily it went straight through without exploding or we should not even have come down in the sea. Then the leading edge of the port tailplane was shot clean away and the port wing badly battered. In fact it was smashed up, but we climbed at plus two and a half pounds boost away from the target, to 10,000 feet, being shot at all the time. We were a bit out of luck. We set course to avoid all that dirt and a bit later went over Bremen. We didn't have time to see much of what had happened there because we were shot at again. Then we flew towards home, passing through a very severe front.

'We could still see no land for four hours after we had left the Neukölln gasworks blazing merrily and that meant that we were about an hour overdue. We had gone through a lot of very bad weather. It seemed as though our petrol tanks had escaped damage, but we were beginning to calculate our fuel, just the same. Off the Dutch coast we got our location. We were somewhat north of the track. We had had to take quite a lot of avoiding action. When we heard our location we came down through the cloud, working on the estimated time of arrival at a particular point. We got down to 1,500 feet and found ourselves still over the sea. There was no land in sight. We flew on for a little more than half an hour. I thought we must have overshot England and we were over the Irish Sea. We turned again and sent out an SOS which was received and acknowledged. The trouble was that there had been a great change in wind speed and direction, of which we, of course, knew nothing. Besides which our air speed was very much slower than normal because of the damage. Then one engine cut out because of lack of petrol and while the other engine was going I turned the aircraft head into wind in case I had to land in the sea.'

At this point Pilot Officer Carless added: 'The captain had taken over the aircraft from the second pilot [Sergeant Hubert Charles Gerard Brook] some time before and asked to be strapped into his seat. They did that and the navigator [Sergeant William Gordon McAllister] came back to see that the rest of the crew were OK. Orders were given to prepare to abandon aircraft and to land in the sea. So the dinghy was got ready and the Very lights and pistols were collected. The navigator began to hack away the door to use as a paddle.'

'I brought the aircraft down into wind and the nose hit the crest of a wave,' continued Millson. 'It crumpled straight up on the crash and I was drenched. That didn't matter, because I was going to be drenched in a couple of minutes anyway. The rear gunner threw out the dinghy which didn't open at once. I climbed out of the escape hatch and walked along the top of the fuselage to see the rear gunner and second pilot in the water tearing the dinghy open with their hands. It opened upside down so we couldn't throw the bag of Very lights into it. They were thrown into the water in the hope that we could pick them up later; but the sea was so heavy they drifted away.

'Two got into the dinghy and with the help of another member of the crew we pulled it on to the mainplane when both of us clambered in. The navigator was still in the water, hanging on while we recovered our breath. We were pretty well humped out. He said he was all right, but after a moment he let go of the line and clung to the door, intending to hang on to the aircraft. Then the dinghy was swept against the tailplane and half of it burst and we could not right it. The navigator, still clinging to the door, drifted away and disappeared. We were helpless and couldn't reach him. There was too much swell. The aircraft floated for about five minutes in all and then went down tail first. We first hit the water at 0720 and after we were in the dinghy tried to organize ourselves. It was only half inflated and we were not very successful in getting it straight, but we sat and kept watch and after about an hour opened up the emergency rations and found the rum and malted milk tablets. But we were very seasick and only the rear gunner could keep anything down. At about 1245 we saw the first Hudson aircraft above us, so we fired the only good emergency rocket we had. The aircraft saw us and circled round but lost us - we were so low in the water.

'By six o'clock I decided that we should have to spend the night in the dinghy and we started to bail it out. We had a pump that didn't function too well what with one thing and another and we all sat in the middle and the sides lifted up. I think that saved us. It was just the merest fluke really, but when we got the sides up a Sunderland flying boat spotted the dinghy, dropped sea markers and attracted another Hudson that was looking for us. The Hudson signalled with a lamp, "Help coming - launch." And the rain simply streamed down and browned us off.

'After half an hour the launch came up to us and tried to throw us a line. The wind was so strong it blew it back. So the crew of the launch tried another tack. They went up wind and drifted down and got us a line which we tied to the dinghy. Then a heavy wave knocked the launch on to us, which tipped us over and we were in the water again, stiff with cramp and most of us nearly exhausted. That was six-forty-five and we had been adrift for eleven and a half hours.

'We were bundled down into the cabin and stripped. They put us into sleeping bags and blankets and gave us hot tea, massage and respiratory exercises. The wireless operator was all in. He had passed out. The rear gunner had paralysed legs. But for two hours we slept, dead to everything and the sea was so rough that it bounced me off on to the floor. Yet, through that sea the launch had come at its top speed, which was over thirty knots and had travelled one hundred and thirty miles from land. There isn't enough to say about the way they did their stuff. They got us back to hospital and into warm rooms with heated beds where they simply cooked us for about four hours. The officers lent us their lounge suits and we had a very good party in the mess and the station commander sent his car for us and brought us home.' The crew on returning to Dishforth were given fourteen days' sick leave.[20]

On Monday, 14th/Tuesday, 15th October, Air Marshal Peirse sent seventy-eight Hampdens, Wellingtons and Whitleys to Berlin, Stettin, Böhlen, Magdeburg and Le Havre. Two Hampdens were shot down. X2910 on 44 'Rhodesia' Squadron, piloted by Sergeant Leonard John Burt, was shot down by Leutnant Hans-Georg Mangelsdorf of 2./NJG 1 who was killed in the aerial combat. X2993 on 50 Squadron, flown by South African Pilot Officer Arthur Howell Davies, was claimed by Hauptmann Werner Streib commanding 1./NJG 1. Burt and two of his crew were killed, one being taken into captivity. Davies and one of his crew were killed, two others being taken prisoner. The next night 134 aircraft attempted to bomb many targets in Germany. A Hampden on 83 Squadron at Scampton, which force landed at Southwold in Suffolk, was the only loss.

---

20  The two other members on the crew were Sergeants Hubert Charles Gerard Brook and E.A. Young. Flight Sergeant Brook was posted to 90 Squadron at Polebrook and given his own crew. He was killed on 28 July 1941 when the Fortress I that he was piloting on an air test crashed at Wilbarston, Northants.

The next major operation was on Sunday, 20th/Monday, 21st October when 139 bombers went to many targets in the occupied countries, Italy and Germany. Berlin was the largest raid with a visit by thirty Hampdens. An Irish sergeant pilot, who was recently awarded the DFM, spoke about the raid on Berlin on the BBC.

'If a bomber crew are to be successful in all they undertake it is essential that they should work as one man. My crew are an excellent team and that is one of the main reasons why we were able to pull this attack off satisfactorily. When I was at school I was often told that if an Irishman, a Scotsman and an Englishman lived together in one room it would not be long before they fell out. I am glad to say that this does not apply to my team, perhaps because there are two Irishmen to keep the peace.

'So much depends on the navigator that it is just as well that I should tell you straightaway that it is he who comes from the same country as myself. The rear gunner is the Scotsman and the wireless operator the Englishman. The rear gunner and myself are more or less RAF "veterans". We have both been in the service about five years. The navigator joined up straight from school and the wireless operator gave up his job as a clerk to undertake what he calls "more exciting work".

'This was my first official visit to the German capital. I was over it once before, but that was after I had been attacking a target at Stettin. Afterwards we all thought it would be rather fun to make the Berliners go underground, so on our way home we flew over the city and made the ground defences waste a lot of energy and ammunition for nothing. But the flight was a great deal more thrilling than the raid on Stettin. This time on our arrival over Berlin we ran into a fierce barrage; shells were bursting all over the place, but in spite of this we spent about forty-five minutes over the capital before we dropped our bombs. We explored the city thoroughly and eventually found the target we were after. All the time I was manipulating the stick, the navigator was busy getting a decent pinpoint, while the other two members of the crew were giving me advice on which way to go in to avoid the ack-ack. We were then fairly high up, but the shells were still bursting pretty close to us. None of them actually rocked the aircraft, but two were close enough for us to hear them burst. There was a slight ground haze over the city, but the moon penetrated it and showed up all we wanted to see. Suddenly, through the intercommunication system and above the roar of the engines, I heard the navigator say: "I am sure that's the target." Having complete confidence in him, I had no hesitation in shoving the stick forward and the nose of the aircraft down. Just before we went down I said to the crew: "All right, down we go," and just as we started I thought of my crew hanging on for dear life. We had been talking about dive attack for at least an hour before we got to Berlin. During the dive, which was made at a good speed, I had the target in the gunsight and I held it there. All the time the target was getting bigger and bigger. Then I shouted, "let them go" and the bomb-aimer pressed the button. As soon as the bombs burst all the anti-aircraft guns opened up and every ten or twelve seconds we felt the most colossal bumps and the machine was jockeyed about all over the place. At first I started to climb, then to avoid the shells I had to dive again, then climb, then go from side to side, then do stall turns, then up, then another dive. This business of going up and down went on five or six times. One thing I am certain of is that I wouldn't dare to throw the aircraft about in daylight as I did that night.

'At one moment I saw a balloon go up in flames. Fire from the guns on the ground must have hit it. Actually, I did not see the balloon until it caught fire; there was a flash and the whole thing was ablaze. We were only thirty yards away at the time and the cable down, whilst some of the burning fabric was sliding right in front of us. One of the chaps said that it reminded him of the Indian rope trick. In the end the cable fell clear of us and we all thought afterwards what a good thing it was that a shell had hit it. Twenty minutes later we were right out of the barrage and setting course for home.'

A Hampden on 44 'Rhodesia' Squadron was shot down with the loss of all the crew on the raid on Berlin. Two other Hampdens force landed, at Colchester in Essex and near Veryan, Cornwall.

A new 'winter' directive was issued on 30th October in which oil targets remained 'top priority' but they were to be attacked only in bright moonlight when there was some chance of hitting them. In the words of the directive 'regular concentrated attacks should be made on objectives on large towns and centres of industry with the primary aim of causing very heavy material destruction which would demonstrate to the enemy the power and severity of air bombardment'. The reality however was that the Order of Battle numbered only 532 aircraft - 217 Blenheims in 2 Group, 100 Wellingtons, 71 Hampdens, 59 Whitleys and 85 obsolete Battles, so only about 230 aircraft were suitable for night operations in winter. While mainly Hampdens, Wellingtons and Whitleys carried out night raids on targets in Germany and the occupied countries throughout the rest of October and into November, numbers rarely totalled more than a few score unless other types - notably Blenheims - helped to swell the force. Bomber aircrew though were particularly keen to 'dish out' some form of retribution for raids on British cities in the Blitz. On 14th/15th November 1940 Robert Kee never forgot seeing the bombing of Coventry from Upper Heyford airfield where he was learning to fly twin-engined bombers. Born on 5th October 1919 in Calcutta where his father ran a jute business, Kee read Modern History at Magdalen College, Oxford before leaving in 1940 to join the RAF. He trained as a pilot and in July 1941, was commissioned and joined 44 'Rhodesia' Squadron at Waddington, flying Hampdens. 'The feeling was, I wish I could bomb Berlin and get our own back a bit,' he wrote. He did bomb Berlin twice. 'I think there was pleasure in the thought that we were reciprocating after the bombing of places like Coventry and London.'[21]

'As the Berlin raids stepped up,' recalls Sergeant A.L. Chapman, a Whitley pilot on 102 Squadron, 'the Germans began pulling guns away from Cologne to Berlin.' Chapman had joined the squadron on 15th August 1940. 'The first twenty-four hours I spent in shelters - we were bombed by thirty Ju 88s and a lot of aircraft were destroyed.[22] On 15th/16th December 1940 I had Squadron Leader D.A. Morris, the acting CO of the squadron flying with me on the trip to Berlin. We completed the trip but when we arrived back, there was a thick fog, something like two hundred feet of it. Above it you could see quite clearly and looking down straight through it you could occasionally see the ground. We even found the aerodrome, but as soon as I made an attempt to come down into this fog, the whole thing disappeared! It was impossible to land.

'We couldn't communicate with the ground although we could hear them talking to other aircraft. So we had to fly around and try and find some other place to land. It was unfortunate because in 1940 any field of any size had ditches dug in it or poles sticking up - anti-invasion measures.

'Then I remembered that in my lectures somebody had told me that if I flew over an English ack-ack battery and gave a certain signal, they would

---

21  On the night of 18 February 1942 Kee took off to lay mines off the Frisian Islands. His Hampden was hit by flak at 8,000 feet and he ditched the aircraft off Schiermonnikoog. Two of his crew were killed. Kee and his navigator were taken prisoner.

22  Driffield airfield was attacked at around 1320 hours and the attack lasted for about 45 minutes during which time about 100 bombs were dropped on the aerodrome and the surrounding area. Ten Whitleys sustained damage resulting in all of them being written off. There was also damage sustained to four of the five hangars, the living accommodation and other buildings. In total thirteen military personnel and one civilian lost their lives. ACWm2 Marguerite Hester Hudson WAAF, aged 19, of Wadley, Sheffield was the first WAAF to be killed by enemy action in the UK.

lay down their searchlights in a line with an aerodrome which would be clear and would receive me.

'I flew over this battery and gave this signal. It didn't seem to work at first but after a while it did.

'All the lights came down and pointed in one direction. Fine! I'm going to get down now and I flew along the beams right out to sea! What happened I don't know, whether they thought, this is a German intruder! Maybe they were trying to deceive us.

'Anyway, out to sea. Well, that was no good. And then I suddenly remembered Flamborough Head, maybe I can get down there? I tried and actually touched the ground, but then I saw something looming up in front, out of the fog, so I had to pull up again, right over the cliff and out to sea. I started climbing, thinking hard what am I going to do next? By this time I'd been in the air eleven hours twenty-five minutes!

'Finally, the fuel ran out so I had to ditch in the sea. The aircraft manufacturer said they would float for five minutes. By the time I got out, the last one, the tail was under water. The dinghy was in the tail so I had to decide if we should dive in and get it or not, but the plane was going down. Better try and hang on together. We were under water to the shoulders. Every now and again I sent off a Very pistol - we must have been about two or three miles out to sea.

'Eventually we heard the sound of an engine coming towards us - I don't know how long we'd been there - maybe two and a half, three hours? Suddenly everything went silent and we thought, oh hell, they can't find us in the fog! Later on we heard the splash of oars. We hailed and they found us. As we were getting aboard, the plane's aerial snapped, wound itself round the observer and we had a heck of a struggle getting him unwound! He nearly drowned.

'When we landed we were sent off to hospital to check we were OK. We'd been in the water for several hours. On Christmas Day morning we were walking down Bridlington promenade and lo and behold there was my aircraft on the beach - it hadn't sunk!'

By the end of 1940 the 'Big City' was bombed on ten occasions, the last on 20th/21st December when 125 aircraft were dispatched to the capital, Gelsenkirchen and the Channel ports. Flying Officer Geoffrey Leonard Cheshire, a Whitley pilot on 102 Squadron at Topcliffe wrote: 'Once again "met" reported severe icing conditions reaching up to 15,000 or 16,000 feet. This time I adopted different tactics. I put my faith in the forecast and flew all the way below it at 1,000 feet. Unfortunately, we passed clear over Den

Helder where the guns were unusually active, but they missed us. The clouds broke, but not before we had begun to think we were going to look stupid; none the less they did break and we climbed up to our height without so much as hearing the rattle of ice off the airscrews. The others were not so fortunate: they tried a straight climb and ran into more than they had bargained for. In fact all of them except "Jackie" were forced to turn back. "Jimmy" [Ross James] suffered the most. He lost both engines fifty miles out to sea and was down to 2,000 feet before they picked up again: what was more, he nearly lost his nose through frostbite. Poor old "Jimmy".'[23]

From January to early March in 1941 there were no further trips to the city, but Berlin was never left untouched for long, weather permitting. On 12th/13th March, Bomber Command flew 257 sorties against targets in Hamburg, Bremen and Berlin. These raids came after the second Blitz on Portsmouth on 10th/11th March when over one thousand people were rendered homeless by thousands of incendiaries and hundreds of HE bombs dropped on the city. The raid, like the one on Coventry which had remained uppermost in Robert Kee's mind, had a profound effect on George Carter, a Whitley navigator. He was on one of the fourteen Whitleys bound for Berlin with another thirty Hampdens and twenty-eight Wellingtons. Using sheets torn from his log, at 2020 hours he began writing a few paragraphs to his girlfriend Nicole. 'As you can see from the address, I am on the job. It is the first time I have been to the "Big City" and as I have nobody else to tell the great news, I tell you. We are at present sixty-four miles off the English coast, a lovely night, moon as near as dammit full. We are punching the old kite along at about 8,000 feet to get full benefit of a favourable wind over this long sea crossing (three hours) and I have not a lot to do. I started to write this note in ink, but the reduced pressure up here has forced it all out and the pen won't work, so I'm reduced to pencil now. I shall have to break off for a while now as I have to work out some wireless bearings and switch on one of the auxiliary tanks and check our drift by flame float. It's getting cold - 0° on the clock now, and a cold white moon lighting up the plane... I hope we knock the blazes out of the target (which incidentally is the post office in the centre of the city). Before, I have always felt sorry for the people down below, but the other night I came over Portsmouth on the way home and saw it afire. I saw an explosion about 2,000 feet high. So now I feel different about it and I shall not be too careful to hit the post office.

---

23  *Bomber Pilot* by Group Captain Leonard Cheshire VC OM DSO DFC, first published in 1943 by Hutchinson & Co Ltd.

I have got one bottle, one brick and one piece of concrete to throw out with some personal messages to the Hun.'

At 0120 Carter continued: 'Well that was Berlin that was. Their AA was mustard - shook me rigid. We appear to be doubtful about our position so some work must be done ... The flak over Berlin was very accurate and the searchlights held us at 18,000, AA going off all around us - I bet we're full of holes. The shells keep bursting in front of us, and me being in front with the bomb sight, kept getting the smoke in my eyes. Was I scared? I'll say I was scared! I let our bombs go in the middle of the city. I hope they helped our war effort. I could not see where they landed...' The bombing was very scattered, sixty buildings were hit but none was considered destroyed. Three aircraft, including a Whitley on 102 Squadron piloted by Flight Lieutenant Frank Hugh Long DFC, which crashed at Denekamp, failed to return. Long, a tall New Zealander known as 'Lofty' to his crew and three of his crew members were killed. The navigator, Sergeant William Edward Van Klaveren, one of seven sons born of a Dutch farmer who married in England survived the crash of the aircraft but died of diphtheria in captivity on 4th May. Another Whitley on 102 Squadron returning on one engine crashed at Ringstead in Norfolk trying to land at Bircham Newton killing the skipper, Pilot Officer Fred Malin and one of his crew and injuring the three others. Four bombers were lost at Hamburg and Bremen. A further raid on Berlin, on the night of 23rd/24th March by thirty-five Wellingtons and twenty-eight Whitleys fared little better.

'In the spring of 1941 our people were doing very little offensive,' wrote 'Jimmy' Malley, a Wellington navigator on 149 Squadron at Mildenhall who completed thirty operations. 'We were the only people that were taking any offensive action at all. I think we went to Hamburg about three or four times. Hamburg raids always were frightening efforts, absolutely. The noticeable difference was the intensity of ground fire. We were hit over Hamburg; nothing serious, and the crew remained uninjured. But most of all we hated Berlin. That was because of the length of time we were in the air. Flying time to Berlin was about nine or ten hours in a Wellington. If you saw fire on the ground, you checked to see if you thought that was the target. We were so spread out by the time we got to the targets, that we weren't really an awful lot of help to each other; we weren't communicating at all with the other aircraft. You usually had about two hours' spare petrol. The long trip home was the worst thing of the lot. Sometimes, if my navigation wasn't quite good enough we would come under fire on the way out. But by then I had learnt the major areas to miss. We were learning the whole time.

You went more on what you experienced than on what you were briefed. The trouble about the Wellington was, once it got to about 8,000 or 9,000 feet it froze up. All heating went because it was water heating. We were over Berlin one night when we ran into thick cloud. We were an hour and a quarter over the city, waiting. Stupidly I had taken off my glove and I hadn't even a window below me; it was open. The temperature was probably about minus 5° or 6° at that height. When eventually I saw a small gap in the clouds, I got ready to bomb and I suddenly realised I couldn't press the tit with my right hand at all. I had to use my left hand to press the tit and my right hand has never really recovered from that.'

At Waterbeach on Wednesday, 9th April Sergeant Alfred Jenner, a wireless operator-air gunner on 99 Squadron who had flown twelve operations since joining the squadron from 15 OTU (Operational Training Unit) at Harwell in mid-November 1940 was 'on' that night. 'At Waterbeach we played a guessing game,' he recalled later. 'If there was a "breeze" that an op was on that night we would watch the petrol bowsers refuelling the "Wimpys" and note the number of gallons. If it was about 400 gallons that meant a trip to the Ruhr; if it was over 650, it must mean Berlin! Everyone was worried but did not show it. We had things to do to pass the rest of the afternoon. The wireless had to be checked and guns cleaned. At 5 o'clock that afternoon we entered the briefing room and sat down. At the end of the room was a large map, covered with a curtain. The Briefing Officer dramatically pulled the curtain aside and we were startled to see a red ribbon that seemed to go on forever! It meant a four and a half hour trip to Berlin. We all thought, "Jesus Christ! Why me?" '

Eighty aircraft - most of them Wellingtons (36) and Hampdens (24), as well as seventeen Whitleys and three Stirlings on 7 Squadron (on this bomber's first raid on Berlin) – set off in perfect visibility and nearly a full moon.[24] During March-April, 7 Squadron operated from the famous Rowley Mile strip because Oakington's grass runways had many soft patches and were unsuitable for the operation of heavy aircraft. The famous racecourse had been used as a landing ground for aircraft in the First World War. HRH the Prince of Wales landed at the strip in 1935 before travelling by road to attend the Jubilee Review at Mildenhall. After the Munich Crisis, in 1938, the Air Ministry took an interest in the area as a satellite for bombers at RAF Mildenhall. The Rowley Mile course, in about 300 acres north of the

---

24  Other aircraft attacked Vegesack and Emden and also dropped mines in the East Frisians. The operation on Vegesack cost two Wellingtons.

Beacon Course and Cambridge Hill, offered one of the largest grass landing and take-off runs - 2,500 yards - in an east-west direction. Although long and flat, crews had to remember to hurdle the twenty foot high Devil's Dyke running along one boundary. Accommodation for air and ground crews was in the racecourse administration buildings, the grandstand and requisitioned housing locally until new huts could be built.

At Waterbeach this operation - his thirteenth - would be 'Alf' Jenner's first with a new crew captained by Squadron Leader David Torrens, their new Flight Commander. 'As he was new to Bomber Command,' continues Jenner, 'it was decided to give him the most experienced crew. I was by now something of a veteran with twelve ops and I became Torrens' front gunner. First WOP was Arthur Smith; a splendid wireless operator who had served in the pre-war RAF in Iraq. The second pilot was Eric Berry, who came from a well-off Yorkshire family and who had flown private aircraft before the war. His wartime training had been short; converting straight from a Tiger Moth to a Wellington. Although he had only flown two or three ops he was well thought of and was about to skipper his own crew. Our rear gunner was Pilot Officer Palmer and our observer, Flying Officer Goodwin, who was from Ipswich.

'After briefing finished we ate our Flying Supper in the mess. It was rather poor fare, usually corned beef and chips, bread pudding and tea. Everyone was in a high state of nervousness and excited hysteria, although no one showed any sign of despondency. We were quite well trained and highly motivated.'

Although Jenner was not superstitious, he felt prompted to write to his wife. At 1900 hours the crew truck nicknamed 'Tumbril' took the crew to the infamous 'R-Robert' waiting at dispersal. Jenner recalls: 'It was really dark, cold and clear. A bomber's moon shone overhead. I climbed into the astrodome area and stowed my parachute. Our pilots wore theirs in flight. As we taxied out and lined up on the new tarmac runway I gripped the astrodome hatch clips, in case I needed to get out quickly, as I always did. We were away first. Torrens thundered down the runway (our bomb load was small because of the need for extra fuel). With flaps full on we climbed slowly into the sky above Waterbeach. I climbed into the front turret immediately (enemy fighters might already be about).'

'Grinding away slowly we headed for Southwold, our point of departure,' continues Jenner. 'Nearing the coast of Holland I exclaimed, "Enemy coast ahead!" There were a few shots then all was quiet again. The captain talked quietly to us, telling us to keep our eyes peeled. Then the fun began. A succession of searchlights picked us up and passed us on from one to another until we could see the multitude of coloured flak bursts over Berlin. We had been told that there were 1,000 guns at Berlin. They couldn't all fire at us but it felt like it. Down below, Lake Wannsee shone in the moonlight. Buildings, or imagined buildings, appeared in the Berlin suburbs below.

'We could actually smell flak. The Germans were very good gunners. A shell knocked out one of the engines. Fortunately, it did not catch fire. Torrens feathered the prop. We dropped our bombs and droned away. Nearing Brunswick Torrens came on the intercom. "Sorry to tell you chaps but we will not make it back. You will each have to decide if you want to bail out or stay in the aircraft for a crash-landing."

'I had previously decided that should such an occasion occur, then I would jump. I looked at the altimeter. It read 1,100 feet (300 feet less than recommended). The ruddy bulkhead at the front prevented me from turning the turret door handle. (To bail straight out of the turret would have taken me into the turning props.) To my relief, Eric Berry opened it from the other side. Goodwin and I bailed out. The four remaining crew stayed with the aircraft which crash-landed at Wolfenbüttle near Hanover. They set fire to the aircraft before being taken prisoner. Goodwin and I joined them.'

Another two Wellingtons, a Whitley and a Stirling I flown by 20-year-old Flight Lieutenant Victor Fernley 'Farmer' Pike DFC on 7 Squadron, which was shot down by Feldwebel Karl-Heinz Scherfling of 7./NJG1, were lost on the Berlin operation. Pike and five of the crew, including 19-year-old Sergeant William Edward Osterfield, one of the three WOp/AGs, were killed. The only survivor was the 23-year-old flight engineer, Sergeant Charles MacDonald, who was taken prisoner. The Stirling crashed near Lingen, Germany. Stirling N6009 skippered by Flying Officer J.F. Sachs had returned early to Newmarket with engine overheating after developing a propeller fault over the Dutch coast and N6005 captained by Flying Officer Graham Baptie Blacklock, having been damaged on the outward journey from an attack by a night-fighter, bombed Emden.

Flight Lieutenant 'Ken' Batchelor on 9 Squadron had taken Wellington 'S-Sugar' off from Honington, Suffolk at 2025 hours. 'The mist cleared to perfect visibility and there was a full moon. Just after crossing the Dutch frontier we could see the searchlight barrier running right down from Emden. As we got closer we could see also that they were coning one or two of our chaps with about thirty searchlights. We saw five aircraft downed in about ten minutes. Later, another crew reported having seen six parachutes from one. On and on we went on track, over the huge lakes and on to the north of Hanover, which was very busy pasting someone. We came in south and saw plenty of activity over Brandenburg. We stooged on, fairly unmolested, picking up a railway line to follow it to the target. Over the centre of Berlin, with the Wilhelmstrasse plainly visible, suddenly - ching! A wandering master searchlight found us and immediately thirty more coned and caught us perfectly. It was as bright as daylight in the cockpit and we were completely blinded. We bombed and then began weaving round and round and up and down to lose them, but still they stuck fast, and then the apex, with us in it, was filled with all the heavy flak that they could put up. We could see the yellow bursts everywhere with red-hot shrapnel, the puffs lit up by searchlights and the concussions bumping us all around as the close ones crumped and cracked in our ears, above the roar of the engines. We could not get out. After what seemed like hours we cleared and got out south. We had been thoroughly pasted and it scared all of us more than any of us had been scared before!'[25]

The German official communiqués admitted that the three-hour raid caused 'considerable damage'. The Berlin News Agency said that 'The RAF bombed up and down the Unter den Linden. High explosives and incendiaries were dropped on residential areas and public buildings and two hospitals were hit. Incendiaries gutted the attic of the famous Prussian State Library and the Staatsoper Unter den Linden (State Opera House), which firemen reported was "a complete loss".[26] Several people were killed and injured.' It went on to claim that, 'flak and fighters shot down eleven bombers, seven before reaching Berlin'. Dense smoke hung over Berlin long after the raid and attracted hundreds of spectators but the fire was roped off. Hundreds of yards of hose criss-crossed the Unter den Linden in the heart of the German capital where incendiaries apparently came down in bundles and fell on many other buildings in the famous thoroughfare. Bombs also hit William I's Palace, the University and the Schlöss Bellevue in the Tiergarten district and also damaged office buildings.

An Air Ministry communiqué stated that 'Large fires were started in the centre of Berlin, where powerful explosives also burst... The raid was made under a moon that was almost at the full. As our bombers neared the German capital all the defences of the city sprang into action... Before midnight bombs were seen to burst near the main railway station and others exploded in a large goods yard. As the attack progressed then the number

---

25   See *Out of the Blue: The Role of Luck in Air Warfare 1917-1966* edited by Laddie Lucas (Hutchinson 1985).

26   It was rebuilt during the Cold War period, under the German Democratic Republic government.

of fires increased and in the third hour of the raid a great fire spread in the heart of the capital, from which tremendous clouds of smoke surged high into the air. Most of the pilots came under very heavy fire, but there were moments when the weight of the attack baffled the defences and a few British aircraft were able to slip through unscathed. There were barriers of searchlights to catch our bombers and after one bomber had almost cleared one of these walls of light, a German fighter came in from astern and opened fire. The British rear gunner held his fire and then answered with a short burst. The enemy held on to his course until he had passed the bomber, but before he had time to turn the British front gunner had got him in his sights and loosed a burst. A second or two later the fighter was silhouetted against the moon and then dropped like a stone with smoke pouring from him.'

A follow-up raid on Berlin by 118 aircraft on 17th/18th April was largely thwarted by haze over the two aiming points. Eight aircraft failed to return from the Berlin operation and two Wellingtons were lost from the ten that set out to bomb Cologne. Five of the aircraft that were lost were Whitleys, three of them on 77 Squadron at Topcliffe, one of whose crews ditched sixty miles off Blyth in Northumberland. They and a 58 Squadron crew skippered by Pilot Officer Andrew A. Law that also came down in the North Sea, were both rescued. A Wellington crashed near Combe Martin in Devon returning from Berlin. This was the largest total lost on night operations so far in the war, but raids on the German capital and other cities were having an effect. In Berlin deep shelters away from buildings and water mains were being hastily constructed. The Unter den Linden district was suffering severe damage and the Opera House, the War Museum (which contained the death mask of Hindenburg) and the old Royal Stables had been hit.

'You will direct the main effort of the bomber force, until further instructions, towards dislocating the German transportation system and to destroying the morale of the civil population as a whole and of the industrial workers in particular.' In these words Air Marshal Sir Richard Peirse, Commander-in-Chief of Bomber Command was instructed on 9th July 1941 to open a new phase of the air offensive against Germany.

# Chapter 2

# The Point of the Spear

*'We accepted the fact that as a necessary part of the prosecution of the war there were civilian deaths. It occurred in Britain, it occurred in Germany. One got used to the fact that civilians were suffering and they were suffering all over the eastern front and the Jews in eastern Germany. Everyone accepted that this was total war. We were doing the job we were asked to do and we thought it was essential under the circumstances we were in. Without America in the war the only way we could hit at the Germans was through Bomber Command. The whole attitude of Bomber Command was that we were the point of the spear and we had a job to do. It was highly dangerous. We had to accept that in modern war civilians were killed. In our eyes we were in a desperate situation and we knew it. The trials of the German nation did not worry us an awful lot.'*

**Flying, Farming and Politics (2004) by Squadron Leader George Mackie, Lord Mackie of Benshie DSO DFC. At the outbreak of war and standing 6 feet 4 inches in his socks, he was a strapping trainee farm manager in East Anglia. When war was declared in 1939 he volunteered for the RAF and became an observer/navigator, surviving three operational tours - more than seventy operations - in Bomber Command. On his squadron (115), only seven out of thirty crews survived their first operational tour of twenty-five raids and he admitted that drink had a large part in keeping the tension down. Many beery nights were spent in the 'Cutter Inn' in Ely, near 115 Squadron's Witchford, Cambridgeshire base. He would say that the landlady made a major contribution to the war effort by looking after the airmen so well. By the end of the war,**

**115 had the distinction of being the squadron with the
most operational service, most losses by any one single
unit and the most tonnage of explosives dropped.**

In July 1941 Air Marshal Sir Richard Peirse had, on paper, a nominal
strength of forty-nine bomber squadrons, or almost 1,000 aircraft, but eight
of these squadrons were equipped with Blenheim light bombers. There were
eight squadrons of the new twin-engined Manchesters, but four were not
yet operational. On 13th April 1941 all Manchesters had been temporarily
grounded due to a higher than expected number of engine bearing failures.
On 16th June a second grounding of the type was ordered due to continuing
engine troubles. The Manchester was only just capable of remaining in the
air on one engine, as Flight Lieutenant 'Kipper' Herring on 207 Squadron
discovered one night. After throwing out everything that was not bolted to
the airframe, including the machine guns and the Elsan, 'Kipper' Herring
brought his Manchester back from Berlin, below 1,000 feet all the way and
received an immediate DSO. Rumour was that at one point Herring's crew
had nothing left to throw overboard but their trousers and were starting to
dismantle the airframe to save an extra pound or two of weight to make
it back over the North Sea.[1] The unserviceability of the Vulture engine
forced squadrons to make use of obsolete bombers such as the Hampden in
its place. Upon the restart of operations that August, additional issues with
the aircraft were encountered; the problems included excessive tail flutter,
hydraulic failures and faulty propeller feathering controls. So for the time
being at least, Peirse had to rely mainly on the Wellington squadrons, for so
long the backbone of Bomber Command operations.

Another new aircraft, the Halifax, was just coming into service and
on 25th/26th July two of them on 35 Squadron at Linton-on-Ouse took
part in a raid on Berlin for the first time. One of the seven Stirlings that
were dispatched ditched in the North Sea and all on Flight Lieutenant
F. Thompson's crew were taken into captivity after being adrift in their
dinghy for four days. A second Stirling piloted by Flight Lieutenant
M.C. Sherwood on 7 Squadron at Oakington was hit by flak over Berlin
and crashed at Ouddorp in Holland. All the crew was taken into captivity.
The Halifax skippered by 26-year-old Pilot Officer Ernest Ronald Peter
Shackle Cooper was shot down. All of Cooper's crew died.

---

1  Jack Bushby quoted in *Bomber Group At War* by Chaz Bowyer (Ian Allan Ltd, 1981).

# THE BERLIN BLITZ BY THOSE WHO WERE THERE

In August 1941 a record sixty-seven RAF bombers were shot down by flak and fighters. On 2nd/3rd August, fifty-three aircraft - forty Wellingtons, five Stirlings and eight Halifaxes - were detailed to bomb Berlin. Flight Lieutenant Leonard Cheshire (later Group Captain Cheshire VC DSO DFC), who having completed his first tour of operations on 102 Squadron in January had immediately volunteered for a second tour, was piloting one of the Halifaxes on 35 Squadron. 'It was the first raid of the season and therefore the defences were not prepared, which as it happened, was just as well, because of the four aircraft scheduled to be there at the same time three failed to take off.' He had only got a new crew together the night before and they had not had time to get used to one another. Martin, his rear gunner was a wiry bus conductor from Tunbridge Wells who had only done three trips but already could boast a DFM. Then there was 'Jock', once a customs official from Leith, now a wireless operator with the experience of thirty-four trips. 'Paddy' from Londonderry, as yet no trips to his credit, but six years' service in the RAF was the flight engineer. In the nose was Crock. Tall, crinkly dark hair and good-looking, from London town. Second pilot was Stead. Young and fair and until you grew to know him, shy, but nothing violent seemed to bother him. Before the war he was studying to be a vet. Then, most important of all, there was Sergeant G.J. Henry, the navigator. On the night of 8th/9th September 1939, six days after war had been declared, he was on a Whitley on 102 Squadron that was forced down at Nivelles aerodrome in Belgium during a 'Nickeling' raid.

All of Flying Officer W.C.G. Cogman's crew were interned, first of all in police headquarters in Brussels and then in a fort in Antwerp. They remained there until the Germans invaded. After many days of walking and hitch-hiking and camping in the open Henry reached Boulogne and crossed to England on the Isle of Man packet.

Writing about the Berlin raid Cheshire said: 'It was a curious sensation being over Berlin alone and we were glad to escape with only a few holes. That was the start and so on it went: Berlin, Cologne, Berlin, Duisburg, Berlin, Essen and again Berlin. All of it routine and most of it unexciting.' Cheshire was to become legendary in the annals of the RAF. At Woodall Spa later in the war some American officers from a nearby airfield had been invited for a few drinks and to compare tactics. One rather boastful young American pilot was telling anyone who would listen, that he had now completed six missions over Germany and he appeared to think that this was something of a record. He turned to Cheshire who had been leaning against the bar listening politely and enquired, 'And how many missions have you done Sir?' Cheshire thought for a moment and then said, 'Let me see, I think it must be over a hundred by now…'[2]

On 12th/13th August seventy aircraft were detailed for another raid on Berlin. Forty 'Wimpys', nine Stirlings, nine Manchesters and a dozen Halifaxes were on the Battle Order. The aiming point was the Reichsluftfahrtministerium or RLM (Ministry of Aviation), built in 1935-36 and bounded on the north by the Leipzigerstrasse and on the east by the Wilhelmstrasse and the south by Prinz-Albrechtststrasse. On the western side was the building of the former Prussian House of Representatives, but by 1943 this housed the Aero Club. The site of the ministry covered 400,000 square feet, 250,000 of which was the building itself. It had 2,800 rooms and offices, 4,000 staff and had extensive bomb and gas proofing.[3] But only thirty-two bombers reached and bombed in the Berlin area and the Ministry was untouched. Three Manchesters, three Wellingtons, two Halifaxes on 76 Squadron at Middleton-St-George and Stirling 'N-Nuts' on 15 Squadron, which crashed at Berxen near Bremen, were lost.[4] Sergeant J.D. Jeffrey was taken prisoner but three of his crew, two of them Canadians, were killed.

'F for Freddie' on 142 Squadron piloted by Flight Lieutenant Alexander 'Doug' Gosman was one of the 'Wimpys' that failed to return. He and Flight Lieutenant R. McD Durham the navigator and Sergeant Leslie 'Pinky' Frith the wireless operator had flown Fairey Battles in the disastrous air campaign in France in May 1940. Gosman's Battle was the first operational aircraft to land at Britain's newest airfield at Binbrook, opened only days after the evacuation from Dunkirk. Sixty per cent of the squadron did not return to England and the demoralized survivors were sent to Binbrook, eleven miles south-south-west of Grimsby to re-equip with Wellingtons. Frith was almost at the end of his tour. Born in Bradford, he had joined the RAF as a regular in 1938. When the German armies began their attack on Holland and the Low Countries in May 1940 his squadron had been at Berry-au-Bac near Rheims. 'It was like flying in a bus after the Battle,' he recalled. 'It was also a totally different bombing concept for us. We had been trained in dive bombing and low-level attacks and we found ourselves as part of a strategic bomber force in 1 Group.' 'Les' met and married a girl from Grimsby and

---

2  Quoted in *A Bird Over Berlin* by Tony Bird DFC.

3  *Bombers Over Berlin* by Alan W. Cooper.

4  Four Wellingtons failed to return from the raid on Hanover by 65 Wellingtons and thirteen Hampdens.

they had settled into a pleasant cottage in Stainton-le-Vale, just a short cycle ride from RAF Binbrook. Now, over Berlin, he had swapped the delightful vale for the valley of death. 'The flak was terrible,' Frith says. 'We had never seen anything like it. We managed to drop our bombs and had just turned for home when we saw another bomber hit by flak and blow up. Then we were coned in the searchlights. The port engine was hit and we began to lose height. We tried everything we could do to keep her flying but it was useless and the pilot gave the order to bail out.' Frith remained at his wireless set relaying to Binbrook what had happened until, with the aircraft at 1,500 feet, he bailed out, landed in a cabbage field and within a few hours was captured, so beginning almost four years of imprisonment. He was joined in captivity by Sergeant K.S. Holman the front gunner and Sergeant J. Jackson RNZAF the rear gunner.

On return a Stirling on 13 Squadron flown by Pilot Officer J.E.M. Conran, crash-landed at Honington. A Halifax on 35 Squadron captained by 24-year-old Pilot Officer Jack McGregor-Cheers crash landed at Salhouse in Norfolk. (McGregor-Cheers and crew were killed a fortnight later on 24th/25th August at Düsseldorf). The Halifax skippered by Sergeant John McHale on 35 Squadron crash landed on return to Middleton St. George. All the crew was killed. One of the two missing Halifaxes on 76 Squadron was piloted by Sergeant C.E. Whitfield, which crashed at Wesermünde with five crew dead. The other was flown by Flight Lieutenant Christopher Chevalier Cheshire. When war broke out he was in the middle of his second year at Oxford, studying law. Leonard, his older brother by two years, was certain that he saw his brother shot down by flak less than a mile away. 'As the flames broke out, most of the guns closed down,' wrote Cheshire, 'but some of them - twenty or thirty or so - went on firing and their shells were bursting right among the wreckage. Fifty-five minutes we were under fire and then we left the defences behind. As on the way in, the route was free from guns but away on the starboard the barrage never ceased and all around the clouds were menacing. Twelve thousand feet: what a height to bomb from! [5]

'The weeks went by and the succeeding trips grew less eventful. "Jimmy" [Flying Officer Ross James DFC] was shot down over Berlin [on 2nd/3rd September] and I thought, "Well, really this is too much."' Then one morning came the news that he was waiting for so long. His brother

---

5  *Bomber Pilot* by Group Captain Leonard Cheshire VC OM DSO DFC, first published in 1943 by Hutchinson & Co Ltd.

was safe. 'What wild rejoicing there was that day and what a weight off my heart! "Willy" [Flying Officer G.S. Williams, shot down on Turin on 10th/11th September] was safe too, in the same camp, but "Jimmy" was dead. Then came a letter from Christopher - safe and sound [in prison camp] and soon after his engineer [Sergeant P.H.T. Horrox] wrote describing what had actually happened.'

'We were flying fairly high through a barrage of AA fire when a group of searchlights caught and held us. We tried to get out of them but found we could not. Things were getting bad and to settle everything, an explosive shell burst on the tail wheel, which set the machine uncontrollable and a deathly silence from the rear gunner [Flight Sergeant William Woods]. The machine started into an ever-increasing dive when the captain gave the order to jump. The wireless operator [Sergeant E.C. Gurmin] and observer [Sergeant "Reggie" Wash] and second pilot [Flight Sergeant G.J. "Slim" Smalley] jumped in turn; the captain happened to be at the next escape hatch, with me very close behind. By this time the machine was diving steeply and the captain, regardless of himself, stepped over the hatch and let me go first, which I did. The rest of the crew landed safely by 'chute, but I regret we presume both rear gunner and front gunner [Sergeant Alexander Thompson Niven] dead, because we had not seen or heard anything of them. We think the rear gunner was killed by the explosive shell and the front gunner had not time to get out.'

On 7th/8th September, Leonard Cheshire's third wartime birthday, 197 aircraft - 103 Wellingtons, forty-three Hampdens, thirty-one Whitleys, ten Stirlings, six Halifaxes and four Manchesters were given three aiming points in Berlin. The weather was perfect and the moon was full. 'Who could ask for a finer set of circumstances?' wrote Cheshire.

Sergeant J. Ralph Wood, a Canadian navigator/bomb-aimer (Observer) from Moncton in New Brunswick, would never ever forget his introduction to 102 Squadron, thirteen months after joining the RCAF. 'Arriving at Topcliffe around midday on 25th July, the officer commanding informed me that I would be on that night's raid to Hanover. Who? Me? Why, I hadn't even unpacked my kit bag. Our commanding officer was a queer one. We called him "Curly", but not to his face. He was RAF permanent force and had been stationed in India too long. We thought he'd gotten too much sun out there. He was baldish and had a remarkably long, red handlebar moustache, which he took great pride in. I noticed during my stay that anytime he put himself down to fly, the operation would be a comparatively easy one. How unlike Pilot Officer Cheshire, who was later to become Group Captain Cheshire, winning the vc and other decorations. He was described as a mad man who always picked the dangerous targets like Berlin for himself. Some say this was partly because his brother was shot down over Berlin.

'I watched the flight's chief navigator go through his routine preparing for the flight. I watched him prepare his flight plan, get the meteorology report, go to the intelligence office for his secret coded information, on rice paper so you could eat it if necessary and other pertinent things to do before going off into that treacherous looking sky.

'That navigator and crew never returned.[6] He had suggested that he go in my place. That was a hell of an introduction, especially when stories were circulating about washing out the remains of a tail gunner with a hose; there was so little left of him.'

Ralph Wood, his two pilots, a wireless operator and a tail-gunner arrived back at Topcliffe without incident, which gave the Canadian sergeant a great feeling of relief and satisfaction. He found it hard to believe that he had been over Germany but harder to believe that he was back in England. 'At this stage of the game we didn't fly as a set crew. The members were interchangeable for various reasons. For my part I always made a quick appraisal of the pilot I was to fly with. How much confidence could I place in him? For that matter, how much would he have in me? We all had to depend on each and every crew member. We were a team - each relying on the other to do his job to the best of his ability. On three ops in October 1943 we had another Sergeant Wood as a crew member. He was a Scotsman. During my stay overseas my nickname was usually "Timber" or "Chips"; or just plain "Woodie".'

The trip to Berlin on 7th September was his eighth op. On his first trip he had found himself in the briefing room nervously preparing his charts for the raid and trying to appear calm and nonchalant, not wanting to appear to be too much of a greenhorn. After the briefing, the navigators gathered around the huge plotting table in the operations room and worked out their D.R. (dead reckoning) courses to get their crews to the target and far more important, home again. The dead reckoning was based on the predicted

---

6 The crew skippered by Squadron Leader Eric Alliott Verdon-Roe were one of two that were lost on 102 Squadron that night. They crashed west of De Kooy in Holland. All were killed. The skipper's famous father was Sir Edwin Alliott Verdon-Roe OBE HON FRAeS, FIAS the first Englishman to fly an all-British machine. His other son, Squadron Leader Lighton Verdon-Roe RAFVR DFC, died in action on 13 May 1943. With his brother Humphrey, Alliott founded the A.V. Roe Aircraft Co. on 1 January 1910.

winds as supplied by the met section, the airspeed, the groundspeed and the drift, as well as other information so important in their navigation.

'Before taking off we usually had a nervous pee beside the aircraft. This was much easier than trying to manipulate in the air. Many course corrections and adjustments were made during the trip from new information obtained in flight. The only navigational aids in these early days were from fixes obtained from the wireless operator and good only up to a limited number of miles from the English coast. As a matter of fact I soon learned to jokingly call my navigation - guestimation!'

Leonard Cheshire's rear gunner Richard 'Revs' Rivas agreed with his skipper that everything was perfect and he was able to map-read their way across Germany to Berlin. 'I had never seen the ground so distinctly at night before. Fields, rivers, lakes, railways, roads, all showed almost like day: I was even able to distinguish cornfields.'

When 21-year-old Bernard John Kemp joined the RAF in May 1940 he 'put in' for an observer's course, although it was his ambition to be a pilot. Above that ambition, however, was an impatient desire to get really flying and into the war. The authorities had informed him: 'You can get an observer's course in six months, but you will have to wait a year to go for pilot.' Kemp, therefore, went through all the normal routine agony of the Initial Training Wings at Hastings and the observer's course at Prestwick. Completing training at Louth in Lincolnshire on the first course to be held there, he remembered with some vividness the remark made by the officer who finally pinned upon him his observer's brevet. Said the officer: 'This is too easy. If I had my way, you chaps would do ten operational trips before you got one of these.' Precisely why any member of an aircrew, except the pilot, should be denied a brevet before having 'gone operational' escaped Kemp. The officer concerned however, need not have worried about young Kemp's justification of his badge in any way whatsoever. He was shortly to have more excitement than is normally crammed into ten operational trips, however arduous. At twenty-one he was a quick-thinking, highly imaginative man with a keen sense of observation. In the early days of his operational flying on Whitleys on 58 Squadron at Linton-on-Ouse, he noticed that some of the girls around, locally known as 'chop' girls, seemed to have a 'jinx' on aircrews. More than one of them was known to have been the special girlfriend of quite a string of men who went off in their aircraft and never came back. Kemp forced himself to go out with the one who had the most impressive list, just to show that he was not scared and felt as jumpy as the devil about it for some time afterwards.

Meanwhile, he was keen on his job and found astro-navigation absorbingly interesting. Much of the time when the other boys were beating things up at dances or at parties, he would be hanging out of the window of his billet, shooting star positions with his sextant. As a result of this practice, there came a certain evening - 7th/8th September 1941 - when he was the only man on 58 Squadron to get his aircraft over its objective (Berlin) on time. The rest of the aircraft were delayed in reaching the target area owing to inaccurate wind-forecasting.

Kemp was observer on Whitley V Z6947 GE-S flown by Sergeant Kenneth McIntosh Newton, which took off from Linton at 2015 hours. Fortunately, it was a warm, balmy evening, Kemp's lively imagination had been bothering him. When he went to draw his Irvin suit, he noticed that the storekeeper had issued him with a second-hand one on which was marked the name of a man he knew to be dead. He tried to hand it back and asked for another, but the storekeeper inquired what all the bother was about and was there anything in that to make anyone 'windy'? To accept any such suggestion, or admit it even by inference, was more than any 21-year-old of self-respect could face. Kemp, therefore, took the dead man's suit without another word and went off. But he didn't take it to the aircraft; he stuffed it in a kitbag in his quarters and left it there when the time came to take to the air.

At this time Kemp was a seasoned man with seven completed operations behind him. He was not suffering from 'beginner's twitch' and, as he went out to the aircraft at its dispersal he was in a normal frame of mind. Kemp was probably one of the most normal types of people you could have found in circumstances of this kind. He was a stable character who did not regard himself as any form of hero and would be both horrified and embarrassed if anybody suggested any such thing. Nevertheless, a lively imagination is not always a pleasant thing to have and once again that evening Kemp found his own inconvenient. As the big Whitley aircraft started rolling and then began to gather speed down the runway, he saw a line of people standing at the grass edge. Undoubtedly they were just the ordinary people who either by duty or normal curiosity are on hand at any time of operational take-off in war. But, as the aircraft gathered speed and flashed past them, Kemp saw that they were all waving and he had a sudden desolate conviction that they were waving the aircraft and its crew a final farewell.

Those who like to deal in omens may find food for thought in this. Kemp admitted that he never remembered having had that impression on any previous take-off. He excused him by saying that at the time he was 'a bit keyed up' or the point at which the stable man finds added strength and the unstable has hysterics.

From that point however, Kemp was far too occupied with the business in hand to let omens and superstitions trouble him. The Whitley had as heavy a bomb load as was possible for its long trip to Berlin and back. It was carrying two 1,000lb bombs, four 500-pounders and a rack of sixty incendiaries weighing four pounds each. By later standards of the war, such a load was a pip-squeak, but the Whitley had been designed long before the war when targets at such a range as Berlin were not thought of seriously as objectives. Meanwhile, Kemp concentrated on his navigation.

The Whitley arrived over the German capital dead on briefing time - 2355. It was the only aircraft on 58 Squadron to get there with such perfect punctuality. But directly it arrived, the welcome it received from the ground gunners was more than enthusiastic. As Newton steadied the aircraft to make the run-up to his target, Kemp was conscious of a tremendous noise of bursting flak all around, constant flashing explosions and clouds of smoke wreathing back in the strong moonlight. The reception was as hot as he had yet known in his experience and he privately reckoned that they were going to be lucky if they got away without serious damage after they had spotted their precise target and dropped their load. Then, suddenly, he reared violently in his seat and hardly knew what had happened when he found he had collapsed back again. The first sensation had been as though some unseen giant had given him a terrific kick in the backside, but apart from the stunning impact which knocked his senses askew, he felt no pain. He realized that he was bleeding and a gingerly investigation showed him that he had been wounded in the right buttock. This was unpleasant, but as he began mentally to 'get back' to his surroundings, he realized something that was positively uncanny. All the noise, which had previously been so deafening, had now stopped. There was an eerie silence. It was suddenly borne in upon him that even the engines had stopped their strong, heavy drone. For a moment he had the unreal impression that the aircraft was empty. Then he saw that Newton and co-pilot, Pilot Officer F.R. Wilbraham, were still in their seats. At the same time he realized that the plug which connected his helmet earphones with the intercom was dangling clear. He saw that, in the wild jerk he gave after being wounded, he must have dragged the plug out of its socket. And as a result he had not heard his pilot's order, which had obviously been given, for the crew to bail out.

As clear thinking came back to him, Kemp decided that since the disabled and impotent aircraft was plumb over the centre of the city of Berlin, it was time for him to see that the object of the flight was carried out. Therefore, he released the bombs. As the aircraft lifted to the loss of their weight, he saw Wilbraham throwing him down his parachute pack. After which the 'second dickie' took a firm hold on his release ring and dived away. Kemp dragged himself close to the captain's seat and yelled out to know if there was anything he could do. Newton had his feet braced up in the 'crash' position. He shouted back that there was nothing anyone could do and told Kemp to get away as quickly as he could. Kemp dropped down to sit in the edge of the escape hatch with his feet dangling into space while he tried to tighten his straps. He took a dive but jerked at his ripcord almost too soon. As he turned head over heels in space he had the alarming sight of his pilot - chute narrowly missing the tailplane of the aircraft as it whisked overheard. A few minutes later Newton was dead, killed in the final crash when the Whitley struck the ground and disintegrated in flames. Pilot Officer Wilbraham and Sergeants L.E. Proctor and J. Ford were taken prisoner.

Meanwhile, for a few moments, Kemp went through a spasm of rather sickening pain. This was because the parachute harness around his body was looser than it should have been; the result of wearing no Irvin suit, because he would not wear one that had belonged to a dead man. The webs of the harness which passed down between his thighs therefore caught him awkwardly when the speed of his free fall was checked by the opening envelope above. The resulting pain was just as bad as many a rugger player or cricketer has had cause to remember. When a man's weight is almost entirely depending upon thigh straps of this kind, it isn't too easy to alter position and gain relief. Kemp heaved and hauled himself on his shoulder straps as best he could through sickening moments until he found some sort of ease. He realized that he was as brightly lit up as any music-hall star on the stage of the palladium. First, one searchlight found him. Then, as it steadied on the white mushroom of his parachute, others came swinging in vast sweeps across the sky to join the focus of the first. The pyramid of searchlights gradually followed Kemp down to the ground. He had a feeling of helpless nakedness in that glare as he came down the last few thousand feet. The AA guns were now thudding and banging a ferocious chorus all over the city as the rest of the raiders began dropping their bomb loads. As the vague darkness of the ground approached, he tensed himself, waiting for the sudden barking of machine guns, which he more than half expected would open up and riddle him with bullets when he came within range.

However, for once the German gunners restrained their well-known sense of humour. Not a shot was fired at him as he dropped down below the trajectory of the searchlight beams and fell quickly into what appeared like a mass of sea anemones, an area of thin, waving fronds which seemed to reach out to grasp him.

Kemp used his common sense and decided that it must be a forest. But it wasn't. As an example of the extraordinary tricks that the eyes of a sorely-strained man can play, it was just ordinary medium-length grass, with very hard, solid earth directly beneath it. Kemp hit the earth with a force that knocked the breath out of him, long before he reckoned he was within 20 feet of it. The thud caused him to bite his lip, heavily and painfully. But he still kept his head, plunged and struggled to free himself of his parachute harness before dropping down, relaxed, to regain his breath.

He was very quickly surrounded by a group of men who had evidently watched his descent in the searchlight display and were ready at his point of landing. From what he could see of their dress, they were farm workers. They treated him decently enough, helping him down into the cellar of a house nearby, where they were soon joined by some of the women of the establishment.

The place where Kemp had landed was just east of Berlin, in agricultural country. He spoke very little German but found it easy enough to make the farm folk understand that he was wounded. One of the men glanced at his blood-stained seat and gestured to him to take his trousers down but this he refused to do in front of the women. Somehow, there was a difference between making a public show of oneself and being treated by a trained hospital nurse. Both the men and the women seemed amused at his modesty, but they helped him to another cellar where a couple of the men undressed him. Then one of the women appeared with hot water and rough bandages and did her best for him while he was lying on his face. This woman earned his undying gratitude, for, during the four hours that he stayed there, and before men of the Luftwaffe arrived to take him away, she smuggled some chocolate to him. The men treated him decently too, to his surprise. They all gave him cigarettes and when he indicated he was hungry, brought him black bread, a coarse jam and some ersatz coffee, which was peculiarly bitter to his tongue. Apparently there was no sugar or milk available.

At last, a very young and smart officer of the Luftwaffe put in an appearance and saluted him with considerable ceremony. This man spoke fair English and remained just as polite and pleasant when Kemp announced that he was a sergeant and not the holder of a commission.

Throughout all this the shrewd Kemp suspected the usual build-up in which the confidence of captured men was very carefully gained by pleasant treatment in order that they might be persuaded to talk. He was not far wrong, for after humane treatment of his wounds he was taken to Dulag Luft near Frankfurt-on-Main, where, after refusing to give more than his name and number according to regulations, he was forthwith clapped into solitary confinement. Here he got very thirsty and asked for water. The guards brought him a rough-looking wine, but having heard about such things, he refused to drink it, knowing that it probably contained a relaxing drug that would put him off his guard. Later on he discovered that others were given the same treatment but made the mistake of drinking the wine and to discussing the type of aircraft in which they had been flying. It is a measure of Kemp's character that, even after three and a half years in Stalag Luft I at Barth near the Baltic coast in Pomerania, he was still periodically up for questioning and never disclosed any further details.

Of his life in prison camp throughout the years that followed, Kemp had little to say, other than a general description given by most men who have endured it. 'Oh well - it was hell, but somehow we got through.'

Sergeant Kemp got down on to British soil at Ford in Hampshire at 3 o'clock in the afternoon of 14th May 1945 and walked into his home in the district of Addington, Surrey at 3 o'clock in the afternoon two days later. He became a civil servant, happily married and the father of two young daughters.[7]

When 'Revs' Rivas had neared Berlin the suburbs appeared, getting gradually thicker until they were over the city itself. 'We cruised around - almost like a "Cook's tour" - he wrote, 'and I could see the houses, streets and parks as clearly as though I was looking at an aerial photograph. The moon was so bright that the searchlights were almost ineffective in their attempts to compete with its brilliance… The guns left us alone that night, too. Whether the shells were not bursting at our height, or whether we were just lucky, I don't know, anyway, we got off scot free. After we had dropped our bombs we cruised around a bit more before turning north on our long journey home!'[8]

Ralph Wood sat at his navigator's table behind the pilot's seat in the cockpit. As he neared the target he unplugged his oxygen lead, his intercom, and dragging his parachute with him, made his way to the bombsight in the nose of their flying coffin. 'I never used a bomb aimer during my tours. They appeared later on in the war and there weren't always enough to go

---

7  Adapted from *Jump for it! Stories of the Caterpillar Club* by Gerald Bowman (Evans Brothers London 1955). Gerald Bowman was a novelist who wrote *Sawdust Angel, Pattern In Poison Ivy* and *The Quick and the Wed.*

8  *Tail Gunner* by Squadron Leader R.C. Rivaz DFC, first published in 1943.

around. I felt that if I could get us to the target I should have the pleasure of bombing same. It was a long crawl in the darkness and without oxygen the going was tough. Reaching the bombsight and front-gunner compartment, I searched frantically for the oxygen connection to restore my strength. With the aid of a flashlight, partly covered so as not to attract any wandering enemy fighters, I found my connection and began breathing easier. I was now lining up the target with the bombsight as I directed the pilot on the bombing run - Left - Left - Steady - R-I-G-H- T - Steady - Left - Left - Steady - Bombs Gone! The aircraft leapt about 200 feet with the release of tons of high explosives. Now we flew straight and level for thirty seconds, the longest thirty seconds anyone would ever know, so that we could get the required photo of the drop for the Intelligence Officer back at Topcliffe. Picture taken; "Let's get the hell out of here". Still in a cold sweat with the flak bursting around and the searchlights trying in vain to catch them I crawled back to my plotting table. The pilot was still taking evasive action as I gave him the course for home. The black blobs of smoke surrounding the aircraft were flak and when I could smell the cordite it meant they were bursting "too damn close". On our homeward journey we got into our thermos of coffee and sandwiches of spam.'

The crew on Wellington 'S-Sugar' on 40 Squadron at Alconbury flown by Pilot Officer John 'Jo' Lancaster had problems after the target as he recalled: 'Weather was clear over the target and by the standards of those days the attack was successful. On the way home however, together with a number of our other aircraft, due to a big change in the forecast winds, we drifted too far north over ten-tenths cloud and flew back over Hamburg, Bremen, Emden, Wilhelmshaven et al. This route suffered almost continuous flak and eventually, down on our port side, we could see the causeway which crosses the entrance to the Zuider Zee. Just as we were all distracted by this sudden glimpse, a great shower of red tracer shot just over the top of us, followed by an Me 110. We quickly went into a tight defensive left-hand turn. The Me 110 went round in a wide left-hand turn and tried another attack. We went into a steep spiral dive, and in attempting to follow us the 110 presented a view of its belly to our rear gunner, Keith "Kiwi" Coleman, who raked it from end to end. It disappeared vertically into cloud at about 4,000 feet. Now, the limit in speed of a "Wimpy" Ic was 266 mph - officially. In the recovery from our dive, our airspeed was indicated as 330mph! We sustained no damage, either from the 110's efforts or by having exceeded our "limiting speed" by twenty-five per cent and arrived back at Alconbury after eight and a quarter hours in the air without overload tanks.'

'We landed back in the early light of dawn with the moon still light in the sky,' wrote Leonard Cheshire, 'and "Revs", as had been his wont in the past, carried my chute out of the aeroplane. He set his jaw at an angle, clamped his teeth on his pipe and smiled contentedly, like a cow.'

'Magnificent Leonard. Magnificent. The best trip I have ever done.'

'Yes "Revs", life's just starting. But I never thought I'd live to see Berlin as clearly as that.'

'It's the first time I've heard you sing down the intercom since last December. What were you circling round for after dropping the bombs?'

'I lived in Berlin once for four months, with Admiral von Reuter; I was looking for his house.'

'Did you find it?'

'No, but I saw the street, right by the Potsdam Lake. It stands out quite well.'[9]

Two Whitleys that were lost were claimed north of Berlin by Leutnant Rudolf Altendorf of 2./NJG3. Thirteen other aircraft - eight Wellingtons, two Hampdens, two Stirlings and a Manchester - also failed to return. That same night attacks on Kiel (where three aircraft were lost) and Boulogne (where forty-seven aircraft claimed excellent bombing results without loss) took the total effort to 303 sorties for eighteen aircraft shot down. This was the highest loss in one night thus far in the war. Good bombing in clear visibility was claimed at Kiel and by 137 crews attacking Berlin where it was reported that most bombs exploded in the Lichtenberg and Pankow districts, east and north of the centre. Damage was also reported to several war-industry factories, transport and public utilities and public buildings as well as a zoo, sixteen farms and 200 houses. Thirty-six Berliners were killed, 212 injured and 2,873 people were Ausgebombt [bombed out], some only temporarily.[10]

Arriving back without incident at Topcliffe, which they had left ten hours' earlier, Sergeant Ralph Wood felt quite elated. 'We had actually bombed the capital of Germany. But the trip wasn't that pleasant. Berlin in a Whitley! I don't believe it!' he wrote. 'At debriefing by the intelligence officers, accompanied by a cup of coffee laced with over proof rum, I was tired, but happy. Our real treat was the flying breakfast of bacon and eggs

---

9   *Bomber Pilot* by Leonard Cheshire. Flight Lieutenant R.C. Rivas DFC was killed on 13 October 1945 when his Liberator VI transport he was flying in crashed on take-off at Melsbroek in Belgium.

10   *The Bomber Command War Diaries; An Operational reference book 1939-1945* by Martin Middlebrook and Chris Everitt (Midland Publishing Ltd., 1985,1990,1995).

and our discussions of the attack with the other crews on the raid. Bacon and eggs were otherwise scarce as hen's teeth. At the ritual breakfast after every mission, there were empty tables - chairs, dishes and silverware aligned - for the men who weren't coming back.'

As he settled into squadron life he found that the best way to keep one's sanity was to separate your pleasures from your work. He didn't want to become one of those casualties found walking around the airfield talking to himself. 'There was the odd one who cracked up mentally and you really couldn't blame him,' he wrote. 'For relaxation we would frequent the pubs in the village of Topcliffe, Thirsk, Ripon and Harrogate. The nearest meeting place was the 'Black Swan' pub, or as we called it, the 'Mucky Duck', in the village of Topcliffe.'

In all Ralph Wood would fly thirteen operations on Whitleys. After completing his tour, finishing it on Halifaxes and surviving a very bad crash on a training exercise which killed his pilot, he flew another fifty trips on Mosquitoes in 1944, which included no less than seventeen operations to Berlin.

A follow-up raid on Berlin on 20th/21st September by seventy-four aircraft ended in failure when the force of Wellingtons and Whitleys was recalled because of worsening weather. Ten aircraft did not receive the signal and bombed alternative targets. None reached the capital. Three Wellingtons and a Whitley failed to return and a dozen more bombers crashed in England, including two in the North Sea and one in the Humber. Two Wellingtons on 75 Squadron RNZAF crashed in Norfolk trying desperately to get back to Feltwell. Pilot Officer Arthur Sidney Raphael crash-landed at Horning on the Broads without injury to the crew.[11] Sergeant John Anthony Matetich, 28-years-old, from Salisbury, Rhodesia and crew on 'X-X-ray' who had not received a recall signal had gone on to Berlin alone. Sergeant Lawrence Alan 'Joe' Lawton RNZAF the observer recalled: 'We returned to find that fog had closed all the airfields in our Group. We did not have enough fuel to go further so we were told to head the aircraft out to sea and bail out.' Lawton's aircraft had been hit by a Ju 88 over Boulogne in September 1940 and he was badly wounded by a 20mm cannon shell and was not expected to live but he recovered and by April 1941 was back again on ops. He was on the crew of Squadron Leader Reuben P. Widdowson on the night of 7th July when the second pilot, Sergeant James Ward RNZAF with a rope tied around

11    While on 467 Squadron RAAF, Squadron Leader Raphael DFC and crew were KIA on the Peenemünde raid on 17/18 August 1943.

his waist went out on the wing of their burning aircraft and extinguished the flames, an action which earned him the VC. Now, as Matetich gave up trying to reach an airfield before the fuel gave out, he ordered the crew to bail out. 'Joe' Lawton recalled: 'It was dark and I did not see the ground before I hit, cracking a couple of vertebrae. I eventually found a farmhouse. As I was carrying a parachute the farmer, who had opened the window, immediately produced a shotgun and was going to give me both barrels. However, I persuaded him instead to take me to the police station.'[12]

Twenty-one-year-old Sergeant R.F. 'Freddie' Whitehorn was a second pilot on Whitleys on 78 Squadron at Middleton St. George in the early autumn of 1941. Memories of his first trip, on Berlin, were not ones to cherish. 'I can't profess to be one of these brave types for whom it was all a great adventure. I think that went for most of us - actually, we were all scared stiff. Berlin shook me up a bit. As soon as we got over the French Channel coast, the flak opened up. That gave you your first taste of it. When you got within reach of Berlin they had a hell of a defence, guns and searchlights - searchlights everywhere. Particularly a blue one which searched till it found an aircraft: when it got you about twelve others coned you! You tried evasive action but you felt like you were walking into a public place without any clothes on, that's the feeling - completely naked and defenceless. Luckily we were never attacked by a fighter but I saw others of the squadron shot down by fighters go down in flames there. The flak was very heavy - it came in and ricocheted through the plane.

'The pilot used to scare me a bit. He'd have a few drinks in the mess before we went and keep dropping off to sleep, leaving it on "George" (the automatic pilot). We flew long distances on "George". It saved a lot of strain, but he was dozing there and I thought, suppose a fighter comes up? They gave us tablets to keep us awake - we used to take handfuls and hope for the best. The Whitley was a slow old thing. It flew along with its nose down. You felt very exposed because you were going so slowly. You could see the flak following you up and think that's bound to catch you - you see it start behind and keep bursting nearer and nearer. That's going to get me soon!

'We were usually told to bomb from about 16,000 feet so there'd be a lot of aircraft in a small space! We were told which target to hit - the navigator had all the details. He used to get it in the bomb sights, give the details of the

---

12  See *Out of the Blue: The Role of Luck in Air Warfare 1917-1966* edited by Laddie Lucas (Hutchinson 1985). 'Joe' Lawton was not on John Matetich's crew on their next operation, on 15 October 1941 when they were all killed.

run-up and let the bombs go. It was very easy to get lost. After one raid we got back to England next morning about six o'clock. It was getting light, but we hadn't the faintest idea where we were! We flew around for a while, getting short of petrol, we even considered ditching in a field with the undercarriage up. We were turning all these things over, discussing what we should do, when a Spitfire flew up alongside us. He saw we were an English plane so we followed him in. The first thing we did when we got down was to open our bomb doors and we found a thousand-pounder hung up! It had been triggered, so if we had crash-landed there would have been quite an explosion.

'I wouldn't say that the navigator was all that good. Once we nearly bombed Sweden. We were meant for Berlin and the navigator said, "Oh, there are lights over there, shall we go and bomb those?" That was Sweden! Lucky we didn't! We generally decided if there were lights on there must be some catch somewhere. They used dummy targets. They'd set a few things on fire hoping that you'd go and drop your bombs there and some probably did.

'If you had a fighter on your tail you'd be inclined to jettison your bombs there and then and get the hell out, or get into cloud if there was some about. The thing was the nights chosen for bombing raids usually had a moon and not much cloud. You could even have a few days' leave, go home and you'd get a telegram saying come back straight away because there's a moon period, with good visibility. They wanted as many crews as possible. So to hell with your leave, back you went to take advantage of the moon period.

'Berlin was one of the longest trips and Turin, over the Alps. But Italian flak was about 5,000 feet below us so we weren't bothered. In fact we laughed at it, took the mickey out of the Italians. We just cruised around at our leisure and dropped our bombs where we hoped was the right place. When you'd done six trips on Halifaxes as a second pilot you went back to Whitleys as a captain.'

By mid-October 78 Squadron was using Croft airfield as well as their home airfield and on 16th October Whitley Z6646 is believed to have been in the circuit of Croft when the starboard engine failed at low height during the NFT (Night Flying Test). 'We went out just as it was getting dusk to do two or three circuits and bumps,' says Whitehorn, who did the first couple of circuits without any incident, 'and then Pilot Officer "Bert" Smith took over.' Bertram Owen-Smith was born in Liverpool in April 1922, but when he was young he moved with his family to Swansea.

'On his first take-off he swung right off the runway - which could happen with twin-engined aircraft,' recalled Whitehorn. 'The torque is trying to push you one way and if you don't keep your rudder on the back stick you will swing off. That's what he did. We tailed through the rough. Whether he did the props in I don't know but we staggered off the ground and got to about five hundred feet.

'He said, "The undercarriage is not coming up!" "We'd better do a quick circuit and go in again if we can!"

'As soon as we said that the port engine started banging and cut right out. We tried to make a circuit as quickly as we could but with the one engine it was a bit difficult - we got into a sort of a flat spin. As I say, it was dark, we lost our bearings! We thought we saw the lights of the flare path but judging by where we ended up it must have been a railway siding. We were still trying to straighten it up but we hit the ground. Immediately, the starboard engine where I was sitting burst into flames. Then it was all fire, just like that, as quick as that! We were scrambling to get out. I was sitting next to the pilot.

'I didn't see him but apparently we both did the same thing, which was to try and get out by the pilot's escape hatch over the pilot's seat. I couldn't find it and I thought I'll go back down the fuselage - I wasn't too keen - you thought very quickly - all these thoughts run through your mind. To get down the fuselage you had to crawl under the fuselage petrol tank - I'm not too keen but I could only see that way out!

'The starboard side of the aircraft had broken open as we hit the ground - there was a river and we caught the undercarriage in the bank which took most of the shock off for us. I stumbled out and found myself on the engine that was on fire - got up quickly! It seemed the other pilot and the wireless op came out almost immediately. The rear gunner was down the other end away from the flames. He turned his turret and got out the back. He came up out of the darkness and we were wandering around for a minute or two like idiots until the ammunition and the flares started going up. Then we moved a bit further away. We found our clothes were on fire - we walked up to the river and splashed it over each other. Some locals came up to us and said are you English or German? We soon told 'em but they were very good actually. They took us down to a little village and the doctors gave us a drop of whisky and an injection for the pain.'

'Freddie' Whitehorn had been severely burned, especially his face, ears and hands. Pilot Officer 'Bert' Smith and Sergeant 'Gerry' Dufort, the Canadian observer, had also suffered serious burns. Sergeant Kidd the WOp/AG was only slightly injured.

'The RAF ambulance turned up and took us to hospital, which was quite near. Part of it was a mental hospital. They took us into the wards there and dressed our burns. They were wondering how to treat us and they were saying, well, the last burns they had, they'd put on treacle and flour! Luckily they didn't use it on us - they thought about it - they didn't realize how serious it was. They said in three weeks it'll be healed up, you'll just have pink skin there.

'Well, it was all quite a painful operation! They decided to put our hands in bunion bags which were a new thing then, sort of like plastic bags. They used to flush it through with a solution of milk and inflate it with oxygen. It's supposed to keep the plastic off your hands and enable you to move them at the same time. I must say we didn't think much of them. The bags didn't stay up; they came down on your hands which were extremely painful.

'They put gentian violet on our faces - my wife came to see me and she didn't know who was who. She saw three people sitting there with gentian violet all over their faces! But the nurses were very nice; they wanted to do their best for us. They had to feed us and they were very gentle and understanding how to feed us and do the usual functions for us. They couldn't do enough.

'After a while an RAF MO came to see us and he got us transferred to an RAF hospital. We were put in the newly opened burns ward there which was actually in the officers' wards. Some of the other patients were a bit "off" because we weren't officers, only NCOs.

'They had just got these newly introduced saline baths which were a great thing. They put us in and took our old dressings off. The relief was marvellous! We were there a few weeks until Sir Archibald McIndoe came along to see us. He said he'd take us down to East Grinstead for plastic surgery. I was there for the next two and a half years.'

All told, Berlin was attacked five times by RAF Bomber Command before the end of 1941. 'Winter began to show her traces and the Germans began to demonstrate what store they set by ground defence,' wrote Leonard Cheshire. 'The guns, it is true were much the same as ever, a little more powerful and a little more accurate, but where there used to be one, there were now two, three, four and in places even ten. And as for the searchlights, the change was remarkable. Once they had been ineffective at 8,000 feet, now they were effective as high as 18,000. I have never flown as high as that, so I rely on someone else's word, but at least they held us at 11,000 feet over Berlin. And this is only half the story: where before there were fifty or sixty, there were now two or three hundred and on a front reaching from Denmark right down south of Abbeville and stretching many miles inland; where once we had gambolled around in utter freedom, there was a festering bed, not of dozens or hundreds, but, whether you like it or not, of thousands. Yes, night bombing was indeed very different from what it had been eighteen months ago: night-fighters, and a continuous barrier of shells and searchlights, and, more aggravating still, a host of knobs and technical instruments which we would have scorned in summer 1940. But in spite of all this, the trips were no more interesting than before, nor were they any more exciting. For the simple reason that the work was no longer a novelty and that more technical skill was required; the first carefree, exultant joy was, perhaps, gone, but in its place appeared an atmosphere of quiet enjoyment.'[13]

On thirty-nine nights between 30th July and 31st December RAF bombers operated in weather variously described as 'bad', 'extremely bad', 'very poor visibility', 'thick cloud', 'icing' and 'ten-tenths cloud.' Conditions were never worse than on 7th November when the Battle Order for the 'Big City' totalled 169 aircraft: 1 Group, twenty-two Wellingtons; 3 Group, sixty-nine Wellingtons and seventeen Stirlings; 4 Group, forty-two Whitleys, ten Wellingtons and nine Halifaxes. This was the biggest force sent to Berlin up to that time. A further 200 Hampdens, Manchesters, Halifaxes and Wellingtons were dispatched to Cologne, Essen, Mannheim and smaller targets including the Channel ports. While weather forecasts spoke of cloud over the Ruhr the more severe weather lay to the north and especially in the area of the Bight and northern Germany generally. For the return conditions were expected to be good with clear visibility at the bases.

The noon weather forecast on 7th November showed that there would be a large area of bad weather with storms, thick cloud, icing and hail over the North Sea routes by which the bombers that night would need to fly to Berlin, Cologne and Mannheim and back. Even so the aircraft were allowed to take off. It was an important milestone for Bomber Command, the C-in-C, Air Marshal Sir Richard Peirse, having ordered a major effort with Berlin the main target. On the morning before the raid, the various bomber group planners got together over the conference telephones to consider the forthcoming night's work. First they heard what the met officers had to say. The forecast was by no means optimistic. Clouds would be building up to 15,000 feet over Germany and icing conditions were prevalent. A strong wind would be helping the bombers towards their targets, hindering then on the way back. It was not a good forecast, but it was typical of many nights during that appallingly bad winter of 1941/42. It did little

---

13 *Bomber Pilot* by Leonard Cheshire.

to allay the fears of many, Squadron Leader John Searby commanding 405 'Vancouver' Squadron at Pocklington, which was equipped with Wellington IIs, among them. This airfield in 4 Group in Yorkshire was like most others in Bomber Command country. Set in a small farming community, it had three pubs, an old Anglican church and two rather ordinary hotels, which would serve customers a very restricted wartime meal for five shillings. This was the top price allowed by the Government to any restaurant in wartime. The station itself was not a comfortable billet and in the bleak days of early November 1941 men shivered in the hutted accommodation common to many wartime airfields. 'It was a dreary camp,' wrote Searby. 'The Officers' Mess was short on warmth and comfort: I slept in a wooden hut where the draughts from the cracks between floor and wall caused my jacket, which hung on a peg, to swing gently to and fro until I plugged the gaps with newspaper. Accustomed to a dry cold the bitter winds of that first week in November tried the Canadians sorely and relief was found in bottle form - the party spirit was well to the fore and everyone joined in. A long way from home and stuck in a situation over which they had no control they accepted the weather, the wooden huts and the war with a cheerfulness which did them credit!'[14]

Born on 23rd April 1913 at Whittlesey, Cambridgeshire, and commissioned at the outbreak of war in 1939, Searby would become legendary in the annals of the Pathfinder Force. As he sat in the briefing room he listened to the Intelligence Officer armed with the latest information on the gun and searchlight zones. 'It was all matter of fact and nobody batted an eyelid. The ten crews of 405 Squadron sat passively accepting a repeat of that which they already knew. On the big wall map of Europe the green tapes crossing the North Sea to Denmark and on to eastern Germany, where the huge splodge of hatched green and red areas surrounded the target, drew their attention - and it seemed a very long way to travel. There were no questions - it was old stuff, anyway - and we passed on to the Met briefing. Outside it was a bitterly cold day with the sun occasionally breaking through yet there was no hint of bad weather so that when the Meteorological Officer hung up his chart showing a cross section of what was expected I received a jolt - just one thing caught my eye - the pillar-like cu-nim clouds standing in regular formation over the sea route to Jutland.

'Forecast temperatures were low and there was evidence of frontal activity off the Danish Coast. All in all I thought it likely to be a rough night.

---

14    *The Bomber Battle For Berlin* by John Searby (Guild Publishing 1991).

The convection clouds were not expected to rise much above 10,000 feet and there was risk of ice in such clouds. Over Germany heavy cloud could be expected with occasional breaks: this cloud could extend to 10,000 feet. Bomb loads for the Wellington IIs on 405 Squadron were 1 x 1,000, 4 x 500, 1 x 250 and two small bomb containers each holding ninety of the little incendiary bombs: no bad effort considering the distance to the target. The route to the target lay directly east from the Yorkshire coast to Denmark - for all 4 Group aircraft - whilst 1 and 3 Groups flew almost directly east from the Wash and Norfolk coast to the "Big City" following what was to become a well-worn track skirting the major cities of Osnabrück, Hanover and Magdeburg.

'Only the previous night I had attended a party in the ante room to welcome two visiting members of the Canadian Parliament - an occasion for everyone to speak up without fear or favour - and heard not a single voice raised in complaint... A different mood prevailed at our pre-flight supper and there was no enthusiasm for the task ahead. The weather map had done the trick; those tall "thunderheads" over the North Sea spoke a language well understood by all save the newest arrivals - and the latter were not represented in the tally of ten crews headed by Flight Lieutenant John Emilius "Johnny" Fauquier in command of "B" Flight.'[15]

Born in Ottawa, Ontario, on 19th March 1909 and educated at Ashbury College, Fauquier had entered the investment business in Montreal, Quebec, where he joined a flying club. After earning his commercial pilot's licence he had formed Commercial Airways at Noranda. A splendid flyer who had flown in all kinds of aeroplanes in the northern territories, he was really experienced and was regarded as a true warrior. Later known as 'The King of the Pathfinders', he made a name for himself as a tough individual of few words. His curt manner meant that he did not have to say a great deal. Few people knew 'Johnny' Fauquier off duty, partly because he was always 'on duty'. He had the reputation of being a terrific fire-eater, but if he trusted anyone, he trusted them completely. But a man only let him down once! Fauquier wrote: 'At briefing we were told our target was to be Berlin. When the Met Man came along with his chart I immediately smelled a rat: he was nervous and seemed unable to make up his mind about the wind velocity for the return to base.'

The risks in reaching Berlin, involving a round trip of 1,200 miles for British bombers, were great at any time and many of the aircraft that night,

---

15   Ibid.

with a full bomb load, would have very little range to spare. Aircraft in general use at the time were the 'old guard' of Bomber Command: the slow, tough and very reliable Whitley, the equally dependable Wellington and the Hampden. There were only a handful of the newer Halifaxes, Stirlings and Manchesters. The planning conference that morning must have considered all this and particularly the fact that the limited range of the Whitley made Berlin a critical target in the best of weather. Even on good nights the bombers normally based in northern England often took off from southern airfields to save fuel. The planners must also have discussed the probability that these aircraft would use up extra fuel by climbing to clear the forecasted cloud tops. There was little chance of flying through the clouds because of the severe icing forecast.

One who recalled the events of this dramatic day was Air Vice-Marshal (later Marshal of the RAF Sir John Cotesworth) Slessor, Air Officer Commanding 5 Group. 'I had been away visiting Bomber Command HQ that afternoon and on returning to my headquarters was met by our senior meteorological officer, Mr. Mathews, who told me in no unmeasured terms that in his view we should be undertaking a quite unjustifiable risk in sending the Hampdens to Berlin in the icing conditions to be expected. I had the utmost faith in him - he knew the aircraft and the crews and what could be expected of them almost as well as I did and I had no hesitation in diverting my group from Berlin to a closer alternative target and so informed Command.' Slessor telephoned the C-in-C that afternoon and stated that his Hampdens lacked the range to fly to Berlin and back given the forecasted strong westerly winds. No doubt frustrated by the recent long run of bad weather and poor bombing results, Peirse wanted to mount a major effort against Berlin but he allowed Slessor to withdraw his sixty-one Hampdens and fourteen Manchesters from the Berlin force and send them to Cologne instead. The target for fifty-three Wellingtons and two Stirlings of 1 and 3 Groups was Mannheim, which left 169 aircraft of 1, 3 and 4 Groups: a hundred and one Wellingtons, forty-two Whitleys, seventeen Stirlings and nine Halifaxes, to drop their bombs on three aiming points in Berlin. Just over ninety more bomber crews were given targets as far afield as Essen, Ostend, Boulogne and Oslo, where thirteen Halifaxes sowed mines.

Labouring under a maximum load of bombs and fuel they took off from airfields all over Eastern England and climbed painfully up through the gloom. Many had been briefed to land at southern airfields as there was little chance of them getting back to their own home bases. The first difficulties came soon. The weather had worsened in one slight respect; there were some cloud tops which were higher than the 'solid top' forecast. The slender margin by which the bombers would reach Berlin was cut and the heavily loaded aircraft were faced with a problem. They could fly through the clouds and risk icing up, which with their heavy load might prove critical, or they could fly round the cloud tops and use up their precious fuel.

'Johnny' Fauquier was one of many who carried vivid memories of that night. He wrote: 'Take-off was around 11 o'clock. All went well on the way out until we climbed out of the overcast which was solid all the rest of the way so that we had nothing but dead reckoning and forecast winds to get us to the target. Finally, we reached the point where we thought and hoped Berlin lay beneath - dropped our bombs and turned for home. It wasn't long before I realised we were in trouble because the winds had increased greatly in strength and were almost dead ahead. Eventually, I lost height down to a few hundred feet - to avoid icing conditions and to save fuel since the headwind would be less strong.'

Pilot Officer Harry Drake, who later became an Air Correspondent in London, was making his second operational trip as second pilot in a 10 Squadron Whitley and carried equally vivid memories of that night. Drake recalled that on the outward trip they were able to get their Whitley about 1,000 feet above the solid cloud. But stretching at least 4,000 feet higher were other cloud tops. 'We knew icing to be heavy and decided to go round the clouds. But we lost so much time and fuel in doing this that, by the time we had crossed into Denmark and the solid cloud had begun to break up, we knew that it would be useless trying to reach Berlin as we hadn't enough fuel left. Instead we searched along the north German coast and found Lübeck sufficiently clear for a visual bomb run and we bombed there.' What happened to Drake happened to many others and aircraft which should have gone to Berlin diverted to Lübeck, Warnemünde, Rostock, Kiel, Schleswig, Sylt and other towns because they knew they would have insufficient fuel to reach the German capital. But their difficulties were not over. 'We were still worried about the development of upper cloud,' says Drake of the return journey, 'and of the difficulties of making a descent through cloud when we got back home. It would have been more than tricky making a straight down blind approach with hills round the airfield, so we looked for a hole off the Danish coast and luckily found one. We spiralled down through it and found the bottom of the cloud only 500 feet above the sea. We returned all the way at 200-300 feet, met frequent thunderstorms and grand displays of St. Elmo's fire, although we were in no position to appreciate it! Most of our crew were sick all the way back.' But Drake and most of the others who had diverted from Berlin had the fuel reserves left to make a British airfield.

For those who struggled through to Berlin it was a different matter. In the first place, most of them flew straight through the cloud tops on the outward journey; they had to, otherwise they would not have had sufficient fuel left for the return journey. In the high cloud tops many iced up. Some got into difficulties and by the time they should have flown out of the cloud tops they were below the level of the solid cloud. At Berlin another surprise was waiting. A clear area had been forecast for the target region, but Berlin was far from clear. Not that this had any bearing on the ability of the aircraft to get back. Its main effect was to make bombing difficult. It was on the return journey that troubles began in earnest. One of the men who got to Berlin and back was Sergeant D.K. Brearey, who after the war ran his own business in Ipswich. Brearey made the trip in the rear-turret of a Whitley on 102 Squadron. He recalled that there was light flak over the target but no sign of enemy fighters. After a fairly successful bombing run Brearey's aircraft ran into bad weather. It was blown off course and lost its way and drifted over Hamburg where it was met by a lively flak barrage. 'Near the Dutch coast,' recalls Brearey, 'we ran into dense cu-nim cloud, iced up and both our engines cut out. My captain, Sergeant "Tony" Wickham, took the Whitley down in a rapid glide from 12,000 to 2,000 feet. In the centre of the cloud the wireless operator got a shock from his set, great chunks of ice flew off the props and wings and hit the fuselage. My turret was completely frosted over and I could see nothing. It suddenly became very cold and very still.' The Whitley levelled off at 2,000 feet and Wickham managed to nurse the engines back into life. It was bad weather all the way back to base, but they made it safely. Others in the squadron were, according to Brearey, so tired after the trip that they crashed on landing. One ploughed through a group of Nissen huts. 'These casualties were in addition to those officially listed as missing,' he said.

Stories of the hectic night of 7th November came from all over Bomber Command. Crew members were unable to touch metal parts without their gloves. A navigator who laid down his gloves for a few moments was unable to put them on again as they had become frozen solid. Sixty-six degrees of frost was recorded inside cabins and icicles grew around chins like brittle white beards. But the crew managed to overcome these hazards in one way or another. They used their superchargers to climb quickly above the icing level, they spiralled down to sea-level, or they tried to fly around the worst areas. And all these manoeuvres used up valuable petrol.

Pilot Officer Charles Acton Chaplin Havelock on 77 Squadron at Leeming reported 'severe icing from 2-10,000 feet' but he made it home.[16]

Halifax crews on 76 Squadron at Middleton St. George described the weather thus: 'as a result of the extreme cold Air Speed Indicators and compasses were made unserviceable'. The alcohol in the compass bowl was adjusted to withstand very low temperatures indeed. The powerful four-engined Halifax Is, not long in squadron service, rode above the threatening cu-nims but out of the six aircraft detailed only two, Pilot Officer Charles Cranston 'Jock' Calder and Sergeant George Racine Herbert, reached the Berlin area and bombed from 15,000 feet. Herbert put down at West Raynham in Norfolk on the return. Squadron Leader Walter Stanley Hillary and Sergeant Eric T. Borsberry both abandoned their sorties, the former because his port outer engine ran continuously on rich mixture and the latter because his instruments were frozen up. Squadron Leader John Theodore Bouwens abandoned his primary target and bombed Flensburg.[17] Calder and Herbert flew for eight hours that night whilst the humble Whitleys struggled on for eleven hours before reaching their home airfields.[18]

Sergeant Lloyd-Jones and his Whitley crew on 78 Squadron at Croft, just over four miles south of Darlington, County Durham, were fortunate in lobbing down at RAF Coltishall in Norfolk with only two gallons remaining in the petrol tanks after throwing various items into the sea. This included the four Brownings from the rear turret 'owing to a misunderstanding by the rear gunner'. Nevertheless, the action saved the lives of the crew.

The Whitley flown by South African pilot Ernest Johnston Sargent and 'F for Freddie' flown by 25-year-old Pilot Officer George Marshall McCombe, from Castlerock, Northern Ireland, did not make it home. McCombe's last message stated 'task abandoned at 0225' which was the time they would be over Berlin or near it but could see nothing owing to the dense cloud. 'F for Freddie' was shot down over the West Frisians by Oberleutnant Ludwig Becker of 4./NG 1 in a Bf 110. Sergeant John William Bell, the 21-year-old second pilot, bailed out first but landed in the water and drowned. His body was washed ashore at Lemmer harbour on 19th November. He left a grieving widow, Christine in Kessingland, Suffolk. McCombe and the rest of his

---

16  Havelock and all except one of his crew were killed on 27/28 December on the operation on Düsseldorf.

17  Squadron Leader Bouwens was killed flying a Blenheim on 11 Squadron at Galkanda in Ceylon on 22 April 1942 when he flew into a hill in bad weather,

18  Pilot Officer Herbert DFM was shot down and killed on 11/12 June 1943 while on 35 Squadron.

crew died when the aircraft crashed on the lake shore.[19] Ernie Sargent's Whitley was hit by flak and crashed at Rhinow at 0455 hours and he was killed. His crew bailed out safely and were taken prisoner.

At Dishforth 51 Squadron lost two Whitleys. Only one member on 25-year-old Squadron Leader Peter George Scott Dickenson's crew on 'F for Freddie' survived to be taken prisoner. Dickenson left a widow, Cynthia Clare of Letchworth, Hertfordshire. Sergeant A.W. MacMurray RCAF and crew on Z6839 crashed near Bierum in Holland and were taken prisoner. At Topcliffe 102 Squadron lost three Whitleys. On 'B-Baker', captained by Sergeant Reginald Charles Matthews, his wireless operator called for a QDM (What is my magnetic course to steer to base airfield?) at 0726 hours, when they must have been only a short distance from the Yorkshire coast, since other aircraft on his squadron landed at 0700 and 0743 respectively. Matthews and his crew were lost without trace. The two other Whitleys on 102 Squadron that were lost were flown by 23-year-old Pilot Officer Bruce Buchanan Percival Roy of Palmer's Green, Middlesex and Sergeant Thomas Henry Thorley. All ten crew were lost without trace. On 58 Squadron at Linton-on-Ouse the Whitleys piloted by 24-year-old Pilot Officer Kenneth Monckton Tuckfield and Pilot Officer Douglas Edwin William Brown failed to return. Tuckfield's last known position put him sixty miles due east of Scarborough heading directly for base before he no doubt ran out of fuel. All five crew were lost without trace. Brown's Whitley was shot down by flak over the Kiel Canal returning from the operation. He and his crew are buried at Kiel War Cemetery.

1 Group contributed twenty-two Wellingtons for the Berlin attack and a further sixty were detailed to attack Mannheim and the Channel ports. Only nine crews on the Berlin operation claimed to have bombed anywhere near the 'Big City' and four 'Wimpys', all from the four Polish squadrons operating under Air Vice-Marshal Oxland's command, failed to return. Three Wellingtons were lost on Mannheim. At Binbrook, only Pilot Officer P.J. Oleinek and Flight Lieutenant Donald Teale Saville - 'The Mad Aussie' from Portland, NSW - succeeded in getting to the target area out of the five aircraft on 12 Squadron that were dispatched. Oleinek was engaged by heavy flak fired through 10/10th cloud, from which evidence he deduced that they were in the vicinity of Berlin since it coincided with the navigation plot. He then flew around the area at 12,000 feet but all to no avail and he contented himself with dropping his bombs at intervals wherever the

---

19  *Lemmer & Bakhuizen* webpage by Willem de Jong.

flak was most concentrated before turning for home. This 'Wimpy' flew for eight and half hours before landing safely back at an airfield in Lincolnshire. Pilot Officer Alexander James Heyworth, captain of one of the Wellington IIs carrying eight 500lb bombs to Berlin, flew in cloud with tops at 19,000 feet; he experienced bad icing trouble and extreme cold and was forced to return short of fuel. Pilot Officer C.A. Barnes, with a battle-tried crew, found his guns frozen up and ice so heavy on his Wellington that to continue was impossible, while Sergeant C. Voller experienced oxygen failure. Wing Commander Saville DSO DFC later commanded 218 'Gold Coast' Squadron. He was 'anti-bull', enjoyed a pint and had a rather twisted sense of humour. He and six of his crew were killed on the fire raid on Hamburg on 24th/25th July 1943 when his Stirling was shot down by Feldwebel Hans Meissner of 6./NJG3 near Neumünster.

In 3 Group, 7 Squadron at Waterbeach dispatched eleven Stirlings for two aircraft missing. Twenty-two-year-old American, Flying Officer Douglas Byrd Van Buskirk RCAF, crashed near Duisburg with the loss of all the crew, they were buried at Reichswald Forest. Van Buskirk left a widow, Lilias, in Houston, Texas. 'K-King', piloted by 25-year-old Sergeant James William Cooper Morris RAAF was hit by light flak and crashed near Hekelingen. All the crew perished in the crash and they were interred at Crooswijk. The remaining aircraft captains attacked alterative targets or abandoned due to icing or mechanical failure. At Wyton four Stirlings on 15 Squadron reported bombing Berlin on ETA and one bombed Münster. At Feltwell, 75 Squadron RNZAF dispatched eight Wellingtons. Twenty-seven-year-old Sergeant John William Black RNZAF was last heard transmitting on the Group frequency at 2236 hours – 'target not attacked'. The New Zealander's Wellington crashed at Oldebloom with the loss of all six crew. Pilot Officer W.R. Methven's wireless operator transmitted an SOS at 2228 hours before the Wellington went down. Methven and four of his crew were taken prisoner. Sergeant John Cuthbert McKechnie Gibson RNZAF, the navigator, was killed and he was later interred at Reichswald Forest. At Honington, of nine Wellingtons on 9 Squadron that were dispatched, five reached the target area but none claimed to have attacked the primary due to cloud and severe icing conditions. At Waterbeach, 99 Squadron dispatched eight Wellingtons, none of which succeeded in identifying Berlin owing to thick cloud and severe icing. Flight Lieutenant John Patrick Dickinson and all but one of his crew, who died when his parachute failed to open, were taken prisoner. Dickinson was sent to Stalag Luft III where he took part in three escape attempts and four more from Colditz Castle where he helped on a fifth! Pilot Officer W.D. Moore and crew, and Pilot Officer Charles George Gilmore, who crashed at Beilen in Holland with the loss of all the crew, also failed to return.

On 101 Squadron at Oakington, three Wellingtons attacked Berlin, one abandoned the sortie and Pilot Officer William Dave Clayton Hardie and crew were lost without trace. At Marham, five Wellingtons on 115 Squadron attacked through thick cloud and two more unable to reach Berlin attacked alternative targets. Its parent squadron on the station, 218 Squadron, dispatched thirteen Wellingtons, all of which went the distance, though none were successful identifying the target and there were no early returns. At Mildenhall, one 'Wimpy' on 149 Squadron attacked Berlin and three abandoned the operation owing to severe icing. Sergeant Stanley William Dane and his crew failed to return. Only one member of the crew survived. At Stradishall, 214 Squadron detailed five Wellingtons for the raid. One bombed on ETA, two returned early due to engine failure and one was reported 'missing'. The fifth 'Wimpy' failed to find Berlin owing to cloud. At East Wretham, 311 (Czech) Squadron dispatched ten Wellingtons, seven of which claimed to have attacked Berlin. The other three abandoned the operation owing to weather and engine failure.

Only seventy-three aircraft in total reached the general area of the German capital, where bombing was scattered. The Spandau Power Station was hit and damage was caused to a considerable area of Moabit, one of the working-class quarters of Berlin. In all, twenty-one Wellingtons, Whitleys and Stirlings failed to return and there seems no doubt that most, if not all, of these were forced down through lack of fuel. Losses on the Berlin raid were high at 12.4 per cent (twenty-one aircraft). Total losses for the 392 sorties flown were thirty-seven aircraft (9.4 per cent); more than double the previous highest for a single night.

It was between six and seven o'clock next morning that the extent of the night's losses became apparent. Most of the attacking aircraft were by this time nearing the North Sea. SOSs began to come into the bomber bases. 'Running short of petrol; Ditching' was the gist of these messages as, one by one, pilots realised that they would never have the fuel to get back to England. Understandably, the most critically placed were the aircraft which got to Berlin. Forty-three aircraft claimed to have bombed Mannheim as ordered. Seven Wellingtons, including two 'Wimpys' on 300 (Masovian) Squadron failed to return from this raid. A few bombs fell on Cologne also, but all sixty-one Hampdens and fourteen Manchesters returned safely.

One brilliant piece of airmanship and bravery was denied the full credit it deserved because the Wellington ran out of petrol. Pilot Officer Lucian

Ercolani on 214 Squadron had reached Berlin and dropped its high explosive load successfully through a gap in the clouds, but before the incendiaries could be released the gap closed. Knowing that they would fly over other worthwhile targets on the way back from Berlin, Lucian Ercolani kept the incendiaries, unfortunately, as it happened. Over Münster a lucky flak burst hit them and set the incendiaries alight. The bomb release gear was smashed and there was no getting rid of the burning load. The wireless operator took ten minutes to fight his way through the smoke and flames to reach the rear of the Wellington, whence he could let out his trailing aerial. This would give him a greater range and increase the chances of maintaining contact with base. Before long the Wellington was ablaze along the whole length of its bomb bay. The crew used fire extinguishers and coffee from thermos flasks to try to put the fire out, but to no avail. The intercom had failed and Sergeant Fry, the rear gunner, was effectively cut off from the rest of the crew by the flames, but the aircraft still flew. After a while the fire subsided but the incendiaries still burned in the bomb bay. Realising that it must have been a great help to the AA gunners who continued to shoot, Ercolani closed the bomb-doors to hide the tell-tale light. Still with the fire in its belly, the Wellington crossed the coast and started out over the sea. It lost height steadily but there seemed a hope that they would make home. But they ran out of petrol and were forced down off Thorney Island, Sussex. When the aircraft hit the water Ercolani was injured and he went down with the sinking bomber, but the cockpit section floated to the surface, allowing him to join his crew in the dinghy, which then floated into the North Sea and eventually along the English Channel. The six crew drifted for fifty-seven hours in their dinghy before they were washed ashore near Ventnor. Flying Officer Ercolani was awarded an immediate DSO, a very rare accolade for so junior an officer, 'for outstanding courage, initiative and devotion to duty.'[20]

At Pocklington John Searby observed that the Canadian crews on 405 Squadron returned 'utterly fatigued, half frozen and disgusted.' 'Winston Churchill's succinct phrase about not fighting the weather as well as the enemy' came to mind. It was a view shared by Flight Lieutenant

---

20  Ercolani's father, born in St. Angelo, Tuscany in Italy on 8 May 1888, was a picture frame maker who migrated to London in search of work. He married in 1915 and took British citizenship in 1923. Lucian Brett Ercolani was born at High Wycombe in Buckinghamshire on 9 August 1917 and educated at Oundle where he excelled at sport. He left school in 1934 to work at his father's company, Ercol. When war broke out Lucian joined the RAF and trained as a pilot in Canada, returning in May 1941 to join 214 Squadron.

'Johnny' Fauquier. His 'Wimpy' was heavily damaged by flak but he succeeded in returning to a crash landing. 'I have seen the North Sea in many moods but never more ferocious than that night,' he wrote. 'Huge waves of solid green water were lifted from the surface and carried hundreds of feet by the wind. After what seemed like hours in these appalling conditions I realised we were unlikely to make base. I had little or no fuel left and told the crew to take up ditching positions, though our chances of pulling off a successful ditching in darkness amid that hell of strong winds and blown spray were practically nil. It was then I saw briefly one of those wonderful homing lights and made a beeline straight for it, crossing the English Coast with all gauges knocking on zero. In a few moments we found what I thought was Driffield but it proved a non-operational airfield. I could just make out the runways - as it was early dawn - and slapped the wheels and flaps down whilst I still had power, only to find at a hundred feet the runway blocked with railroad iron to prevent the enemy making use of it. They had erected pylons of this stuff all down the runway but, of course, they forgot to put any kind of obstruction on the grass surfaces. I landed but swerved to port and damaged the starboard tailplane. All in all we were lucky and nobody was hurt, thank God. As soon as we climbed out of the aircraft we were surrounded by the Home Guard, who were most hostile in spite of our uniforms and the RAF roundels on the fuselage. They were going to lock us up! I asked repeatedly for the colonel, or whoever was in charge, to make contact with Pocklington, but he was still suspicious. He asked me when we had left England and when I said, "11 o'clock last night," he replied: "no aircraft can stay in the air that long." Finally, everything was smoothed over and we were picked up and returned to Pocklington.'[21]

'Fauquier's luck,' recalled John Searby, 'held on this and other occasions but he was still a bit sour when I met him in the Mess the night following the Berlin raid, expressing himself forcefully on the subject of Air Staff planning at Headquarters Bomber Command. Although he makes no mention of it his Wellington was heavily damaged by flak: the misery of that North Sea crossing with a 70 mph headwind eating up the scant fuel reserve and the expectation of a ditching in darkness and a wild sea, was shared by all save the Halifax crews who had no fuel worries and whose new four-engined bombers carried them over the weather.' What happened to the other nine Wellingtons? The weather encountered is summed up briefly as, 'Bad; 10/10ths cloud with few breaks,' yet six crews battled their way to

---

21  *The Bomber Battle For Berlin* by John Searby (Guild Publishing 1991).

the target area and two – 'Q-Queenie' captained by Sergeant Sutherland and 'G-George' captained by Sergeant Suggitt caught a momentary glimpse of the city: whilst others bombed on the estimated position. Flight Sergeant Alexander Lawrence Dennis Hassan RCAF, flying Wellington 'D-Dog' dispatched a signal to base at 0223 'Operation completed', but of this gallant crew nothing more was heard and they may well have fallen victims to the fury of the North Sea, as did others when the petrol ran out. Sergeant A. N. McLennan's 'Wimpy' was hit in the front turret, tailplane and starboard engine by flak, but the Canadian pilot made it home.[22]

Sergeant Edwin John Williams RNZAF, born 1913 in Timaru, Canterbury, New Zealand, abandoned his sortie with zero oil pressure on one engine but jettisoned his bomb load over what he believed to be Wilhelmshaven before staggering back to Pocklington on one engine. 'An attractive personality,' wrote John Searby, who had flown with him on his 'second dickie' trip a week earlier on the night of 31st October/1st November to Hamburg. 'He was the very stuff of which bomber captains were made - determined to force his way through regardless of weather and enemy opposition to drop the 3,000lb load of high explosive on the docks which lined the River Elbe. Now, the New Zealander estimated the wind at height to be 80 mph with an outside temperature of -42C. Their slow crawl back to base with the Wellington capable of not much over a hundred and ten with one engine feathered and tending to overheat called for skill and determination but as he put it, "it was nothing to write home about - the alternative was a ducking." Williams jettisoned his bomb load over what he believed to be Wilhelmshaven before staggering back to base on one engine.' Determined to force his way through regardless of weather and enemy opposition, Williams was killed just over a month later, on the night of 28th/29th December when his Wellington was shot down on the trip to Emden.[23] He left a grieving widow, Alice Selena Williams, who lived in Devonport.

Canadian, Flight Lieutenant Wilfred John 'Mike' Lewis DFC, one of the six original pilots on 207, the first Manchester squadron, was piloting 'W for William', one of the four Manchester Is on the raid. Lewis, who had joined the RAF on a short service commission in 1939, hoping later to have

---

22  *The Bomber Battle For Berlin* by John Searby (Guild Publishing 1991). Sergeant Hassan and his crew were killed.

23  Williams, Sergeant D.J. Gordon, navigator; Flight Sergeant Jack Cecil Donkin RCAF, wireless operator; Flight Sergeant Joseph Raymond Frederic Bourgeau RCAF and Sergeants Ronald James and Willis Langhom, the two gunners, were interred in Sage War Cemetery.

'a very good shot at becoming an airline pilot', had flown a first tour on Hampdens. He had recently returned after a week's leave having finished his second tour and was expecting to be posted to 44 'Rhodesia' Squadron, but his squadron commander had asked him to do one last trip (his sixty-first) because they did not have a captain to fly 'William'. Sergeant Charles Hall, his WOp/AG recalls, 'The outward flight was uneventful until about midnight when at about 13,000 feet over the sea near Tönning in Schleswig-Holstein, Sergeant "Dusty" Miller the rear gunner shouted, "Night-fighter astern!" This was accompanied by a stutter of machine-gun fire, which hit our aircraft in the area of the port engine. As Miller opened fire the night-fighter continued over the top of the Manchester enabling me, from my mid-upper gunner's position, to fire into the belly of the enemy aircraft at very short range. Flight Lieutenant Lewis had immediately dived our aircraft and sought cover of thick cloud and contact was lost with the enemy fighter. There were no casualties, but we had a serious fuel leak, so after dropping our 4,000lb bomb and incendiaries on a searchlight concentration at Wilhelmshaven (which had given us much trouble in previous operations) we set course for Waddington. The port engine cowling began to glow red-hot and then white-hot in turn. Lewis shut down the engine, feathered the airscrew and activated the fire extinguisher within the engine cowling. This seemed to extinguish the fire but thereafter twelve very anxious eyes were focused on the port engine for signs of further trouble! It soon became apparent that we were not capable of maintaining height on the one remaining Vulture engine so we gradually lost height. With the gunners keeping a sharp lookout we descended through cloud emerging at 1,500 feet over Holland with the inhospitable grey-black waters of the North Sea clearly visible. At this point Lewis decided that we were not going to make the English coast and turned south aiming to reach the Friesian Islands. The Friesians eventually came into view and turning westward again Lewis kept the aircraft parallel to the shore. We took up our crash positions. Amidst noise, water and mayhem we hit, bouncing several times before settling in what turned out to be the surf of the north coast of Ameland.

'The only evidence of anger was a lot of holes in the engine cowling and the wing and a great stream of gasoline coming out of the main port gas tank. None of the crew was damaged; no shot actually entered the fuselage. Probably one bullet went through the radiator and shortly thereafter the engine temperature suddenly started to go and bang! It ceased and that was it. We feathered the engine and started back home but we were just slowly losing height. I crash-landed the aircraft on the beach of the Dutch Friesian island

67

of Ameland about 0100 hours. I was fortunate. The whole crew survived. No injuries other than a broken bone in one hand of the rear gunner and one who hit the windshield and had concussion. Very short, nothing dramatic except for that ten seconds and it's all over.' After Lewis put 'W for William' down safely on the beach in about five feet of water the crew took to their dinghy and got ashore. As they had previously agreed not to compromise any Dutch civilians, they were taken prisoner. Their attacker was Feldwebel Siegfried Ney of 4./NJG1 who successfully claimed his fifth Abschuss.

In all, 137 crews claimed to have bombed their allotted targets in Berlin. Fifteen bombers were MIA and at least ten, including two Wellingtons on 115 Squadron are thought to have been shot down by night-fighters.[24] A great number of fighters, not far short of a hundred, were seen over Germany and the invaded countries. A Wellington was held in a cone of searchlights over Holland; suspiciously, there was no anti-aircraft fire and the suspicion was confirmed when the rear gunner suddenly saw tracer bullets coming from 300 feet above and astern. He could not see the enemy fighter at all, but he fired back, three bursts in all, in the direction from which the tracer was coming. No more tracer came after the first burst, but instead, the gunner saw small objects, black and smoking, fall down through the searchlight beams. Evidently the enemy fighter had been severely damaged, but nothing was ever seen of it, though its defeat must have been seen from below, for the anti-aircraft guns on the ground at once began to put up a fierce barrage. At other times the presence of enemy fighters was only detected when they fired coloured lights as a signal. One such fighter got itself into a barrage, signalled to the gunners to cease fire, but was hit and fell in flames.

Over the northern outskirts of Berlin a Hampden was held by searchlights and dived to 4,000 feet to get away. At that height a fighter approached and fired from 100 feet away. The Hampden pilot went on with the dive until he was within fifty feet of the ground, but even at that height the bomber was still held by the searchlights and it was not until it had flown several miles just over trees and rooftops that it got away from the lights and from the pursuing fighter. Sometimes the enemy appears to have been less persistent. Over Holland a Junkers 88 circled round a Wellington and then at once

---

24  R1772 piloted by Sergeant Rowland Bertram Dunstan Hill was shot down over Kiel Bay by a Bf 110. Hill crashed to his death. Five crew bailed out safely and were PoWs. R1798 was shot down on its return from Berlin by Oberleutnant Helmut Lent of 4./NJG1 as his 23rd Abschuss at 0458 hours near Drachtstercompagnie in Friesland province with the loss of all Sergeant Ian Patrick McHaffie Gordon's crew.

made off; a Stirling turned to attack a Messerschmitt 109 and the enemy at once turned and fled. Over western Germany a bomber was being engaged by anti-aircraft fire; a Junkers 88 approached, did not like the look of the barrage and would not come up to the attack.

A Junkers 88 attacked a Wellington four times over Berlin and got in one or two hits. But when it made its fourth attack the Junkers flew right through a stream of bullets pouring from the Wellington's rear turret and as soon as it was through the zone of fire it caught alight and fell to the ground. The Wellington crew were able to see the wreckage burning on the ground for some time. In all, four enemy fighters were claimed destroyed that night and several more were damaged. Ten Wellingtons, nine Whitleys and two Stirlings were lost on Berlin.

Nowhere were searchlights more concentrated than at Berlin and the flak was always very heavy. 'There seemed to be about fifty searchlights in one bunch alone,' said the navigator of a Halifax. 'Shells burst close, some of them sending out clouds of smoke which, in the night sky, looked almost like barrage balloons.' Fifty out of sixty-five postal wagons were destroyed in the Potsdamer railway station, which was severely damaged. The railway lines leading to the Anhalter and Friedrichstrasse stations were hit in many places and traffic was dislocated or brought to a standstill for some time. Warehouses were burnt to the ground near the Ost Kreuz station. A 4,000lb bomb completely demolished five large buildings in the Pariser Platz at one end of the Unter den Linden and killed more than a hundred people. Two hundred more were reported to have been scalded to death by the hot water system, which burst and flooded the basement in which they were sheltering.

One by one the returning bombers landed back at their stations in eastern England. Pilot Officer Mike Evans and crew on a 149 Squadron Wellington returned to Mildenhall after what was an eventful trip, as Sergeant Jim Coman the wireless operator recalls. 'All went fairly well until we were making our bombing run, straight and level, when we were coned in searchlights and received numerous hits by flak. After releasing the bombs at 9,500 feet we took evasive action but were unable to get out of the searchlights, so we dived to rooftop level and moved out of the target area as quickly as possible. The AA gunners were actually shooting bits off their own buildings trying to hit us. We gained height as soon as possible to regain our bearings and arrived back at the Dutch coast short of fuel. All the main tanks were empty so we had approximately twenty minutes flying time on the engine nacelle tanks. We were attacked by a Ju 88 over the Dutch coast south of the Friesian Islands and north of Rotterdam, which our rear gunner engaged, and the fighter broke off trailing smoke from one of its engines. We made an emergency landing at the nearest airfield on the English coast, at Martlesham Heath, a fighter 'drome. As we landed the engines cut out. They had been running for nine hours after take-off. We counted 150 holes in the aircraft before we left for Mildenhall but we failed to spot the most serious damage, which must have happened over the target when a shell must have penetrated the main spar when the bomb doors were open.'

The public learned something of what had happened from the BBC news bulletin at nine o'clock the following evening. 'Reports are now available from our aircrews,' read the announcer, Joseph MacLeod, 'on last night's freak weather which interfered with the biggest offensive our bombers have yet launched against Germany... It was not only phenomenal weather, it was unexpected...' In one respect however, this report was not entirely accurate. The bad weather was not unexpected. The met officers had known what conditions were likely to be as early as the morning of the seventh. No less than thirty-seven aircraft - twenty-one of them lost attempting to attack Berlin - had failed to return from a total of 392 sorties. This loss was more than double the previous highest for night operations but only about two per cent greater than the average losses of the period. But what must have worried the planners at Bomber Command was the staring fact that most of these aircraft were not lost through enemy action. They had not been shot down by night-fighters, nor by flak. They had run out of petrol. Over a pitch-black and cloud-covered continent and over an icy, misty North Sea, twenty-five bombers had glided silently in to crash. Others were practically within sight of the British airfields when their engines stopped and an immediate crash-landing was the only chance left. And there were hundreds of telephone calls between airfields as other crews - the luckier ones - phoned up their bases to say they had just managed to scrape in at a coastal airfield.

The 3 Group officer who wrote up the following plain statement of fact with a cynical overtone made no bones about the fact that the Berlin operation proved a failure. '...This attack was not successful owing to 10/10ths cloud over the area. Quite a number bombed on the estimated position; others bombed alternative targets and a number joined in the rover's party around the Ruhr on the way back... one hundred and twenty-seven aircraft took off on this mainly unsuccessful expedition and twelve are missing. About 200 tons of bombs were dropped somewhere in Germany or Occupied France, however.' Losses on the Berlin raid were high at 12.4 per cent (twenty-one aircraft). In 4 Group ten out of fifty-four Whitleys (nine on Berlin and one on a 'Rover' patrol) failed to return. In 1 and 3 Groups nineteen out of

161 Wellingtons (nine of them on Berlin) were lost. Ironically however, the highest percentage loss of the night was suffered by the Hampdens of 5 Group which had been diverted from Berlin to Oslo and the Ruhr. Here the losses were five out of nineteen.

That the Berlin raid was unusually costly is not in doubt, nor are the factors which contributed to the losses: the extraordinarily bad weather; the limited range of the aircraft then available; and the comparative inexperience at that time of mounting such large-scale bombing attacks. The losses were referred to by Winston Churchill as 'most grievous' and in a note to the Secretary of State for Air and Sir Carless Portal, the Chief of the Air Staff, after the raid he said, 'There is no particular point at this time in bombing Berlin... There is no need to fight the weather and the enemy at the same time.' Portal was unwilling to forward the preliminary reports to Churchill since he disputed the arguments and explanations given by Sir Richard Peirse who was summoned to a meeting with Churchill at Chequers the Saturday evening after the Berlin raid, and the situation was discussed by the War Cabinet. Peirse had presided over a large expansion in the bomber force but, in the face of increasing losses and no evidence of significant impact on Germany, it was obvious that RAF Bomber Command did not possess the numbers or type of aircraft necessary for immediate mass raids. On 13th November, the Air Ministry informed Peirse that only limited operations were to be carried out in the coming months.

Though still classed as a 'heavy', the Whitley did not have the same range as the other aircraft and 7th November proved to be practically the Whitley's swansong. Five months later the Whitley was at last retired from Bomber Command, though it was to continue in service long afterwards in Coastal Command. The Hampden followed the Whitley into retirement in September 1942. Alone amongst the 'old guard' the much-loved 'Wimpy' was destined to continue into battle for many long months to come. The raid on 7th/8th November 1941 would be the last to be made on the German capital for fourteen months, by which time the first of the four-engined bombers, the Stirlings and Halifaxes, would be available. Unfortunately, the Stirling had a dismal ceiling of between 12,000 and 15,000 feet. The Merlin-powered Halifaxes, which equipped many of 6 Group RCAF's squadrons as well as those of 4 Group could fly a little higher, but not much. The situation would only improve with the introduction of the first Avro Lancasters from the spring of 1942.

'The winter of 1941-42 was viciously cold,' wrote Phyllis 'Pip' Beck, a WAAF radio telephone operator in Flying Control at Waddington, where the routine was always the same. 'Stack them up, bring them in.... Sometimes it seemed as if the bitter east wind would never stop blowing and I railed aloud and quite futilely as I trailed across the airfield convinced that I was being dissected by a thousand icy knives.'[25]

At RAF Bomber Command headquarters in January that year the knives were out too for Sir Richard Peirse and he was relieved of his duties. On 22nd February, Air Marshal Sir Arthur Travers Harris CB OBE arrived at High Wycombe to take up his duties as the new Commander-in-Chief. Eight days earlier the famous 'area bombing' directive, which had gained support from the Air Ministry and the Prime Minister, had been sent to Bomber Command. Harris was now directed by Sir Carless Portal to break the German spirit by the use of night area rather than precision bombing and the targets would be civilian, not just military. Sir Arthur warmed to his task, announcing: 'The Germans entered this war under the rather childish delusion that they were going to bomb everybody else and nobody was going to bomb them. At Rotterdam, London, Warsaw and half a hundred other places, they put that rather naive theory into operation. They sowed the wind and now they are going to reap the whirlwind.'

---

25   *A WAAF In Bomber Command* by Pip Beck (Goodall Publications Ltd., 1989).

# Chapter 3

# 'Burning His Black Heart Out'

*'On 15ᵗʰ January 1943, a week before my 16th birthday, my class of 15 and 16-year-old boys was called up for duty with the Flak. Our battery was a heavy one with four, later six, 10.5cm guns, in an emplacement at Spandau-Johannisstift on the western suburbs of Berlin. The battery establishment consisted of two officers, thirty NCOs and other ranks, about a hundred of us boys and some thirty Russian prisoners. The soldiers and the prisoners did the heavier manual jobs. The boys carried out nearly all the other tasks, from radio operator to gunner - even the K3 [gun loader]. You can imagine that it was hard work for a 15-year-old boy to load a gun with 10.5cm ammunition during rapid fire [each shell weighed 90lbs complete with cartridge case] often with the barrel pointing upwards at an angle of 40 degrees or more. The most skilful job was that of rangefinder, often a boy too. Sometimes the commander would allow one of us to give the fire commands, the most exalted position of all: Achtung! Gruppe! Achtung! Gruppe! [Attention! Salvo!].*

*'If the battle was only a short one the fire discipline was usually very good. But woe if the battery fired more than eighty or a hundred rounds! Each gun crew had the ambition to be the best and to fire the most ammunition. Instead of a fine unison crash there would be guns firing off all over the place. We boys were most enthusiastic, and it was a bad day when there was no British activity. Our feelings were not completely selfless, since after a night raid we were allowed to sleep-in in the morning and did not have to go to school. I clearly remember that on one occasion towards the end of 1943 our battery fired about forty salvoes at a very mysterious*

*target; it had been detected by radar moving very slowly, and our commander thought it might be a glider with enemy agents on board. We afterwards learnt that the easy target which had refused to be shot down was in fact a large cloud of Window.'*

**Luftwaffenhelfer Hans Ring. In the defence against daylight high-altitude attacks, the co-operation of flak and fighters and the operation of the Grossbatterien proved successful. In spite of the continual loss of young personnel to the fronts, Germany found it possible to double the numbers of personnel, principally by decreasing the personnel per battery and using the Reichsarbeitsdienst (The Reich Labour Service) approximately 75,000 Luftwaffenhelfer from higher schools. After the German disaster at Stalingrad when thousands of soldiers were needed for frontline duties, all schoolboys in Germany at age sixteen had to enter the flak school in their neighbourhood and approximately 15,000 women and girls, 45,000 volunteer Russian PoWs and 12,000 Croatian soldiers were drafted in to the air defence of the Reich. The Luftwaffenhelfer had the same duties as soldiers but their teachers had to continue their education as well as possible.**

Air Marshal Sir Arthur T. Harris, known variously as 'Butch', 'Bomber' or 'Bert' (as Churchill, using naval slang would often address him in private conversation), has been described as 'a rough, tough, vulgar egomaniac'. To his crews whom he fondly referred to as his 'old lags', he was simply 'the 'guv'ner'. 'If he had put out the word, his squadrons would have flown up to and through the gates of Hell,' wrote one of his pilots. 'What stopped us in our tracks was the speed at which he was asking our crews to ride up to one of those gates.' The last visual crews had as they left the Briefing Room, was a huge coloured portrait of the leader of Bomber Command hanging above the exit. A telling message printed in bold lettering underneath assured them: 'When he says you go, YOU GO!' Whether you liked him, whatever the appellation, or despised him, Harris was just what Bomber Command needed. He feared no foe, senior officers or politicians. He brooked no arguments from juniors and pooh-poohed any from those of equal or senior status who held a contra opinion. Harris knew what he was going to do and proceeded to move Heaven and earth to do it. Woe betides anyone who stood in his way. He was a firm believer in the Trenchard doctrine and with it he was going to win the war. According to Professor Solly Zuckerman, technical advisor to those responsible for the bombing policy, Harris 'liked destruction for its own sake'.

Air Marshal Sir Robert Henry Magnus Spencer Saundby KCB KBE MC DFC AFC who became Deputy AOC in Chief under Harris in 1943, had distinguished himself gaining five victories during the First World War. Saundby was a supporter of the strategy of area bombing against German civil population. On behalf of Harris he selected ninety-four German towns which were ripe for carpet bombing. A keen fly fisherman, he gave codenames to each of them known as 'Fish code'. For example, Nuremberg was 'Grayling' and Berlin was 'Whitebait'. Harris and Saundby knew that hitting Berlin was good for British civilian morale. It was something which bomber crew members like Robert S. Raymond, the son of a Kansas City, Missouri furniture dealer, who had joined RAF Bomber Command while America was still neutral, agreed with. Raymond had gone to France in 1940 and drove an American ambulance with the 9th French Army. He was in the retreat from Sedan when the American Ambulance Unit was disbanded. He went through Spain and Portugal intending to return home, but instead he arrived in London to see if there was anything he could do but was unable to find anything suitable. In a doorway while sheltering from the rain, he saw a poster advertising the RAF. He went to the nearest recruiting office and joined up as an AC2. Promoted sergeant and then pilot officer, Raymond began a tour of thirty operations on Lancasters on 44 'Rhodesia' Squadron at Waddington. He wrote: 'We all knew that sooner or later during this winter we should go to Berlin. Nevertheless, although it was not entirely unexpected and everyone wanted to have it on a line in his log book, I felt rather weak in the knees when I walked into the Briefing Room on 16th/17th January and saw that name on the big board. Price, my Canadian wireless operator from Brockville, Ontario; said, "I'd rather go to Essen than Berlin and I hate Essen as a target."'

In a message to his crews that was read out at briefings for the raid on Berlin, 'Bomber' Harris announced in quiet but forceful tone: 'Tonight you are going to the "Big City". You will have the opportunity to light a fire in the belly of the enemy that will burn his black heart out.'

The Stirlings were withdrawn from an original plan so that only 190 of the higher-flying Lancasters - mostly from 5 Group - and just eleven Halifaxes would participate in an all four-engined bombing force for the first time in the war. The Stirlings would be missed by many Lancaster crews who were happier when Halifaxes and Stirlings were flying as they always drew the flak at the lower altitudes flown.[1]

'Since Carter has been AWOL [Absent Without Leave] for three weeks,' wrote Robert Raymond, 'we took another rear gunner. It was his first operational flight and he was so excited before, during and after the trip that he wasn't worth much. Much of our report on the trip depended on his accurate observations over the target where he had a better view than anyone else. Before take-off he looked up into the bomb bay and asked if that big cylindrical object was a spare petrol tank! It was the 4,000lb "cookie" [blockbuster bomb] and he had never seen one before. Apart from that one 4,000lb bomb we carried nearly a thousand incendiaries. We took off about dusk and never saw the ground after leaving base until we were over Berlin, which fortunately was in a clear area.'

The Pathfinders, which had been promoted to 8 Group status on 8th January and the Lancasters in 1, 4 and 5 Groups made their way to the 'Big City' with the words of their 'guv'ner's' grandiloquent speech resounding in their heads. In the German capital, meanwhile, thousands of Berliners, wearied after fourteen months of bombing, took their seats in the vast Deutschlandhalle in the west end neighbourhood of the capital, determined to enjoy the annual circus, a major event in Berlin's social life. Built in just nine months and opened by Hitler on 29th November 1935 the huge arena, which could hold 8,764 people, had been a prestige project for the Nazi regime, built primarily for the 1936 XI[th] Olympiad to host the boxing, weightlifting and wrestling events.

The raid started in the middle of the evening show at the Deutschlandhalle but the air-raid warning system failed to report the approach of a large bomber force, only of a few single aircraft, so when the Lancasters and Halifaxes arrived over Berlin hundreds of Berliners were not in their homes. The first bombs coincided with the sounding of the sirens and it was reported that there were many scenes of panic until the police could control the crowds attempting to find shelter. But in the Deutschlandhalle the air-raid police and the fire brigade managed to supervise the evacuation of every person and all the circus animals to the parks around the hall minutes before the large number of incendiary bombs fell on the site. Twenty-one people were slightly injured in the crush as the crowds left the building, yet the vast majority of people who reached the open ground were unhurt

---

1   The Halifax IIs and Vs were permanently withdrawn from operations to Germany after the raid on Leipzig on the night of 19/20 February 1944.

and the fire only took hold after the last person had left. It quickly spread however, until the Deutschlandhalle was completely burned out, becoming the largest ruin in Berlin so far in the war.[2]

Stewart Sale, Reuters Special Correspondent, flew on the Lancaster of 57 Squadron at Scampton piloted by Flight Lieutenant George William Curry DFC, a 'roly-poly, jolly Geordie' from Newcastle who had flown thirty ops on Wellingtons on 57 Squadron RNZAF. His crew consisted of Pilot Officer Henderson, navigator; Flight Sergeant 'Les' Sumpter, bomb aimer; Flight Sergeant Higgins, mid-upper gunner; Flight Sergeant Shepherd, wireless operator; Sergeant 'Bob' Henderson, flight engineer and Flying Officer Longden, rear gunner. Sumpter, born in Kettering in 1911, had joined the army as a boy soldier in 1928 and served two stints in the Grenadier Guards. He left in 1931 and re-joined his old regiment at the outbreak of war, but then in 1941 he persuaded his superiors to let him transfer to the RAF. After training in England and Canada he was posted to 57 Squadron at Scampton in September 1942. He then flew as bomb aimer on thirteen operations on Flight Lieutenant Curry's crew. Sale's report 'at a bomber station, Sunday' was sensationally headlined, 'RAF Left Huge Fires Raging In Berlin: Great Weight of Bombs - one plane lost - Eye-Witness Describes City's "Big Hiding"'. 'I saw Berlin burn last night. From the nose of a Lancaster, one of many scores converging on the city, I looked down upon hundreds of points of fire. Over it all there was the rosy glow started by the planes which opened the attack. By the time my plane had reached the target, although it was probably among the first half dozen to follow the earliest arrivals, the spreading flames had marked out Berlin for one of the biggest hidings of its life.

'"Make a good job of it," the Intelligence Officer told the men at briefing, "and the effects will be felt throughout the land". So these crews of the big machines had neglected nothing to make it a good job.

'"A grand effort" had been the words of the Wing Commander DFC who gave us our orders. "We of this station alone are going to give the Hun something to think about," he said, "There will be many other Lancasters out as well. This is a big job you have been waiting for."

'The fliers, jamming into the big room to the doors, looked at one another and grinned. The Intelligence Officer warned them of the dangers - flak for

---

2  *The Bomber Command War Diaries: An Operational Reference Book, 1939-1945* by Martin Middlebrook and Chris Everitt (first published, 1985). The Deutschlandhalle was rebuilt after the Second World War and from 1957 served as a multipurpose arena and sports venue, in the last years primarily for ice hockey, but also for indoor soccer and again for boxing.

certain, searchlights and night-fighter belts. He warned them to be wary of dummy fires and elaborate camouflage. "Not an easy target," he summed up, "but an immensely important one. Its industries reach out far and wide. It is the capital of Hitler's Germany whose people were promised that Germany would never be bombed. It has had this coming to it for a long time. Now it is going to get it." The Wing Commander's final words were: "Every bomber must find and bomb the target. Make two runs if necessary. Goodbye and a good trip."

'We dashed for the hangars and soon, padded and burdened with gear, eight of us piled into the truck that would take us out to 'C for Charlie' whose acquaintance I had already made on practice flights and rehearsals of escape drills. Presently we were heading out to sea over a floor of white cloud. It would soon be night but as yet the sunset still smouldered. "Look at the Lancs," yelled the rear gunner. I put my head into the astrodome to see them - three skimming specks, black against the whiteness on the starboard side and others forming up to port.

'"Big City here we come," the captain sang.

'Steadily we climbed to the enemy coast. The moon was bright - so bright that when I caught the glare of it on the engineer's harness I thought that someone had left a lamp burning.

'My own captain, a veteran in his early twenties, now on his fifteenth operation, made three runs over the target, twice to bomb and once so that the flight engineer could take photographs.

'The raid, officially described as the heaviest of the New Year, lasted an hour and during that time our aircraft dropped a great weight of bombs, including 8,000 pounders and tens of thousands of incendiaries.

'Only one of the strong force, all of which were four-engined bombers, which carried out the raid failed to return. All the others brought back reports of huge fires in the city's industrial area. Other crews reported that the glow of the fires could be seen from 100 miles away. It was a well-planned and heavy blow, aimed at Germany's very heart.'[3]

---

3 Stewart Sale was killed on duty with the Fifth Army near Naples. Flight Lieutenant Curry was later grounded with ear trouble and his crew was told that they had to break up, but Sumpter and 'Bob' Henderson heard a rumour that a new squadron (617) was being formed in a neighbouring hangar and went looking for David Shannon, who was apparently on the lookout for a bomb aimer and an engineer. They both impressed the young pilot and joined his crew. Les Sumpter and Henderson took part in the famous Dam Busters raid (Operation 'Chastise') on 16/17 May 1943, flying on Lancaster ED929/L. On 14 May 1943 George Curry was awarded a bar to his DFC. On 3 September 1944 he was promoted squadron leader and he assumed command of 627 Squadron. He was awarded the DSO on 17 October 1944. A bar followed on 27 February 1945. He finished the war as an acting wing commander.

# 'BURNING HIS BLACK HEART OUT'

Lancaster 'D-Dog', on 61 Squadron at Syerston near Newark in Nottinghamshire, skippered by 33-year-old Squadron Leader Edward Donald Parker was the bomber that was lost. Parker was from West Bridgford, just south of Nottingham. He had been awarded the DFC in 1940 for completing forty-three operational flights against the enemy and he had received the George Cross for an act of bravery on the night of 8th/9th June 1940 when he had rescued his wireless operator from his burning Hampden shortly after take-off from RAF Scampton. The four RAF and three Canadian crew are buried in Berlin's 1939-1945 War Cemetery.[4]

At the target Robert Raymond saw 'just heavy flak and lots of it; no tracers from light guns, which only reached up to about 8,000 feet, no balloons, no searchlights or night-fighters, etc. They knew what height we were and put up a box barrage all around us. We were straight and level for two minutes for the bombing run and every second seemed like a year. The whole of northern Europe is covered with snow and the moon being nearly full, the ground detail was clearly visible. The only colourful parts of the target were half a dozen flares and the great glowing mushrooms from our four thousand pounders. We got a fairly good photo of our results. Cloud over base when we returned was less than 1,000 feet and I did a short cross-country flight until most of the others had landed. I don't like being stacked up on a circuit in cloud at 500 feet intervals with a dozen other tired pilots.'

This raid saw the first use of purpose-designed Target Indicators (TIs) instead of modified incendiaries, which had previously been used. These were dropped on the aiming point by PFF crews though thick cloud en route and haze over the target caused problems and the bombing was scattered mostly in the southern areas with the greatest concentration in the Reichshauptstadt and especially parts of the Tempelhof district. In all, 1,000 tons of bombs caused fires that were visible for 100 miles, but from an RAF bombing perspective, the raid on 16th/17th January was considered to be 'disappointing'. Early in 1942 'Gee' hyperbolic navigation equipment, which enabled navigators to pinpoint an aircraft's position at the beginning and end of a trip, had come into operation, but Berlin was well beyond the range of 'Gee' and 'Oboe' and $H_2S$ were not yet operational. Thick cloud, which was encountered on the way to the target hindered navigation and

---

4  The Hampden, which had on board four 500lb bombs for a raid on Amiens, crashed at Carlton Hill, four miles NNW of Lincoln. Parker returned to the burning wreckage to save the life of his wireless operator, Pilot Officer Lochhead. The two gunners were also injured but survived. Unfortunately, Lochhead was killed in a motorbike accident on 19 September 1940.

Berlin was found to be covered by haze. The Berlin flak proved light and ineffective and it was assumed that the greater altitude of the attacking force had surprised the German gunners, though about half of the personnel of the flak units were away from the Reich capital, taking part in a course. Berlin Gauleiter and propaganda minister Doktor Paul Josef Goebbels was reported as having been most angry and he ordered an overhaul of the air-raid warning system procedure. Because of the failure, an unusually high number of people (198) were killed, considering the weakness of the bombing.[5] Over the next three months civilian casualties would rise to several hundred people as 600 major fires and damage to 20,000 houses was suffered, partially destroying entire districts.

On the bitterly cold Sunday morning of 17th January crews who barely had eight hours sleep awoke with snow more than a foot deep in places. They were almost certain that ops would be scrubbed but at 'Morning Prayers', Air Marshal Arthur Harris' orders were that his 'old lags' were to be briefed for Berlin again. Ground crews were fully stretched and were only able to get 170 Lancasters and seventeen Halifaxes serviceable for the repeat raid on the 'Big City'. It would mean yet another night of heartache for crews' wives and their loved ones. In Lincoln a mother took her daughter and baby sister on a bus ride to the main gate of RAF Waddington. Theresa Ellen de Silva had spoken to her husband of nine years, 30-year-old Sergeant Joseph Herbert Wejies de Silva, on the telephone and arranged to meet him purely because she missed him so much. A hairdresser in civilian life he had voluntarily joined the RAF after watching an aerial dog fight over Clapham Common. Now he was a Lancaster mid-upper gunner on 9 Squadron on the crew skippered by 19-year-old Sergeant Andrew G. Carswell RCAF. Born in Bishop, California, 'Andy' had lived most of his life in Toronto. His brother, Lieutenant James M. Carswell, was serving in the Canadian Army at the Petawawa internment camp in the Ottawa Valley.

'Joe' de Silva's daughter Jacqueline remembered her father on an old bicycle wearing his flying suit having been, or about to be, briefed for that night's operation. He seemed to have a heated conversation with a sergeant at the guardhouse before seeing his family for about fifteen minutes. Because his daughter was so cold he put his flying jacket around her shoulders. It was a tearful goodbye when he left. Returning to Monson Street, Lincoln, the

---

5  This figure includes 53 prisoners of war - 52 Frenchmen and one Englishman - and six foreign workers. *The Bomber Command War Diaries: An Operational Reference Book, 1939-1945* by Martin Middlebrook and Chris Everitt (first published, 1985).

de Silva family had tea, and in the twilight, together with an uncle and aunt, they stood in the little garden as the crescendo of aircraft engines increased overhead. One of the Lancasters flew directly above and the wings dipped slightly left and right. '"Andy" always does that on the way out, if he can. They are off to Berlin now,' said their uncle. He worked for the GPO and 'always seemed to know what was going on'.

Sergeant 'Andy' Carswell wrote: 'January 1943 was a bad time for Bomber Command. Whenever the enemy brought out some new weapon or improvement in its air defence, we would lose some more bombers. When the RAF countered with an advanced technique like 'Gee' that allowed our forces to navigate in bad weather and bomb through clouds, we would lose fewer aircraft. Then the enemy would counter with another new device, like radar-directed searchlights and more of our crews would be lost. It was like a game of chess, played by generals and air marshals and politicians. We were the expendable pawns.'

Tonight was only his fourth operation and they were taking 'A-Apple'. 'I had been anxious at the ops briefing when I saw that our target was Berlin again, for the second night in a row. Same route, same altitudes, same turning points; exactly the same in every respect as the night before. The rationale was that the Germans wouldn't believe that the RAF would be stupid enough to use the same route two nights in a row. Our route was from a point on the east coast of England, straight across the North Sea to Denmark, with its heavy German flak batteries, and out across the Baltic Sea, to a point more or less due north of Berlin. There we were to turn south and fly directly over Berlin, where the Pathfinder force was to have laid down all sorts of marker flares and drop six or seven thousand pounds of high explosives and incendiary bombs on a given marker. History would later show that most of these bombs never hit a specific target, but when you drop tens of thousands of pounds of high explosives over the middle of a large city, there is bound to be very heavy damage, particularly to the civilian population.

'After the briefing, my crew and I had filed into the mess hall for our traditional bacon and eggs, a big treat in wartime Britain, where the average civilian might see an egg once or twice a month. One of the experienced captains at the next table was expounding to his crew on what a great opportunity this was going to be. He was a flight lieutenant with twelve operational trips to his credit, the crew one of the most experienced on a squadron that had been decimated so many times recently that twelve was a pretty respectable number. Nobody had completed a tour of operations (thirty trips) for quite some time and was not likely to for some time to come, unless we could find a way to keep the Germans from shooting down our squadron members in such numbers. The more inexperienced the crews, the more unconcerned they tried to act. The bravado and the wisecracks only covered up the creeping realization that there was a good chance all of us were going to die. No one on the squadron had finished a tour of ops for a long time, the most experienced captain having survived only twelve operational trips.'

War stories were a large part of Richard Dimbleby's life, but he was seeking human interest tales of daring and courage while not upsetting his listeners. The son of editor and statesman Frederick J.G. Dimbleby, Richard had worked on the *Richmond and Twickenham Times*, a newspaper owned by his family, and several other newspapers before joining the BBC in 1936. Despite reservations, the 29-year-old broadcaster had wanted desperately to fly on a bomber to report a bombing raid for the BBC. His chance came after seeing the war at close quarters in France, Africa and Greece and in the Mediterranean when his editor had sent for him. He told Dimbleby that the Air Ministry was willing to allow an observer on the next big night raid on Germany. 'We want you to go but it's a job for a volunteer.' Dimbleby disliked flying, was frequently air sick and the idea of a night raid scared him, but it would be a unique chance to see the RAF at work and a first-class story. He replied: 'I hate the idea but I'll go. Be it on your head if I don't return.'

Next thing Dimbleby knew he was in a compartment smelling of dusty seats and stale cigarette smoke on an LNER train steaming its way slowly out of London to 106 Squadron at Syerston in Nottinghamshire. It was not a fast train; they seldom were on the routes north-east and east from the capital, increasing speed only by the smallest amount as it reached open country. Reaching the main road that would take him past the Lancaster station, presently Dimbleby saw through driving rain the shapes of camouflaged hangars and near the edge of the road the high, proud Lancasters gleaming in the rain on their dispersals on its eastern side. Others were parked in a field on the opposite side and a level crossing gate folded back against the hedge marked the crossing point. A few men were working on the aircraft, but the long concrete runways were empty and there was little or no movement around the hangars. Dimbleby judged with relief that there would be no operations that night. He was not really a coward but he was glad of a reprieve, however short.

The French Air Force Farman 223.4 *Jules Verne,* which on 7 June 1940 flew a bombing raid on Berlin in retaliation for a raid on Paris four days' earlier by a force of 300 German bombers. This was the first of 363 Allied air raids on Berlin in WW2.

Wellington crews who took part in the first raid on Berlin on 23/24 September 1940 posing with a map for the cameraman.

Wellingtons and their crews who took part in the first raid on Berlin on 23/24 September 1940 when 129 Hampdens, Wimpys and Whitleys were dispatched to 18 separate targets.

Flight Lieutenant James Victor 'Jim' Verran, born in Waipawa at Hawkes Bay of Cornish and Scottish stock, had been disappointed to miss out on a commission in 1939 when the RNZAF recruiting drive had proved so successful that the lists were closed before the letter 'V' had been reached. With a dozen New Zealanders of like mind, he travelled to London via Panama in a Royal Mail steamer and presented himself for interview at the Air Ministry where he was accepted into the RAF. By July 1940 he was flying Whitley V bombers on 102 Squadron, completing 35 operations, attacking targets across France and Germany as well as raiding Milan - the first direct raid on Italy. He was awarded the DFC on 23 April 1941. (via Ian Frimston)

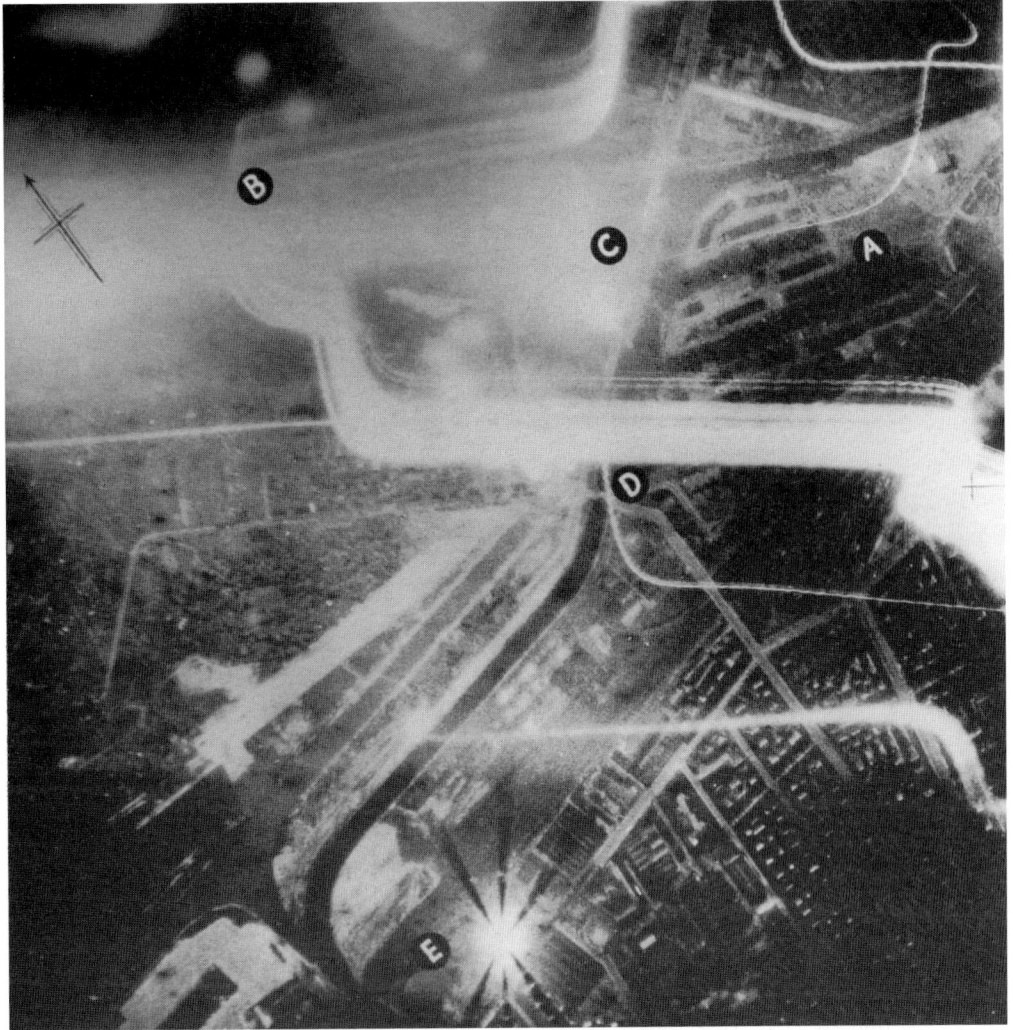

The first photograph released of a Bomber Command attack on Berlin, probably taken on the night of 23/24 September 1940 when 129 aircraft were concentrated against various targets within the city. The Verbindungs Canal is visible running from bottom left to top right, with the Westhafen inland docks and the Charlottenburg gas-holders at 'E'. The first raid on Berlin, on 25/26 August, had been sanctioned by the War Cabinet following Luftwaffe raids on London the previous night. Eight further raids, with varying degrees of success, were dispatched to the German capital during the autumn. The broad strokes of light in the photograph are searchlight tracks and the thin ones tracer.

Whitleys in their characteristic nose-down attitude coming into land.

On 12/13 August 1941 when seventy aircraft were detailed for another raid on Berlin the aiming point was the Reichsluftfahrtministerium or RLM (Ministry of Aviation), built on in 1935-36 and bounded on the north by the Leipzigerstrasse and on the east by the Wilhelmstrasse and the south by Prinz-Albrechtststrasse. On the western side was the building of the former Prussian House of Representatives but by 1943 this housed the Aero Club. The site of the ministry covered 400,000 square feet, 250,000 of which was the building itself. It had 2,800 rooms and offices, 4,000 staff and had extensive bomb and gas proofing. But only 32 bombers reached and bombed in the Berlin area and the Ministry was untouched.

Aerial photograph of Berlin taken on 23 March 1941 when 35 Wellingtons and 27 Whitleys attacked the 'Big City'. Bombing results were not seen because of cloud and heavy flak. All aircraft returned safely.

On 24/25 September 1940 Pilot Officer Karel Trojacek on 311 (Czech) Squadron force landed Wellington L7788 at Leidschendam in the Den Haag area of Holland while on an operation to Berlin owing to engine trouble. The crew initially went on the run but they were soon captured and Pilot Officers' Vaclav Killian Zdeněk Prochazka and Trojacek and Sergeant Arnost Zabrz became prisoners of war, but when German troops attempted to capture Sergeant Karel Kunka the next day he took his own life because he feared his capture might endanger his family in Czechoslovakia. The aircraft was recovered by the Germans and test flown.

99 Squadron crew members Sergeants' Alfred Jenner (left); Eric Berry and Albert Smith at Stalag Luft III shortly after their Wellington was shot down on 9/10 April 1941.

Luftwaffe night fighters, mostly Bf 110s and Ju 88s operating under ground control, were having some success against the bombers, particularly on moonlit nights. Of eighty bombers dispatched on 9/10 April 1941, most of the five lost are believed to have fallen to fighter interception. One fortunate to escape was Wellington T2739 on 99 Squadron at Newmarket, which was raked with cannon-fire near Berlin and lost the top of its fin and rudder, Flight Lieutenant Keith Thomas Alfred Harvey DFC, here examining the damage, was able to bring the bomber back to make a safe landing at Waterbeach. It was the second narrow escape for the crew who crashed on moorland west of Otterburn, Northumberland returning from Berlin on 30 October 1940. Harvey was killed on 30 December 1941.

Squadron Leader H. Budden DFC with his faithful Spaniel 'Michael' that flew on several trips with his master. 'Michael' was wounded in a back leg from shell splinter during the daylight raid on the *Gneisenau* and the *Scharnhorst* at Brest on 24 July. When Budden was married, the first decision of his new wife was that 'Michael' should stay home. On his next flight, Budden was shot down.

Wellington II W5461 EP-R on 104 Squadron at Driffield which FTR from Berlin on 12/13 August 1941. Squadron Leader Harry Budden's DFC MiD crew became a PoWs. Budden spent the rest of the war as a PoW in Stalag Luft III. At the time he was missing a newspaper article was published with the headline: 'The Flying Spaniel' which accompanied him on raids such as the first of the war on Sylt, March 1940, several raids on Norway and Berlin and other German towns. He was awarded the DSO on 2 September 1941.

Flight Lieutenant Christopher Cheshire on 76 Squadron in the cockpit of Halifax I L9530/MP-L at Middleton St. George on 6 August 1941. Painted on the fuselage below is his tongue-in-cheek family crest incorporating various 'Cheshire' elements such as a cheese and grinning cats!

Christopher Cheshire survived when his aircraft was shot down on Berlin on 12/13 August 1941 and spent the rest of the war in a prison camp while his brother, Flying Officer Geoffrey Leonard Cheshire - then serving on 35 Squadron - went on to become one of Bomber Command's most celebrated pilots.

Crew of Wellington Ic W5378 QT-A on 142 Squadron in the spring of 1941 at Binbrook. Back Row L-R: Sgt MacLean, rear gunner; Sgt Les Frith, WOp/AG; Flying Officer Kelly, second pilot; Pilot Officer R. McD Durham, navigator; Sgt K. S. Holman, front gunner; Flt Lt Alexander Douglas 'Doug' Gosman, pilot. In the front are members of the ground crew. Gosman and his crew were shot down on the night of 12/13 August 1941 on the operation on Berlin when they were flying W5433 'F-Freddie'. All the crew were taken prisoner.

Hampden Is AE257 KM-X and AE202 KM-K on 44 Squadron at Waddington in flight. Both aircraft were lost on raids over Germany, AE257 on the night of 21/22 October 1941 on Bremen and AE202 on Hamburg on 26/27 July 1942. During the autumn of 1940 44 Squadron lost ten crews in two months with the Hampdens straining at the very edge of their range to make it to Berlin and back. Throughout 1941 the casualties mounted for the squadron, including at Waddington when a German raid resulted in ten killed including seven women from the NAAFI which was destroyed.

Air Marshal Sir Richard Edmund Charles Peirse KCB DSO AFC Commander in Chief, Bomber Command from 5 October 1940 to late 1941 and Air Marshal Sir Robert Henry Magnus Spencer Saundby KCB KBE MC DFC AFC who became Deputy AOC in Chief under 'Bomber' Harris in 1943.

*Above left*: Air Marshal Sir John Cotesworth Slessor AOC of 5 Group who on 7/8 November 1941 succeeded in convincing the C-in-C that his Hampdens lacked the range to fly to Berlin after studying the weather reports for that night. The raid was a fiasco with 21 Wellingtons, Whitleys and Stirlings lost for little reward.

*Above right*: Flt Lt John Patrick Dickinson and all but one of his crew, who died when his parachute failed to open, were taken prisoner after being shot down on 7/8 November 1941. Dickinson was sent to Stalag III where he took part in three escape attempts with Flt Lt Vincent 'Bush' Parker, an RAF Spitfire pilot who was shot down in the English Channel on 15 August 1940. Four more escape attempts were made with Parker from Colditz Castle where he helped on a fifth! He is pictured (left) with Squadron Leader Geoffrey D. Stephenson, a Spitfire pilot who was shot down on 26 May 1940 while covering the evacuation of Dunkirk and 'Bush' Parker (right) in the courtyard at Colditz Museum. (Author)

On 22 February 1942 Air Marshal Sir Arthur Travers Harris CB OBE arrived at High Wycombe to take up his duties as the new Commander-in-Chief, Bomber Command.

*Above left*: Squadron Leader Edward Donald Parker GC DFC on 61 Squadron at Syerston who was shot down and killed on 16/17 January 1943.

*Above right*: 19-year-old Sgt Andrew G. Carswell RCAF (pictured (right) with brother 'Jim' in Ottawa at Christmas 1941. 'Andy' Carswell was shot down on the night of 17/18 January 1943.

Thirty-year old Sgt Joseph Herbert Wejies de Silva (right) with his father and younger brother. Born 11 July 1912 at East Redford, Nottinghamshire 'Joe' had wed his fiancée Theresa at Brentford registry office in 1934 and they had a daughter, Jacqueline. de Silva was KIA on the night of 17/18 January 1943 when he flew as mid-upper gunner on Lancaster 'A-Apple' on 9 Squadron, skippered by Andrew Carswell RCAF.

*Above left*: Richard Dimbleby of the BBC who flew in Lancaster *Admiral Prune* to Berlin and back with Wing Commander Guy Gibson the commanding officer of 106 Squadron at Syerston on 17/18 January 1943.

*Above right*: Lancaster W4118 featuring nose art of 'Mickey Mouse' and named *Admiral Prune*. On 5 February 1943 *Prune* and another crew went missing after an engine fire near Dijon. Another Lancaster, ED593, then became Gibson's aircraft. This Lancaster carried the same nose art but was named *Admiral Prune II*.

Seen here on an air test in January 1943 Lancaster ED592 was delivered to 50 Squadron on 7 February 1943. ED592/B and Pilot Officer Francis Eric Townsend's crew FTR from the operation on Berlin on the night of 1/2 March 1943. All the crew were killed. (Charles E. Brown)

'T for Tommy's' crew on 57 Squadron with their 22-year-old Canadian skipper, F/O John Fergus Greenan RCAF (in the centre) in front of Lancaster I W4201. Greenan and his crew were KIA on 1/2 March 1943 returning from Berlin when 'T-Tommy' was shot down and crashed near Riseholme.

Dr. Goebbels inspects the damage to the Hedwigskirche (St. Hedwig's Cathedral) in Friedrichstadt, which was reduced to ashes during the raid on Berlin on 1/2 March 1943.

Flying Officer Walter 'Punch' Thompson DSO* RCAF, a Lancaster pilot on 83 PFF Squadron at Wyton.

75 Squadron briefing at Mepal, Cambridgeshire in 1943.

Flying Officer William Selfridge Day, pilot of Stirling 'R-Roger' on 90 Squadron who received an immediate award of the DFC for his actions on 23/24 August 1943.

John Emilius 'Johnny' Fauquier RCAF later known as 'The King of the Pathfinders'.

His chance came on 17<sup>th</sup>/18<sup>th</sup> January when his pilot was none other than Wing Commander Guy Gibson DSO DFC*,[6] the CO of 106 Squadron. Together they would make the nine-hour-fifteen-minute round trip to Berlin on W4118, better known as *Admiral Prune*. It would be Gibson's sixty-seventh op. As the hours passed, activity on the station grew more intense. Briefing was fixed for the mid-afternoon and at lunchtime the public telephone in the mess was disconnected and all leave from the station cancelled. Syerston was cut off from the world outside. In any case, the personnel were too busy to think of anything but the immediate job on hand. Dimbleby wandered about the station, fascinated by the speed and organization of the work. Like so many people, he had come to take bombing operations for granted; a raid on Berlin was simply the dispatch of a few hundred bombers to a certain target. Now on this clear winter morning as he walked over the hardening ground he saw how vast were the preparations necessary before an operation could take place.

When Dimbleby got to the Lancaster he looked at the nose art of 'Mickey Mouse' on the forward fuselage. 'Why *Admiral Prune?*' asked Dimbleby. Although Gibson's Lancaster was coded ZN-L, W4118 was known phonetically as 'P-Prune'.

'Several of the aircraft on the squadron display Admiral-prefixed nicknames,' replied Gibson, 'because in 1942 we often dropped sea mines on "Gardening" operations and at the time naval officers were attached to the unit.'

Dimbleby wondered how he could fit into the space allotted to him on *Admiral Prune*. When he paraded in full kit it drew the typical, 'God - you look like the Michelin tyre man!' It was a fair description. He was not a slim man, corpulent in fact, but he had an imposing visual presence, was self-assured and articulate.

The last light was fading as Guy Gibson brought *Admiral Prune* to the end of the runway. Richard Dimbleby sat beside him in the cockpit, occupying the seat of the flight engineer. Sergeant G. McGregor, a young Scotsman, squatted cheerfully on the floor behind him. Dimbleby was harnessed to the aircraft by his oxygen tube and the wire of his headphones. His parachute lay behind him and on his lap he held his sweet and chewing gum ration, Gibson's cine-camera and a large handkerchief. However controlled his nerves might be he could not guarantee the security of his stomach.

---

6   The award of the DSO had been made in November 1942 and a bar would follow in March 1943.

Guy Gibson was making his last check, calling each member of the crew on the intercom. 'Okay, Johnny?'

Flying Officer J.E. Wickham, the rear gunner replied. Dimbleby had met him in the mess; he was always lost in an illustrated magazine.

Sergeant McGregor, flight engineer; 'Okay.'

'Okay, Brian?'

'Okay,' replied Flight Lieutenant Oliver, Gibson's new gunnery leader and his mid-upper gunner.

'Okay, "Hutch"?'

'Okay,' replied Pilot Officer E.G. Hutchison the wireless operator.

'Junior?'

'Okay,' said Flying Officer 'Junior' Ruskell, navigator.

'Henry?'

'Okay,' responded Sub/Lieutenant Gerard Muttrie bomb aimer, detached from HMS *Daedalus*.

And last, 'Okay, Dimbleby?' Dimbleby stuck up his thumb.

'Right, here goes.'

Guy Gibson pushed forward the throttles, helped by the co-pilot. The *Admiral* roared to life and leapt forward, bumping madly on the runway. Richard Dimbleby held his seat, clenching his fingers under its hard edge. The hangars passed in the dark, the bright lights of the watch office flashed by. They crashed on. The throttles were wide open and Gibson, so small and compact on his high seat, was coaxing the stick back. Back, forward again, back, forward again ... two-thirds of the runway lay behind and still the old *Admiral* thundered along the concrete with the great weight in her belly. Back, pause a second, back again, well back this time. She bumped once and lifted, touched again and lifted further. They surged up and in a trifle of a second the trees of Syerston were under them and gone and the great sky lay ahead and around.

Next morning British listeners tuning in their wireless sets to the BBC Home Service hung on to every word of Dimbleby's broadcast. 'The Berlin raid was a big show as heavy bomber operations go; it was also quite a long raid and the Wing Commander who took me stayed over Berlin for half an hour. The flak was hot, but it has been hotter. For me it was a pretty hair-raising experience and I was glad when it was over, though I wouldn't have missed it for the world. But we must all remember that these men do it as a regular routine job. The various crews who were flying last night from the bomber station where I'd been staying had flown on several of the Essen raids. That means that night after night they've been out over one of the hottest ports of Germany, returning to eat, drink and sleep before going out again. That's their life and I can promise you it's hard, tiring and dangerous.

'Lancasters, Halifaxes and Stirlings [sic] roared out over the North Sea. We flew among them and turning back from the cockpit to look into the gorgeous sunset, I counted thirty or forty Lancasters seemingly suspended in the evening sky. They were there wherever you looked - in front, behind, above and below - each a separate monster, each separately navigated, but all bound by a coordinated plan of approach and attack. Up above the clouds, the dusk was short. The orange and crimson of sunset died back there where the coast of England lay and ahead of us the brilliant moon hung with the stars around her; below us, the thick clouds hid the sea. We were climbing steadily and as it grew dark we put on our oxygen masks when the air grew too rarefied for normal breathing.

'As we approached the enemy coast I saw the German ack-ack. It was bursting away from us and much lower I didn't see any long streams of it soaring into the air, as the pictures suggest: it burst in little yellow, winking flashes and you couldn't hear it above the roar of the engines. Sometimes it closes in on you and the mid- or rear-gunner will call up calmly and report its position to the captain so that he can dodge it. We dodged it last night, particularly over Berlin: literally jumped over it and nipped round with the wing commander sitting up in his seat as cool as a cucumber, pushing and pulling his great bomber about as though it were a toy.

'We knew well enough when we were approaching Berlin. There was a complete ring of powerful searchlights waving and crossing, though it seemed to me that most of our bombers were over the city. Many of the lights were doused: there was also intense flak. First of all they didn't seem to be aiming at us. It was bursting away to starboard and away to port in thick, yellow clusters and dark, smoky puffs. As we turned in for our first run across the city it closed right round us. For a moment it seemed impossible that we could miss it and one burst lifted us in the air as though a giant hand had pushed up the belly of the machine, but we flew on.

'Just then another Lancaster dropped a load of incendiaries and where, a moment before, there had been a dark patch of the city, a dazzling silver pattern spread itself a rectangle of brilliant lights - hundreds, thousands of them - winking and gleaming and lighting the outlines of the city around them. [The Pathfinders again were unable to mark the centre of the city and once more the bombing fell mainly in the southern areas.] As though this unloading had been the signal, score after score of fire bombs went down and all over the dark face of the German capital these great incandescent flower beds spread themselves. It was a fascinating sight. As I watched and tried to photograph the flares with a cine-camera, I saw the pinpoints merging and the white glare turning to a dull, ugly red as the fires of bricks and mortar and wood spread from the chemical flares.

'We flew over the city three times, for more than half an hour, while the guns sought us out and failed to hit us. At last our bomb-aimer sighted his objective below and for one unpleasant minute we flew steady and straight. And then he pressed the button and the biggest bomb of the evening, our 3½-tonner fell away and down. I didn't see it burst but I know what a giant bomb does and I couldn't help wondering whether, anywhere in the area of the devastation, such a man as Hitler, Goering, Himmler or Goebbels might be cowering in a shelter. It was engrossing to realise that the Nazi leaders and their Ministries were only a few thousand feet from us and that this shimmering mass of flares and bombs and gun-flashes was their stronghold.

'We turned away from Berlin at last - it seemed we were there for an age - and we came home. We saw no night-fighters, to our amazement, nor did any of the flak on the homeward journey come very near us. We came back across the North Sea, exchanged greetings of the day with a little coastwise convoy and came in to England again, nine hours after we had flown out. There were so many machines circling impatiently round our aerodrome that we had to wait up above for an hour and twenty minutes before we could land and it was two o'clock in the morning when the wing commander brought us down to the flarepath and taxied us in.

'We climbed stiffly out, "Johnny" from the rear turret, Brian who used to be a policeman, from the mid-upper, "Hutch", the radio operator; "Junior" the navigator - by far the youngest of us all. Then the Scots flight engineer, a quiet calm sergeant; and last the short sturdy Wingco who has flown in every major air raid of this war and been a night-fighter pilot in between times. They were the crew - six brave, cool and exceedingly skilful men.[7] Perhaps I am shooting a line for them, but I think somebody ought to. They and their magnificent Lancasters and all the others like them are taking the war right into Germany. They have been attacking and giving their lives in attack since the first day of the war and their squadron went on that show too. *Per ardua ad astra* is the RAF motto. Perhaps I can translate it "Through

---

7  Gibson, who led the famous Ruhr dams raid in May 1943, was KIA in a Mosquito of 627 Squadron on 19/20 September 1944. Sub/Lieutenant Gerard Muttrie was killed on 15 April on Stuttgart. Hutchison, who was Gibson's WOp/AG on the Dams raid was KIA on 15/16 September 1943 on the Dortmund-Ems canal operation. Pilot Officer G. McGregor was posted on 24 July 1943.

hardship to the stars". I understand the hardship now and I'm proud to have seen the stars with them.'

All the Lancasters on 106 Squadron returned safely, but 61 Squadron, which shared the base at Syerston, was missing one Lancaster. 'J-Johnny' flown by 22-year-old Pilot Officer James Woolford RCAF, an American from Charleston, Illinois, was hit by flak and crashed in the Hohenzollerenplatz behind the Lutheran Kirche, Kiel. There were no survivors. Woolford left a widow, Virginia Thorton Woolford. 'X-X-ray' *Admiral Air Goosk,* piloted by Sergeant Philip Noel Reed on 106 Squadron had been hit by flak and on landing back the undercarriage collapsed, but there were no injuries to the crew.[8] On 3rd February the crew's luck ran out when Reed and his crew failed to return from a raid on Hamburg. Two nights later, *Admiral Prune* went missing with another crew after an engine fire near Dijon. Lancaster ED593 then became Gibson's aircraft. This Lancaster carried the same nose art but was named *Admiral Prune II.*

Over the North Sea Robert Raymond climbed up through layers of cloud tinted with the red glow of the setting sun. In the clear air between them it looked to him like some of those dreamy cloudland shots in *Lost Horizon.* 'Just a space without a horizon except for the banded cloud of soft greys, mauve, purple and grey blues and with "George" [the automatic pilot] flying I had plenty of time to think - odd thoughts as mine always are - how scared I had been in a nearby town two nights before when sitting in a cafe during an Air Raid Alert. Several enemy planes bombed from low-level and one bomb demolished the building across the street. The blast effect even from that small effort was considerable and made me appreciate what we were doing to the enemy targets with our forces and weight-carrying capacity. Verily it is better to send than to receive in this racket. Then I thought about the message from the Chief of Bomber Command which had been addressed to us tonight and read out at Briefing, "Go to it, Chaps, and show them the red rose of Lancaster in full bloom." Someone behind a desk had given an order to a great organization and here we were a few hours later, one of the pawns in the game, sitting up over the North Sea with the temperature at minus 30° Centigrade, wondering if we would ever see England again.

---

8  On the night of 13/14 January in one of the first 'Oboe' raids on Essen, Reed had brought the severely damaged 'G-George' back after being twice attacked by an FW 190 'Wilde Sau' night-fighter shortly after bombing the target. The rear gunner was badly wounded and the mid-upper gunner, Sergeant James Breeds Hood, was killed, but Reed managed to fly the crippled bomber as far as the USAAF base at Hardwick before executing a successful crash-landing.

'Vapour condensation trails were plainly visible in the clear moonlight above cloud, showing that many other planes were a few minutes ahead on the same track. They are always a curious phenomenon and form at the trailing edge of your wings, due to the decrease in pressure there. Out over the sea we pay no attention to them, but over enemy territory they always result in attacks by night-fighters. Conditions over the target were about the same as the previous night, except the visibility was even better. Several members of the crew heard shrapnel from spent bursts bounce off our fuselage and the rear gunner saw five members of a crew bail out and go down on their white silk umbrellas. We passed quite close to them. Flak was more accurate than the previous night and several times I saw the black smoke puffs indicating shell bursts right in front of us as we were leaving the target area... Collected some ice on the return trip, but I have no fear of that now, having studied diligently and knowing why, when and how it occurs. It is only necessary to be able to recognise the type of cloud, the frontal weather conditions and have an accurate thermometer to avoid its cumulative effects. Each time I climbed to lower temperatures or descended to clearer areas and we went through it confidently, although I have reason to believe that it accounted for some that are missing.'

On 9 Squadron Sergeant 'Andy' Carswell, who had taken off from Waddington at 1645 hours had no doubts either. '17th January 1943 was one of those nights when the Germans seemed to have all the cards, including the weather and they were waiting for us all along the route.' Aircraft captains returning to the Lincolnshire station were relieved to hear the silken tones of the duty corporal in the R/T cabin on the roof of the Watch Office, a square box-like building in front of the hangars, where 23-year-old Corporal Maureen Miller, on eight-hour night duty, listened for landing aircraft coming back from ops. Tall, slender and attractive, with thick, honey-coloured hair and green eyes framed with long, black lashes,[9] Maureen would marry a Lancaster captain on 57 Squadron in December that year.

Suddenly: 'Hello Jetty, Lighthouse "J-Jig", over.'

'Hello Lighthouse "J-Jig", Jetty answering,' replied Maureen. 'Prepare to land. QFE 1003. Over.'

'Hello "Jetty", "Maypole B-Baker" over.'

'"Maypole B-Baker", airfield 1,500, over.'

'Hello "Jetty", "Lighthouse Q-Queenie", over.'

---

9  See *A WAAF In Bomber Command* by Pip Beck (Goodall 1989).

'"Lighthouse Q-Queenie", airfield 2,000, over.'

Meanwhile, 'J-Jig' would have called 'Funnels' as 22-year-old Sergeant Arthur Roy Hobbs approached the runway and then called to say that he was down. 'J-Jig' carried Flight Sergeant 'Frank' Goheen Nelson, a 24-year-old American pilot from Wilkinsburg, Pennsylvania as 'second dickie'. Hobbs' crew would be lost without trace on a 'Gardening' trip off the Biscay coast on 8th/9th April. Nelson and his crew were lost returning from Hamburg on 30th/31st January when they crashed in bad weather over the North York Moors, crashing into the Hambleton Hills and all were killed on their second trip together.

'B-Baker' was then told to 'pancake' and started his landing run. 'Q-Queenie' was brought down to 1,500 feet. Fresh aircraft calling up were stacked at heights 500 feet apart above the airfield circuit, given the airfield barometric pressure to set on their altimeters and brought down 500 feet as the lowest aircraft in the stack landed. Presently, eight Lancasters on 9 Squadron got down but four were overdue. One of them was 'P-Peter'. Flying Officer Anderson Storey, a 6 feet 4 inches tall 25-year-old American from one of the oldest and best New England families and his crew were shot down by a night-fighter south-east of Neumünster in Schleswig-Holstein on their way to Berlin. Before the war 'Andy', who came from Jamaica Plain, Massachusetts, had holidayed in England and he had become something of an anglophile. The Berlin operation would have been his thirtieth and last of his tour.[10]

Nothing was heard from 'G-George' piloted by 23-year-old Sergeant John George Bruce Chilvers, all of whose crew were lost without trace, as were 'V-Victor's' crew skippered by 24-year-old Pilot Officer Trevor Leslie Gibson, an experienced Aussie from New South Wales. On 5th/6th October on the Aachen raid, he had flown his way out of an attack by three Bf 109s and he had once flown through the Alps on three engines rather than over. New Zealander, Flying Officer Eric William Mitchell Jacombs. the 27-year-old second 'dickie' who had grown up in Auckland was among the dead. Early in 1942 he had married Joan Winifred Hill of Mount Eden. By the end of the war just under 11,000 New Zealanders had served with the RAF and of this number 3,290, or nearly one-third, lost their lives.

Over Magdeburg on the return from bombing Berlin 'A-Apple' had been hit by heavy and accurate flak which set the starboard engine on fire and

---

10  See *Bombers First and Last* (Robson Books 2006) and *No Need To Die* (Haynes Publishing 2009) by Gordon Thorburn.

the Lancaster went into an uncontrollable dive. 'Andy' Carswell managed to get the crippled and burning aircraft into a more moderate dive and gave the order to bail out in what he hoped was a fairly professional tone. 'Jock' Martin the Scottish flight engineer methodically picked up the parachute chest packs from the rack on the starboard side, reading the names in the flickering orange light of the fire, and handed them out to the navigator, bombardier, radio operator and Carswell who said, 'Considering the careless way some of us treated our chutes in the crew room, I think he wanted to make sure he got his own. "Paddy" Hipson our Irish bombardier pulled the release pin on the forward escape hatch, and the pad on which he had been lying minutes before, as well as the hatch, was ripped downward into the roaring darkness. The front cockpit of the Lancaster was now full of engine noise from the three remaining Rolls-Royce Merlin 1,250-horsepower engines screaming above the roar of the wind with papers, maps and debris being sucked into the dark void. "Paddy" hesitated, then stepped into the black hole and disappeared.

'"Jock" Martin carefully folded up his jump seat on my immediate right, opening up the way to the nose compartment, and proceeded forward. Without a pause he dived head first through the opening clutching his chest pack with both hands. Our English radio operator and air gunner, "Eddie" Phillips, followed him out smartly without even a nod in my direction. I was glad to see them going out so fast, as the aircraft seemed about to explode, with bright orange flames steadily eating into the wing, only inches away from the fuel tanks.

'A strained voice over the intercom from the mid-upper gun turret - "Joe" de Silva, an Englishman, older than the rest of us, married with kids - "I'm stuck! I can't get out!" Then Claude Clemens, our Canadian rear gunner's voice: "Hang on, 'Joe'! I'll go and yank him out!" A long pause, then Clem's voice again: "He's okay now Skipper - he's out of the 'kite' now and I'm right behind him." Then silence on the intercom.

'We were below ten thousand feet now and the altimeter needle was spinning down at an alarming rate. The cockpit was full of noise and wind. I was straining with all my strength to hold back the control column. The airspeed indicator was past the red line and the noise from the open hatch was deafening. The four throttle levers were back to idle, but the props were still winding up. There were only two of us left, John Galbraith, our Canadian navigator and me. John's intercom was unplugged, the cord dangling from his leather flying helmet. I grabbed his shoulder, pulled him to me and screamed in his ear, "Get out, you dumb bastard!" He looked at me with a strange expression on his face and shouted back over the noise, "We can get her back home!"

'I grabbed the dangling wire on his helmet, pulled his head over to mine, and shouted into his ear, "Look at that fire, you fucking idiot! We're going to blow up any second and you're standing there arguing! Get the hell out! The controls are shot and I can't hold it any longer! If you don't get out, I'm going anyway!"

'"Turn onto a heading of two seven zero, due west," he yelled in my ear, "and we'll get out of here."

'"Don't be an asshole!" I yelled. "We're heading straight for the ground!" We were now at about seven thousand feet. He stood there; his parachute chest pack already hooked on and looked at me with a strangely wild stare that I had never seen before. My parachute pack was still on my lap where "Jock" had dropped it. I let go of the control column, picked up the parachute pack and clicked it in place on my chest harness.

'"Out of the way then!" I yelled and pushed by him. I grabbed his collar and pulled his face close to mine. "You'd better follow me now - you've got about ten seconds!" He stared at me with wild eyes. Then I dived through the open hatch into the roaring black hole, clutching my parachute pack to my chest, hurtling towards the ground at more than 300 mph.'

John Galbraith and 'Joe' de Silva were killed after leaving the aircraft and were laid to rest close to each other in Berlin. Theresa de Silva spent over twenty-five years in a psychiatric hospital after receiving the telegram informing her that her husband was 'missing, presumed killed'. Her two daughters were raised by loving grandparents.

'Jock' Martin, 'Paddy' Hipson, 'Eddy' Phillips the wireless operator and Claude 'Clem' Clemens survived and were taken into captivity. So too, a very much relieved 'Andy' Carswell. 'I had heard tales of British aircrew who, when rounded up by the irate German citizenry after a particularly heavy air raid, were strung up on the spot. I heard similar stories about hapless German crews, arriving by parachute in East London after a particularly bloody raid, done in by the local populace. These stories may have been apocryphal, but I suspect there was more truth than fiction in some of them, considering the circumstances.'[11]

German night-fighters had no trouble finding the bomber stream - at Wickenby 12 Squadron too had lost four Lancasters - and the Nachtjäger

---

11  *Seven Thousand Feet and Falling* by Andrew Carswell from his Second World War memoir *Over The Wire.*

claimed all nineteen Lancasters and three Halifaxes (11.8 per cent of the force) that failed to return. To help swell the numbers of attacking aircraft some of the Lancasters that took part were from the Conversion Units. Two of these on 1654 CU at Swinderby and one on 1656 at Lindholme had been lost with their crews. One of the missing 1654 CU Lancasters, 'X-ray' piloted by Pilot Officer Frederick Arthur Read DFC, was probably shot down over the North Sea ten kilometres west of Vlieland at 2339 hours in bitterly cold weather by Unteroffizier Karl-Georg Pfeiffer of 10./NJG 1. Altogether, fifteen night-fighter pilots, four including Oberleutnant Ludwig Becker, claiming doubles, had their claims verified. Becker's claims for two Stirlings over Holland would seem to indicate that they were part of a minelaying operation, but no losses were reported.

Robert Raymond on 44 'Rhodesia' Squadron found it impossible to land back at Waddington and he was diverted nearly 200 miles, by which time the Lancaster was running on the fumes that came from the last drops of petrol that Griffiths, his flight engineer, was squeezing out of the tanks. 'His knowledge of the Merlin engines, due to long experience, was amazing for a young man of nineteen years,' wrote Raymond. 'More and more I find that knowledge is a more valued asset than courage. Each member of the crew is still learning. Griffiths has found the best speeds to fly and rates of climb for most economical fuel consumption. We keep our own charts and are improving steadily.' Interrogation after the trip was always a pleasant time for Raymond and the crew. It was carried out in the warm, brightly lighted mess while they were eating. WAAFs moved about serving food. All of Raymond's own officers were around and usually a number from the Air Ministry looked on. There was much laughter and many enquiries among the crews about incidents en route. There was much kidding if a pilot did not land promptly when it was his turn. The whole scene was a complete contrast to that of half an hour earlier when most of them were stacked on the circuit listening to the others and the WAAF in the control tower 'cursing like troopers if any stooge didn't land on first try.' He added: 'Came back to base today and found many missing and the rest scattered over England in various ways. Two consecutive nights to Berlin leaves me with but one thought when I have finished this letter. To sleep for at least twelve hours. And my stomach reminds me that I haven't seen an egg for nearly a month and our food is very poor.'[12]

---

12   Robert S. Raymond, *A Yank in Bomber Command.* (Pacifica Press1998).

Lancaster ED360 on 467 Squadron RAAF landed back at Bottesford with the body of Sergeant Alvin John Broemeling RCAF, the 20-year-old air gunner from Provost, Alberta, dead in his rear turret. Broemeling was the unfortunate victim of a missing helmet. A few days earlier he had discovered that his flying helmet was missing from the locker room and he was issued with a replacement. Soon after take-off on the sixteenth he reported that the replacement helmet was unbearably tight. He was told to use the spare helmet carried on the aircraft, but this was fitted with an obsolete oxygen mask, without the aspiratory valve fitted to later models to prevent freezing. By the time the Lancaster commenced its bombing run, at a height of 19,000 feet in temperatures around -50°C, Broemeling's mask was frozen up. The skipper concentrated on his bombing run, but immediately his bomb load had been released he dived steeply to 8,000 feet, to below the need for oxygen masks, although they were still over Berlin's heavy anti-aircraft defences. He set the aircraft on autopilot and did what he could for the now unconscious rear-gunner. The Lancaster was hit twice by anti-aircraft fire but managed to limp home and land safely. Broemeling was reported to have been dead for several hours.

The Bomber Command report stated that the Daimler-Benz factory was badly damaged, but it was not clear if this had occurred on this raid or the one on the previous night and it was not confirmed by the German report. However, the BMW aero-engine factory at Spandau was hit by incendiaries and slightly damaged. There was no important damage in any part of Berlin on this raid. Only eight people were killed and forty-one were injured. The experiments with this Lancaster/Halifax force, using target indicators against Berlin, now ceased until $H_2S$ became available.

Heading back to London two hours after leaving Syerston, Richard Dimbleby pushed his way into the night express. One seat was left and swinging his bag into the rack he dropped into it. As the train gathered speed two soldiers looked in and, finding the compartment full, stood in the corridor outside. Dimbleby was the only civilian, other than an elderly woman opposite. She looked at the soldiers and back at Dimbleby and then she spoke.

'I should have thought a lucky young man like you would have given up his seat.'

Dimbleby was too tired to reply. He sat back, steeped in his knowledge and relief.[13]

---

13 *The Waiting Year* by Richard Dimbleby (Hodder and Stoughton Ltd 1944).

# Chapter 4

# A Wave of Terror

*'Berlin was severely damaged. The Unter den Linden Boulevard has suffered greatly. People are saying that this raid was laid on deliberately for "Luftwaffe Day". The official report puts the number of dead at four hundred and eighty, including six youthful anti-aircraft volunteers. This has been the heaviest attack that Berlin has so far experienced.'*

**Diary entry penned on Wednesday, 3rd March 1943 by Hans-Georg von Studnitz, *While Berlin Burns: The Diary of Hans Georg von Studnitz*, 1943-1945, first published in 1964. Born 31st August 1907 in Potsdam, he began his career as a journalist in 1930 and was called up for war service and attached to the German Foreign Office Press and Information Section.**

After the raid on 17th/18th January 1943 Berliners mercifully received a respite in the heavy night bombing of their city and even the cry 'Achtung Moskito' remained absent over the capital at night. It was not until 30th January, on the tenth anniversary of Hitler's usurpation of power, when two formations, each of three Mosquitoes appeared over Berlin in daylight and attempted to interrupt large rallies being addressed by Goering and Goebbels. The RAF scored a great propaganda victory by bombing in mid-morning at the exact time that the Reichsmarschall was due to speak and the speech was postponed for an hour. In the afternoon three more Mosquitoes repeated the feat when Goebbels speech also had to be abandoned just as he was about to speak. One Mosquito was lost. In Berlin 'Lord Haw' claimed that Britain was so starved of materials that she had been compelled to build bombers of wood. 'Bomber' Harris championed the effort, which he summed up by saying, '[The raid] cannot have failed to cause consternation in Germany and encouragement to the oppressed peoples of Europe.' Still Harris was not yet ready to unleash his heavies on Berlin, and in February too, the sky above Berlin remained clear of RAF aircraft. The attacks that did take place were made on other German cities, on French seaports on the Atlantic coast and targets in Italy. However, the Nazis and the people of Berlin knew from past experience that the respite would not last much longer and by March Josef Goebbels was deeply troubled. 'Reports from the Rhineland indicate that in some cities people are gradually getting rather weak at the knees. That is understandable. For months the working population has had to go into air raid shelters night after night and when they come out again they see part of their city going up in flame and smoke. The enervating thing about it is that we are not in a position to reply in kind... Our war in the east has lost us air supremacy in essential sections of Europe and we are completely at the mercy of the English [sic].' A resumption of raids on the 'Big City' finally arrived on Monday, 1st March when 156 Lancaster, eighty-six Halifax and sixty Stirling crews were briefed for Berlin.

On 76 Squadron, which shared Linton-on-Ouse with 78 Squadron's Halifax bombers, Sergeant V.J. Crutch was the 20-year-old flight engineer on the crew skippered by 29-year-old Squadron Leader John Lawrence Fletcher DFM MID who was on his second tour of operations. 'After breakfast I contacted my skipper in his office to see if there were any orders for me. If he had no instructions I would have probably gone to the Link Trainer for some flying practice, or "Tommy" [Sergeant Louis Arthur Trinder, the 19-year-old mid-upper gunner] and I would have collected some ammunition from the armoury together with a rifle and gone to the rifle ranges for practice. The practice with the rifle came in very handy, on days when the aircrews were stood down for bad weather conditions and there were no operations, we would go to York. There was a shooting gallery there with one accurate rifle out of those available. It was easy to collect a full score and the tablet of Lux toilet soap for the prize. I went on leave around Xmas with an attaché case virtually filled with bars of soap and the large shortbread biscuits which were given to us for flying rations. I never found time during operations to think of eating and since I had a brother and two young sisters at home I had saved the biscuits together with those that were given to me by other members of the crew.

'At lunchtime we waited to hear if there was to be an operation that night. February had been a fairly quiet month because of the weather conditions prevailing at that time of the year. After lunch the word began to circulate that something was on for that night. The whole station seemed to step up a gear. Ground crews became feverishly busy preparing the loads for the night. At around three to four o'clock all aircrew were called to the briefing room. There was an air of expectancy in all the aircrews present, the maps on the wall were covered and we were all waiting to find out where the target was for that night.

'Our squadron commander, Wing Commander Leonard Cheshire[1] arrived, the crews were called to order, the buzz of expectant chat disappeared and the map was uncovered and the target, "Berlin", was announced together with the route to and from the target, time of take-off and the time to be over target (usually about a twenty minute period). There was some excitement in the crew since this was to be our second visit to the "Big City". The previous occasion had been on 16th January. We were advised that maximum effort was to be made that night which would mean putting about 300 heavy aircraft in the air for the operation. The intelligence officer gave us what information was available about the enemy defences. This was followed by a report of the weather conditions which were likely to prevail that night. As the flight engineer of our crew my main interest was the weight of the bomb load together with the fuel requirements for the operation, these normally had to total 60,000lbs, which was the all up weight of the Halifax II. The bomb aimer and the navigator joined their individual leaders as the crews were dismissed from the briefing to collect their maps and further information relevant to the operation.

'Now we were off to the mess to have our pre-flight meal of eggs, bacon and sausage and collect our flying rations. It was at this time, in the short interval available before one started putting on flying equipment, that one really came to terms with one's thoughts about the task ahead and the risks involved. Our flying equipment was stored in a locker room on the edge of the airfield and from there we were taken out as individual crews to our aircraft which were dispersed at various locations around the airfield. Tonight we were taking a second pilot [22-year-old Flight Lieutenant Arthur Thomas Wheatley] with us who had just joined the squadron, so that he could gain some experience.

'From this point onwards we all had a job to do and we were all reliant on each other to do it well. I had a word with the ground crews and received their reports in relation to the aircraft's airworthiness. There was the fuel

---

1  Cheshire had completed his second tour early in 1942, having earned the temporary rank of squadron leader. He was promoted to the substantive rank of squadron leader on 1 March and in August 1942 he returned to operations as an acting wing commander and commanding officer of 76 Squadron.

load to check, the photoflash flares to be checked and that they were stowed safely, the fuel cocks were checked to be sure that they were switched to the right tanks, the Very cartridge identification "colours of the day" were checked that they corresponded to the previous information given at the briefing. Now was the time to start filling all the headings of the flight engineer's log. An entry was required for every change in engine revolutions or boost setting and any variation in height of 2,000 feet, all these factors would affect the fuel consumption. Although we had fuel gauges on each tank they were not used except as a cross-check. The fuel consumption was calculated against engine settings and time and the tanks were only switched normally on these calculations. In fact it was normal practice to advise the pilot of the fuel position in a tank and then proceed to the fuel cock levers situated under the two bunks either side of the aircraft between the main spars. Since the four engines were all fed from a different tank it was reasonable to expect the inner engines on the port or starboard sides would use up the fuel from its tank about the same time and similarly with the outer engines, so normally tank changes came in pairs. I would normally wait there until the pilot felt the engine fail, either port or starboard side, and he would advise over the intercom and I would change the tank, this ensured that we were making the best use of the fuel in case our journey proved to be longer than first envisaged due to weather conditions or for any other reason.

'Eventually there was a Very light fired from the control tower and we started the engines, ran them up to maximum power to check that all was well and then left our dispersal point and joined all the other aircraft on the perimeter track and moved towards the end of the runway, to take our turn, on receipt of a signal from the Aldis lamp of the control officer, to take off. The first critical period was over once we had lumbered down the runway and eventually became airborne. For take-off, the engines were run at 3,000 rpm, 12lbs boost, and once we were airborne they were throttled back to 2,850 rpm, 4lbs boost, which was the normal cruising settings for the Rolls-Royce Merlin 20 engines powering the Halifax at this time.

'The course was now set for our first landfall, which was to be in Denmark. We passed over the British coastline with a view of Flamborough Head below us, gradually climbing to our operational height of 20,000 feet. As we flew we were joined in the bomber stream by the other aircraft of the bomber force, the Stirlings reaching their operational height of 18,000 feet and the Lancasters 22,000 feet and so we would fly to the target stacked in three layers. Some nights, if vapour trails were forming, one would be aware of the other aircraft about you, whilst on other dark nights it seemed as though you were completely on your own all the way to the target.

'Our route was across Denmark and over the Baltic to a point north-west of Rostock where we changed course and headed for our target. Over the Baltic I became aware that one of the engines was over heating and it was at this point that decisions had to be made as to whether to continue with the mission or not. It was decided to rest the engine until we were approaching the target, so the airscrew was feathered, and we continued on three engines.'

'It was dark when we got to the North German coast,' wrote Pilot Officer 'Ron' Read, now a Halifax skipper on 78 Squadron, who had flown his first op, to Turin on 18th/19th November 1942 when 'the butterflies were there all right.'

'Flying in hostile skies was a different proposition to the London "Blitz". Highly trained people on the ground and in the air were spending their lives trying to stop RAF bombers from reaching their target. Flying a bomber over Germany in the spring of 1943 was a crude and cynical business. The "Big City" as we knew it, was a feared target and there was no doubt it would be defended fiercely.

'The plan was to fly north along the coast across Schleswig Holstein and turn south somewhere east of Hamburg. It was intended to indicate that we might be going for one of several targets, Kiel, Hamburg, or Rostock. We would pass them closely, before making a last minute turn south to Berlin. Over Germany, the winds were all over the place and we were soon well off track. We flew over Kiel by mistake and got a very hot reception. It even woke "Taff" Lewis up from his job of monitoring and jamming German R/T transmissions by using tinsel. All aircraft carried a microphone in an engine nacelle. When he heard any German broadcast, the wireless operator pressed his key and the noise of the engine was transmitted on the German fighter frequency, to distort any instructions. "Taff" was a thin, dark little Celt from Newport. A clarinet player in a local band before he joined up, we had something in common. He was also a bit of a wit. Coming from a small Monmouthshire village, he was the youngest of a large family of ten and most unworldly. In 1941 he received his call-up papers. His elderly mother was sure the country could win the war without him and fully expected him to be returned to her as unacceptable. But he was accepted for wireless training.

'As we bounced about the sky, "Taff", while listening out, had been reading his musical magazine, *The Melody Maker*. Seeing the title of a popular melody of the day, he came up on intercom: "Hey Skip, it says here that, *Anywhere On Earth Is Heaven*."

'"You're bloody right 'Taff'," I replied through my teeth, hanging on to the shaking control column. "And I wish like Hell we were anywhere on earth now."

'We ploughed on to Berlin, me hauling and coaxing old "C-Charlie" higher than she'd ever been before. Finally, I told them we were at last at 20,000 feet. There were muted cheers all round. When we reached Berlin the Pathfinders, affected by the fickle winds, were late, so we had to stooge around. After a while, some fires and flares appeared ahead and "Harry" led us to them. We were quite close to them when "Mac" McQueen, the rear gunner, who was only seventeen when he joined up, having lied about his age, said that there were other flares going down behind us. I looked around over my shoulder. No doubt about these, they were the real ones and the ones we were chasing were dummies, well east of the target. Now I had to go back against the stream of incoming aircraft. There were over 300 that night. As I turned I saw a few more aircraft doing the same. Making my turn fairly sharp, "C-Charlie" lost a bit of height. By now there were aircraft all around us, going in all directions. It was bloody dicey. Wanting to get over the target, drop the bombs and get out as soon as possible, I pushed the nose down to speed things up.

'We soon had a good view of the correct marker flares, but I now had to go the full distance back across the target, among the heavy flak and against the oncoming stream, before turning once more onto the correct heading. By the time we'd done that I was down to 17,500 feet for the bombing run. Once more I hadn't managed to bomb from the full height. However, the crew weren't complaining now, they wanted to get it all over with and get out just as quickly as I did. It was hot over Berlin all right. We saw several Halifaxes coned in searchlights. Having dropped our bombs in the approved fashion and spent ten long seconds waiting for our photoflash to go off, I turned for home.'

Squadron Leader Alan Donald Frank DFC was flying 'F for Freddie', a 51 Squadron Halifax. Born on 27th July 1917 at Prestbury, Cheshire and educated at Eton, he learned to fly with the University Air Squadron while at Magdalen College Oxford. From September 1939 Frank served briefly on a training squadron for new Fairey Battle pilots, before being posted to the Advanced Air Striking Force in France. Frank wrote: 'Crossing Denmark we pass into the Baltic and swing towards Berlin. Now we are in the thick of the fighter defences and bursts of horizontal tracer show that the Luftwaffe is active. Over to port an aircraft bursts into flames and descends seemingly amazingly slowly to earth. It is impossible to see the aircraft type nor whether any parachutes have emerged. Suddenly, straight ahead the darkness is transformed. A single searchlight sweeps the sky, then another, then in virtually no time hundreds - the flak follows, and the sky ahead is a continuous mass of flashes from bursting shells. Intelligence told us of 400 heavy AA guns in the city's defences, but that looks like an underestimate! Then the flare droppers get to work and perhaps a hundred parachute flares hang in the night sky. The target markers will be dropped by radar but the master bomber will try to assess their accuracy visually. The target markers resemble clusters of brilliantly coloured chandeliers bursting a couple of thousand feet up and continuing to burn on the ground. The first markers down are red. The Master Bomber now picks the most accurate and directs the back-up marker force to aim green markers at it and that is our target. Finally, the main force - 200 aircraft, each carrying many tons of high explosives and sticks of incendiaries and the scene below passes belief. Continuous flashes mark the burst of high explosive and sticks of incendiaries draw incandescent streaks across the city where fires quickly appear to complete a picture which Dante could hardly have visualised.

'By this time we are entering the Berlin defensive ring - about eighty miles across. So long as we are only subject to barrage fire, the best bet is to grit one's teeth and fly straight to get through as quickly as possible, but this time we are unlucky. A searchlight picks us out and almost at once we are at the dazzling centre of a cone with predicted flak coming up at us. Dropping 2,000 feet to keep clear of the incoming bomber stream, I turn through 180 degrees and fly north out of range of the defences. Then I swing south again to join the tail end of the attack and try again. This time we are luckier. No searchlight picks us up and we have only the barrage and the ever present danger of night-fighters to cope with. Fragments of bursting shell rattle against the fuselage and in the general tension I suddenly realise that my mouth is quite dry, but it is now as safe to go forward as back. As the inferno that is Berlin disappears under the nose, I tell "Minch", lying on his stomach in the nose studying the scene below, to takeover. With a voice of absolute calm I hear, "About two minutes to run, Skipper, left, left, steady, steady - bomb doors open please - all bombs gone. Camera has operated - close bomb doors."

'Now "F for Freddie", less half her fuel load and five tons of bombs, feels positively skittish! "Course for home please, 'Toddy'" and we swing westward. Ahead is the frontal cloud which caused us worries on the way out. Now it offers protection from the ever present fighter threat and I fly towards it. Once into cloud we can all relax except "Toddy". From him

I get the usual steady grumble about the unreliability of forecast winds, the lack of pinpoints and the uselessness of the radio bearings but it does not stop me from opening the thermos and enjoying some indifferent coffee. However, we are not home yet. Over the Zuider Zee we run out of cloud and this is a notorious area for night-fighters. Everybody wakes up to peer into the darkness. Nothing is seen but suddenly "Monica" starts to emit a stream of excited squeaks ("Monica" is a device which warns us that we are being tracked by night-fighter radar). Reaction must be quick and I go into a corkscrew - a violent diving turn which spills the coffee and throws loose objects round the flight deck. An equally violent climbing turn to starboard presses us all into our seats. Thankfully "Monica" has relapsed into silence. We have shaken the fighter off.'[2]

The Pathfinders experienced difficulty in producing concentrated marking because individual parts of the extensive built-up city area of Berlin could not be distinguished on the H$_2$S screens. Bombing photographs showed that the attack was spread over more than 100 square miles with the main emphasis in the south-west of the city. However, because larger numbers of aircraft were now being used and because those aircraft were now carrying a greater average bomb load, the proportion of the force which did hit Berlin caused more damage than any previous raid to this target. (On a short flight, the Lancaster could carry well over 11,000lbs of bombs, but the longer the journey, the more fuel that was needed and consequently less bomb load to avoid exceeding the safe permitted level.) This type of result - with significant damage still being caused by only partially successful attacks - was becoming a regular feature of Bomber Command raids. Twenty-two acres of workshops were burnt out at the railway repair works at Tempelhof and twenty factories were badly damaged and 875 buildings - mostly houses - were destroyed and 191 people were killed.

Sergeant John Crutch, on Squadron Leader Fletcher's crew, wrote: 'The target was well lit that night and although there was fierce opposition from the flak and searchlights we managed to make our bombing run without incident. Having now set course for home, which was roughly due west, we assessed the condition of the aircraft. I had checked that all the bombs had been released by visually checking through the inspection panels into the bomb bay. This was standard procedure, as it was possible for the electrical

---

2  *War's Long Shadow: 69 Months of the Second World War* 11 Nov 2002 by Charlotte Popescu. In April 1943 Frank took command of 51 Squadron. Air Vice-Marshal Alan Frank retired from the RAF in 1970. He died aged 84 in October 2001.

release mechanism to fail and in such circumstances the bomb bay doors were reopened at a suitable time and the bomb released by hand operation. The engine which had been restarted during our run in to the target was running again above normal temperature but was remaining stable. Also, now we had another engine temperature rising. Again decisions had to be made as to whether we should feather two engines and conserve them. We decided to keep a close check on them and feather them only if conditions became critical.

'Way ahead of us the early aircraft over the target had started meeting stiff opposition from flak and a great concentration of searchlights in the region of what should have been Hanover. The pilot questioned the navigator in respect of the accuracy of our course; previously there had never been such a concentration of defences north of the Ruhr or south of the Hamburg region. Taking into account the uncertain reliability it was decided to take a course south of the flak concentration and so we set our new course and all the activity was passed on our starboard side.

'After another period when everything appeared to be going well, the engines were still running within reasonable tolerances, we were quite suddenly coned by a vast number of searchlights. The flak became intense and there we were on our own coming across the north Ruhr defences. For what now appeared to be an unending period the skipper put the Halifax through some amazing evasive manoeuvre changing height and direction so rapidly that I can remember being weightless at times and actually floating in the air about my position in the aircraft and then the G forces would be such that I became literally stuck to the floor. We did not receive any direct hits during this period, although we had never experienced flak as intense. The noise of the flak sounded like metal dustbin lids being clashed together above the scream of the engines and the air flow around us. Miraculously we lived through it and eventually the searchlights were switched off as quickly as they had appeared and the flak disappeared.

'What a sense of relief was felt by us all. The skipper started checking over the intercom system that all the crew were OK and checks began for damage sustained to the aircraft. I had made a tour of the rear end of the aircraft for any noticeable damage and had returned to my position to carry on checks of the engine conditions and the fuel state. The air gunners had been advised to keep a sharp look out for enemy night-fighters when suddenly there were several loud thuds, the aircraft seemed to rear up, a fire started in the port inner engine and the pilot gave the order immediately, "bail out chaps we've had it".

'From that point I did everything automatically as I had rehearsed in my mind a thousand times. I tore off my oxygen mask and helmet, grabbed my parachute from its stowage and clipped it onto the harness as I vaulted the two main spars across the centre fuselage. I have a recollection of something flicking past me as I ran aft, whether it was tracer fire or what I do not know. At the mid-upper turret position I passed "Tommy" in the process of clipping on his parachute. Meanwhile I reached the rear exit, reached down, opened it; sat down, put my feet out and out I went. I do not remember consciously releasing the parachute by pulling the ripcord, but the next thing I was aware of was the jolt of my harness as the parachute opened. There followed a strange silence, everything was completely black. I saw no sign of a burning aircraft although I recall that the canopy of the parachute, soon after it had opened, partially closed, as though buffeted by some external force. This could have been caused when the aircraft blew up. In the dark the feeling was strange. It felt as though I was rising rather than falling. I started to search below me in the darkness for any signs of where I might be landing. Suddenly I saw what I thought was a tree, but while the thought entered my mind, I hit the ground and I was sitting on a clump of marsh grass. It was at this time that I really believed that there was a God in heaven, who controlled all things, whether we are able to understand the reasons or not. Since this time I have always been willing to take life as it comes and accept my destiny.'[3]

It was a fairly clear night and when the bombers were returning to their home bases, the crews could still see the fires in Berlin after one hour flying into the west. This was confirmed by Squadron Leader Geoff Rothwell DFC, a Flight Commander on 75 Squadron RNZAF at Newmarket and a second tourist, who wrote that 'it was the heaviest weight of bombs to be dropped on Berlin and fires were still seen 200 miles from the target.'

Rothwell, who was born on 3rd April 1920 in Didsbury near Manchester, had flown Wellingtons on 99 Squadron in 1940 and in mid-1942 had been

---

3   Squadron Leader Fletcher's Halifax was shot down by a night fighter at 0013 hours at Grootrees near Kasterlee in Belgium. Fletcher, Flight Lieutenant Arthur Wheatley; Pilot Officer Harold Barbour Moore the 23-year-old Canadian air gunner, 'Tommy' Trinder and Pilot Officer Grenville Gordon Stanley the 22-year-old wireless operator were killed. Flying Officer Ernest Lawrence Souter-Smith the 32-year-old navigator evaded. Pilot Officer W.P. Blackman, bomb aimer and John Crutch were taken prisoner. A second Halifax on 76 Squadron, skippered by Pilot Officer Norman Scott Black RNZAF was shot down 40 km west of Texel by Leutnant Robert Denzel of 12./NJG 1 flying a Bf 110 from Leeuwarden airfield. All the crew were killed.

part of a delegation sent to Washington DC. On the 1st March Berlin raid the crew were attacked en route by a twin-engine fighter over Fehmarn Island. After shaking off the fighter the crew successfully bombed the target and were en route home when on the outskirts of Osnabrück they were again attacked. Flying at 13,500 feet both gunners were alert to the presence of a fighter manoeuvring into position at a range of 400 yard astern. Seeing the danger both gunners instantly opened fire with a two-second burst and the fighter was seen to dive away. Almost immediately the Stirling was bracketed by flak and severely hit. The skipper had to draw upon all his experience and flying skill to escape the flak which exploded all around his aircraft. Finally, the crescendo of bursting shells began to recede as the range slowly increased until thankfully the crew were in the clear. Rothwell's windscreen had been shattered and the fuselage was badly holed, luckily missing the crew and any vital equipment. It had been a close shave. Twenty-eight minutes later the crew were north of Münster when a Ju 88 was observed on the port bow slightly above. Both the front and mid-upper gunners engaged the fighter at maximum range with a two second burst and the night-fighter went into a steep dive without firing. A few seconds later the crew then observed a red glow below the clouds which slowly disappeared. Unable to land at base the crew diverted to RAF Stradishall, landing at 0300 hours. It had been a real baptism of fire, the crew had performed magnificently. It was later recorded that for the last encounter the crew could claim a 'probable'. Rothwell recalled, 'my impression after this, my first raid over Germany in just over two years was that there had been enormous changes in tactics, technology and the ferocity of the bombing. It was obvious that there had been tremendous developments in attack and defence by both sides.'[4]

'J for Johnny', piloted by Flight Lieutenant James Victor 'Jim' Verran DFC on 9 Squadron, who was on his second tour after flying Whitleys, returned to Waddington at about 0230 hours. They were using 'Gee' lattice lines to aid their navigation and the New Zealander broke cloud near Waddington at 800 feet but the visibility was poor. He was about to land when another Lancaster [captained by a Canadian, Flying Officer John Fergus Greenan on 57 Squadron] came out of low cloud. The ensuing collision left Verran's Lancaster scattered in pieces across a ploughed field. His left femur was broken, his right arm was paralysed, his jaw broken, and there were serious wounds to his face and head, which were the result of him being thrown

---

4 After a stint on 218 Squadron Geoff Rothwell, in May 1944, was operational again on this his third tour, after a posting to 138 (Special Duties) Squadron at RAF Tempsford.

through his Perspex canopy. Pilot Officer 'Jimmy' Geach the bomb aimer, Sergeant 'Ted' Smithson the flight engineer and Sergeant 'Ken' Matthews the rear gunner were killed on impact. Sergeant 'Ken' Chalk the mid-upper gunner was able to climb out of his turret uninjured. 'Frank' Johnston, the Australian navigator survived, though his brain had been partially detached from his skull. John Moutray the Canadian WOp/AG walked out of the torn fuselage with minor injuries. The crew of the other Lancaster was incinerated. Verran's left leg was encased with plaster up to his waist; his jaw was wired up. He developed a lung infection and had part of a rib removed so that the pleura could drain; he was then given cotton wool soaked in eau de cologne to overcome the smell of the septic fluid. Incredibly, he would, in time, recover from his injuries and return to operational flying.[5]

RAF losses were seven Lancasters, six Halifaxes and four Stirlings; 5.6 per cent of the force. Two of the Lancasters that were lost were on 103 Squadron at Elsham Wolds, a comparatively rough-and-ready base seven miles north-east of Brigg. There were no survivors on the crews of Flight Sergeant William 'Frank' Austin DFM or Flight Lieutenant Gilbert William Stanhope. Austin came from the Liverpool area. It was believed that he had close family killed in the air raids in 1940, which may have been the reason why he was so highly motivated and one of the leading pilots at 103 during that hard winter of 1942-43. He and his crew had flown five ops in seven nights and were on their twenty-ninth operation of their tour. The aircraft was lost without trace and the crew are commemorated on the Runnymede Memorial to the missing. Don Charlwood remembered 'Bill' Austin as a 'likeable fellow, plump, rather pale with straight, black hair that often fell across his forehead. He had brown eyes and the casual manner that often accompanies them. Somehow his battle dress looked slightly big for him. Perhaps it was the way he walked'. 'Never curse a scrub,' Austin had always said, 'It might have been the op you were to go missing on.'[6]

---

5 On 26/27 August 1944, now a Squadron Leader on his third tour, flying a Pathfinder Lancaster on 83 Squadron, Verran was shot down on Kiel by Unteroffizier Gerhard Wartenborger of 4./NJG 3. A German doctor saved Verran's life, carrying out skin grafts without an anaesthetic due to the shortage of drugs and with only paper bandages. The Germans had buried Verran's five crew members in a mass grave and the local people later exhumed the bodies and gave each one a Christian burial. See *Out of the Blue: The Role of Luck in Air Warfare 1917-1966* edited by Laddie Lucas (Hutchinson 1985).

6 *No Moon Tonight* by Don Charlwood (Penguin 1988). Main Force crews were then stood down for one night and the only activity was by sixty aircraft on minelaying operations in coastal areas between Texel and the River Gironde. Three aircraft failed to return.

Halifax II 'R for Robert' (DT641) on 419 'Moose' Squadron RCAF, flown by Pilot Officer Arthur James Herriott DFM, was shot down over the North Sea eight kilometres north of Ameland at around 2139 hours by Major Helmut Lent for his fifty-fourth Abschuss. Two bodies were washed ashore; the five others have no known graves. Stirling I 'T-Tommy' on 15 Squadron, flown by 26-year-old Flight Sergeant Harold Stanley Howland, was shot down by Leutnant Wolfgang Küthe of 11./NJG1 at Schillaard with no survivors. Küthe was killed on 14th April 1944 after gaining his eighth victory when his Bf 110G-4 crashed at Leeuwarden airfield. Most likely he had been hit by return fire. At Zuidloo, Oberleutnant Herbert Heinrich Otto Lütje claimed a Halifax II on 408 'Goose' Squadron flown by 21-year-old Sergeant Arnold Wallace Cochrane RCAF of St. John's, Newfoundland. Six crew were killed and one was taken into captivity after bailing out. Cochrane left a widow, Barbara. Three Halifaxes were credited to III./ NJG1. BB223 on 51 Squadron, flown by 21-year-old Flight Sergeant John David William Stenhouse of Forest Gate, Essex, which crashed at Voorst in Holland with the loss of the seven crew and 'O-Orange' on 35 Squadron flown by 25-year-old Squadron Leader Peter Campbell Elliott DFC of Mill Hill, Middlesex were credited to Leutnant August 'Gustel' ('Noble') Geiger for his thirteenth and fourteenth victories. Flight Sergeant G.C.H. Chandler the air bomber was the only survivor on Elliott's crew. Some bombs hit the Telefunken works where an $H_2S$ set taken from a Stirling shot down near Rotterdam on 2nd/3rd February was being reassembled. In early 1943 Geiger was promoted to Oberleutnant and transferred to 7./NJG1, becoming Staffelkapitän in May 1943 with forty confirmed victories.

'Back at Linton, waiting our turn to land,' wrote 'Ron' Read, 'a Halifax came flying along over the runway shooting off red Very flares. We made way for him immediately. It was Henry Coverley, literally coming back from a spin to avoid the searchlights. He managed to pull out at around 2,000 feet. All his radios and electrics were out and he had to make a landing without any communications. He made it OK, the final happening of an eventful night.[7] Counting the cost next day, we found that of the force of 302 aircraft setting out, seventeen were lost: a nasty 5.5 per cent. Six of them were Halifaxes. On 78 Squadron our luck still held but it was a frail thread, as we were to find out. Later that month I was promoted to flight lieutenant and appointed deputy flight commander.'

---

7   Flight Lieutenant Henry Coverley was shot down on the Nuremberg raid on 30/31 March 1944 and was taken prisoner. He was on his tenth operation on his second tour.

# A WAVE OF TERROR

There was no Main Force activity on the night of Tuesday, 2nd/Wednesday, 3rd March. Minelaying was carried out in enemy waters by sixty aircraft while six Mosquitoes attacked targets in the Ruhr without loss. On 3rd/4th March the visibility was clear over Hamburg, which was under attack by the Main Force. Of the 344 crews who had confidently reported bombing, only seventeen of the 417 aircraft dispatched had actually hit the city. Ten aircraft failed to return and a Stirling was lost on 'Gardening' operations off the Frisians. The night of 5th/6th March, when Essen was raided by 442 aircraft, has gone into history as the starting point of the Battle of the Ruhr. On 11th/12th March, the fourth night of attacks on Ruhr targets, Stuttgart was the destination for 476 bombers, but it was unsuccessful and eleven aircraft failed to return. 'Happy Valley was brighter and merrier than ever,' one pilot proclaimed when on 12th/13th March the Main Force attack again fell on Essen. The Secretary of State for Air, Sir Archibald Sinclair, sent the following appreciative message to Sir Arthur Harris: 'Your cunningly planned and brilliantly executed attack on Krupps has destroyed no small part of Germany's biggest war factory. Congratulations to you and all under your command on this achievement in the teeth of Germany's strongest defences.' The *New York Times* found it appropriate to comment in a leader: 'Germany is apparently reaching the point where she cannot cope, materially or physically, with the effects of bombing. Her enemies did not wait to pummel her cities until the population was strained by years of war and the armies were scraping the bottom of the barrel for men and material. They waited because they were unable to hit sooner. But if Allied strategy had been dictated not by necessity but by a plan to reserve its full striking power until German force was spent, the results would be very much like what they are now.'

On the weekend of 27th/28th March another Berlin operation was scheduled, with 396 aircraft - 191 Lancasters, 124 Halifaxes and 81 Stirlings - on the battle order. Signs were that it would be a very long trip. At briefing the ribbon stretched from the Yorkshire coast and headed toward Groningen on the northern tip of Holland. Before reaching the Dutch coast, the stream would change course, flying just north of the Hansiatic city of Bremen to approach Berlin from the south-west. After bombing the 'Big City' the stream would turn north towards Copenhagen and then turn east, crossing the Kattegat, before making for the Yorkshire coast once again and the relative safety of home. So, although Berlin lay about six hundred miles due east of the bomber airfields the chosen route added a detour of about 150 miles in order to avoid the heaviest fighter concentrations across Holland and North Germany.

'The searchlights were turning off in Berlin as we approached,' wrote 22-year-old Canadian Flying Officer 'Punch' Thompson on 106 Squadron at Syerston, commanded by Wing Commander John Searby. Thompson, born at New Westminster, British Columbia in 1920 and christened 'Walter', in later life he liked to be called 'Punch'. He had joined the RCAF in 1941 and after gaining 'his wings' had been posted to Britain in March 1942. He flew his first operation to Stuttgart on 11th March 1943 with his then CO, Wing Commander Guy Gibson DSO* DFC* in command of their Lancaster. Now, over Berlin, he could see the searchlights shutting down one by one. 'The attack was over and the bomber force had departed. Then we crossed the eastern suburbs of Berlin at 19,500 feet. It took six or seven minutes flying from there over the city before we could recognize anything. I strained against my harness, standing up to see the ground while trying to fly at the same time.' He asked his Scottish bomb aimer, 'Pete' Hanratty, 'Isn't that an airfield down off our port side?' "I think it is," he said. 'Probably Tempelhof', I decided, swinging the Lancaster to the right. 'We should be near the Unter den Linden. Let's see if we can hit the Wehrmacht headquarters, Pete'. I was excited by the danger of being over this great city.

'"Well, I can't see it but I know where it should be," he answered, giving me directions to steer. He too was excited. We plodded on. It seemed to take ages. Now some of the searchlights were being switched on again. They knew we were there but as yet no guns were firing.

'Pete, look for the River Spree or the Tiergarten or maybe a wide road,' I said. "I can see a wide road all right but it's dim - they've gone to bed," he said. We were still at 19,500 feet. We entered upon the bomb run, I opened the doors and after a minute or two of telling me where to fly 'Pete' released the cookie and the thousand pounders; I felt them go. I don't know what we hit but it was near the nerve centre of Berlin. We were on a westerly heading which would have been exceedingly dangerous if the attack were still in progress, because of the likelihood of several hundred bombers flying in the opposite direction. But with the attack over there was little danger of collision. Now some of the anti-aircraft guns began to fire and for the first time I felt the elation of battle. It was exhilarating. I wasn't worried about the guns, not when I could see the gun flashes. I changed altitude, dropping 1,000 feet and altering course as I saw the first battery fire. It then became a guessing game. Will the gunners expect one to turn to the right or to the left? Should one lose altitude or gain it? Probably they'll expect a left-hand turn because it is easier for a pilot sitting on the left side to turn left. So we'll turn right instead and climb. Then there were rapid flashes from two or three other six-gun batteries; I swerved again, feeling like a dancer, pleased with the response of the empty Lancaster. This went on for several minutes and then the guns fell silent as we were leaving the city. All we had to worry about now was getting home. The rear gunner said he could see large fires in the city and the searchlights had once again been turned off. I set course due west for base. At least we had a landmark to start from and the flight plan should get us home.'[8]

Thompson was soon back at Syerston, debriefed and eating a good breakfast after a flight of seven hours and forty-five minutes. 106 Squadron's eleven crews had bombed and returned safely. Four Halifaxes, three Lancasters and two Stirlings were lost (23 per cent of the force). Stirling 'X-X-ray' on 75 Squadron RNZAF was flown by Pilot Officer Martin Lord RNZAF who was on his nineteenth operation. Born on 15th February 1922 at Bulls, Manawatu, Lord lived at Roto-o-rangi in the Cambridge district from the age of five. On leaving school he worked on his grandfather's farm when on 23rd September 1940 he was accepted by the RNZAF. His older brother Norman Lord was a sergeant pilot in the RAF and younger brother Clive was in the Navy. After training in Canada, Martin Lord was posted to 75 Squadron RNZAF where he flew Wellingtons until he converted to the Stirling. With him now were Sergeants' David Wellington RNZAF, 'Norm' Young and Jack Oliver as before, but with the addition of Sergeants 'Len' Nash, flight engineer and 'Bob' McKerrell, air gunner and Pilot Officer Thomas Brown, air bomber. This crew took part in two more operations, the first being on St. Nazaire and their final trip on 27th/28th March, when the aircraft was brought down by flak over Germany, crashing at Melchiorshausen, ten kilometres south of Bremen at 2138 hours. All seven crew members were buried at the Russian PoW cemetery at Vechta, but later re-interred to Sage, south of Oldenburg.[9]

The other missing Stirling was 'L-Leather' on 214 Squadron at Chedburgh, flown by 22-year-old Pilot Officer Edward Challis of Stocksbridge, Yorkshire, which crashed at Finkenwerder on the south bank of the Elbe with no survivors. On 35 Squadron at Graveley, Halifax 'M-Mother' flown by American Flying Officer Harl J. Espy, born 1st October 1920, was hit by flak and crashed near Habichhorst with no survivors. Espy and his crew were laid to rest in Becklington War Cemetery but Espy was later reinterred at Espyville Cemetery in Crawford County, Pennsylvania. 'G-George' on

---

8  *Lancaster To Berlin* by Walter Thompson DFC and Bar.
9  Details of this airman's death were sourced from *For Your Tomorrow* by Errol Martyn.

7 Squadron was hit by flak in the target area which damaged the port outer engine. Flying Officer S. Baker got the bomber home but it swung off the runway and its undercarriage collapsed. There were no injuries.

The raid had proved a failure. The Pathfinders marked two areas, but they were short of their aiming points by five miles. Consequently, none of the bombs were plotted within five miles of the aiming point in the centre of the city and most of the bombing fell from seven to seventeen miles short of the aiming point. Damage was relatively light because of poor marking and partly because about a quarter of the bombs dropped failed to explode. Only sixteen houses were classified as completely destroyed, but 102 people were killed and 260 injured when two bombs, which fell on the Anhalter railway station, hit a military train bringing soldiers back from the Russian Front. Despite the poor marking three aircraft were destroyed at Tempelhof airport and a flak position hit, while at Staaken airfield the flying school was damaged and a further seventy service personnel were killed or wounded. By chance a secret Luftwaffe stores depot in the woods at Teltow, eleven miles south-west of the centre of Berlin was in the middle of the main concentration of bombs and a quantity of valuable radio, radar and other technical stores was destroyed. The Luftwaffe decided that this depot was the true target for the RAF raid on this night and were full of admiration for the special unit, which had found and bombed it so accurately. The Gestapo investigated houses nearby because someone reported that light signals had been flashed to the bombers.[10]

The crew, skippered by Flight Sergeant George Alexander Vinish RCAF on 10 Squadron, was relieved to return to Melbourne, as Sergeant Andrew MacDonald Black his wireless operator, recalled. 'Berlin had been attacked, a good picture obtained and the crew's twenty-second operation was thankfully behind.' A Scot and a pre-war stockbroker's clerk in Glasgow, he remembered Vinish, whose parents were immigrants from Rumania, as a 'tall, gentle and quiet Canadian from a small town, Wakaw, Saskatchewan. The following day 10 Squadron was stood down. In the evening Sergeant Robert Alfred Walker RAFVR, the crew's 21-year-old bomb aimer, took a trip into York where he attended a dinner party. 'Halfway through the dinner,' recalled Black, '"Bob" looked at his watch and remarked that "in about half an hour" Berliners would be startled by a loud explosion from one of our timed, delayed-action bombs… Unbeknown to "Bob", an intelligence

---

10   See *The Bomber Command War Diaries: An Operational reference book 1939-1945* by Martin Middlebrook and Chris Everitt (Midland 1985).

officer, who was also at the dinner, heard his remark and reported him to his CO for careless talk. As a result "Bob" was relieved of his duties and put under arrest pending court martial... Our crew went on and completed its tour but "Bob", who was severely reprimanded, had to join another. On their second operation they were shot down and posted as "missing believed killed in action".'[11]

Squadron Leader Francis John Hartnell-Beavis and his Halifax crew on 76 Squadron had returned to Linton-on-Ouse after bombing Berlin following a flight lasting seven hours fifteen minutes. Born in Hong Kong on 8th June 1913, where his father was practising as a solicitor, he was educated at Uppingham School and later spent nine months at Grenoble University and nine months at Freiburg University in the Black Forest, living with a German family. After training and qualifying as an architect at the Architectural Association in Bedford Square, he worked for two years for Sir Herbert Baker & Scott in London, until war was declared. He first flew Blenheims on 82 Squadron, suffering appalling injuries in a crash landing in R3759 on Hendon aerodrome on 9th June 1940, after the aircraft was struck by lightning. His navigator Sergeant Phipps lost both his legs.

'Even though the weather was appalling,' wrote Hartnell-Beavis, 'I never did find out why it was so important to repeat the attack on Berlin on 29th March (when the force of 329 aircraft of Bomber Command was made up of 162 Lancasters, 103 Halifaxes and 64 Stirlings).[12] The answer lay in the available Pathfinder techniques. The long-range targets could not be marked as accurately as those in the Ruhr; that was one reason why the Ruhr was chosen as the objective in the battle but more distant targets had to be bombed also to keep the fighter defences from concentrating in the Ruhr. So Berlin it was. On this, our second trip to Berlin, we were climbing through thunderstorms and the turbulence was particularly violent, especially in cloud which was solid up to about 16,000 feet, when we appeared to get flipped over on to our back; all the instruments went haywire and I instinctively hauled back on the stick, half looped out and lost about 8,000 feet before regaining control. I didn't know what damage had been done to the aircraft as many of the instruments were on the blink,

---

11   See *Out of the Blue: The Role of Luck in Air Warfare 1917-1966* edited by Laddie Lucas (Hutchinson 1985). 'Bob' Walker had been posted to 115 Squadron in April and was killed on 13/14 July when Lancaster DS690 was shot down on the raid on Aachen by Hauptmann August Geiger of 111/NJG1. There was only one survivor.

12   A diversionary force of 149 'Oboe'-guided Wellingtons went to the small town of Bochum, a few miles east of Essen.

so turned back to base, probably jettisoning the bombs over the North Sea, I don't remember. I often think of the strength of the Halifax which could do a half loop with full bomb load and possibly a ton of ice on the wings, without breaking up!'

A total of twenty-one aircraft was lost on the operation. Lancaster ED586 (in which Ken Letford would take Wynford Vaughan Thomas to Berlin on 3rd September 1943) on 207 Squadron was taken off from Langar, Nottinghamshire by Squadron Leader F.J. Woodward DFC survived, as Gilbert Haworth the navigator recalled: 'We did not suspect that we were due for a unique and very trying ordeal. The moment that the nose of our aircraft entered the Berlin defence zone the dreaded bluish tinted beam of a radar-controlled master searchlight fastened upon us fairly and squarely without any preliminary faltering or wavering. Within another two seconds, three supporting searchlights fixed their beams on us and we were well and truly coned. We had no illusions about our probable fate, nor did we even think about trying to shake off the cone. The aircraft cabin was as bright as day and nothing could be seen outside. We knew what to expect. A large number of 88mm heavy flak guns would engage us as a visual target and would not cease firing until they had destroyed us, on the other hand, it might well be that our bomber would be allocated to the night-fighter force, in which case the guns would leave us alone, keeping the airspace clear for a highly trained and competent pilot to close with us and by the gentle pressure of his thumb, cause his cannons to rake us from stem to stern.

'Which was it to be? It hardly mattered, the result would be the same, our aircraft would end in an almost vertical descent, streaming flames and shedding pieces as it fell. Within a matter of a few seconds we had jettisoned our bomb load as there was absolutely no possibility of carrying out a bombing run on our allotted aiming point. Our air gunners strained their eyes in a rather forlorn hope that they might forestall and outshoot any approaching fighter. Squadron Leader Woodward dropped his pilot's seat to its fullest extent and manfully fixed his gaze inside the cockpit so that he could concentrate on instrument flying and doggedly hold the allotted course to steer. He knew full well that many aircraft had been lost in such circumstances for no other reason than that the dazzled pilots had lost control. At least the Germans were going to have to shoot us down.

'We all waited, not a word was said but we were all thinking the same things. Nothing seemed to be happening; true there was plenty of flak bursting in the sky and the flashes were in the areas all around us but, mystery of mysteries, there was no gunfire being directed especially towards us. We knew this because we could not hear the explosions of any shells. Months before, I had heard some wag on the squadron remark that there was no need to fear the flak unduly if you only saw it, as that was merely a waste of good panic, you should at least wait until you could actually hear the bursting of the shells. Easier said than done, in my opinion. However, our conclusion was that the ground defence organization had decided that the target which we provided was to be for the sole attention of the night-fighter patrols. The guns, doubtless, had other fish to fry.

'We settled down to wait, to wait as patiently as we could, to wait for the crash of cannon fire from an unseen opponent. Turning back was quite out of the question, we therefore flew steadily onwards and, as we did so, we found that we were skilfully handed over from one group of searchlights to another. There was nothing we could do in that nightmare situation, it was impossible to see outside our aircraft to any worthwhile degree because of the dazzle and all sensation of speed seemed to vanish. The world had disappeared and we felt as if we were hanging motionless in space.

'The Berlin defence zone extended for about thirty nautical miles, our ground speed was 180 knots and it would take ten minutes to fly clear of the zone. We could increase our speed by diving but to what avail? We could never outstrip a fighter and by losing valuable height, we would provide the murderous light flak defences with a target that would be laughably easy to deal with. The seconds ticked by with agonising slowness, the suspense was a terrific strain on the mind and I, for one, began to wish they would start the shooting and get it over with. Five minutes elapsed and still we had no sign of either flak or fighters. Were the Germans having a little game and just toying around with us?

'I felt myself getting seriously alarmed, I was enduring an overdose of something I didn't want, a combination of an inability to act or to do anything useful and an excess of time to think - time to think of a burning aircraft, of dead and wounded men, of futile efforts to escape by parachute and an unpleasant reception from an aggrieved populace for anyone who managed to reach the ground alive. There was no conversation in our aircraft, none of us had anything useful to say and therefore nobody uttered a word. We all thought the same thing. The minutes which seemed so endless did eventually pass away and, quite unbelievably, the interval of time needed to fly clear of the defence zone expired. The long fingers of the last group of searchlights lost us and once more we were in the blackness of the night, heading for home and completely unscathed.

'How on earth had we got away with that little lot? What had gone wrong with the Berlin defence organization? I found myself trying to imagine the angry recriminations going on between various German staff officers as they argued and bitterly complained about why a good target, so efficiently spotlighted, had been allowed to escape. It seemed to me that the theory of saturation bombing was vindicated, that hundreds of attacking aircraft had disrupted the ground liaison facilities and vital equipment and key personnel being destroyed at the crucial moment, the enemy's defences had been swamped. We had been endowed with a remarkable anecdote that listeners would be disinclined to believe and I could now vouch that it was indeed possible to read a newspaper in the light of the searchlights at 18,000 feet. Nevertheless, methinks one would have to be in the right mood.'[13]

Squadron Leader Francis John Hartnell-Beavis found that night bombing trips really suited his temperament, particularly on clear nights, flying at about 19,000 or 20,000 feet well above the clouds, the tops of which were illuminated by the moon, trimming the aircraft to fly dead straight and level and setting the Sperry gyro so as to fly hands and feet off. 'We would drone on for hour after hour, listening to Ivy Benson and her all girls band which was one of our favourite orchestras at the time, which "Smithy", my wireless operator, would tune in to and connect to the intercom. Vera Lynn was another of our favourites. You could carefully adjust the throttle controls so that the engines were all perfectly synchronized and with the aircraft as steady as a rock, you could well have been sitting in an armchair on the ground.

'One always flew operations at the maximum height possible, most Halifaxes could get up to about 20,000 feet with full bomb load, although they did vary considerably. I always did a shallow dive over the target area, so as to build up speed and minimize the time spent amidst the flak and on the return trip would trim the engines for maximum economy by turning the props to full coarse pitch and giving fairly high boost so as to be able to close the throttles as much as possible, whilst still maintaining adequate cruising speed. It would also help if you could get the aircraft "on the step", as it was called, which meant building up speed in a shallow dive to say 17,000 feet and very slowly levelling off whilst slowly closing the throttles. We usually had a competition running as to who could return with the most fuel in their tanks.

'Whilst we usually bombed from about 20,000 feet, the Lancasters were always above us and the poor old Stirlings could only gain about 14,000 feet and we could see them silhouetted against the target fires below us, as we

---

13   Quoted in *'Unkindly Light'* in *To Shatter The Sky: Bomber Airfield at War* by Bruce Barrymore Halpenny (PSL 1984).

rained down our bombs through them. I never heard how many Stirling casualties there were arising out of this practice.

'My engineer told me later that he was absolutely terrified on the first few raids and it took him about six trips to get used to seeing the flak and fireworks. I felt very sorry for him, but glad that I did not have to report him for "Lack of Moral Fibre", as this was usually a court martial offence. The Air Ministry took the view that they spent thousands of pounds on training an aircrew up to operational standard and this was money wasted if the aircrew failed them at the end of their training.'[14]

At Linton-on-Ouse Flight Lieutenant 'Ron' Read knew it was the 'Big City' again, because 'Jock' Hill told him he was 'on' that night. 'Trying to make thirty Berlin trips, "Jock" only went there. I hoped we'd have better luck than the last time. The briefing was a nail biter. The weather forecast was awful - thick cloud most of the way, with a high icing index, just the formula I hated. Miraculously, the cloud was supposed to clear over the target. At briefing we were told that Churchill particularly wanted an RAF presence over Berlin that night. There was a Nazi Party rally and Goering was to be present.

'It was just two days after our last "shaky do" on our Berlin take-off [when their 240-gallon bomb bay tank had leaked most of the petrol in it and Read had dropped his bombs "safe" in Filey Bay and aborted] and we carefully checked the overload tank cap. At take-off time there were low clouds on the deck and pouring rain. We were all pleased when the red Very light for a "scrub" went up from the control tower. We weren't so pleased when we learned that it was only a postponement. We were to take off two hours later at 2000 hours. At 2000 we went out only to be told to position our aircraft on the taxiway for a 2200 hours take-off. Our nerves by now were pretty taut. At nine thirty we went out again to our pre-positioned aircraft. It was a terribly rough night. The wind was howling, rocking the aircraft as we sat in it. The rain was hammering on the wings and fuselage. We wished Churchill would go and get Goering himself.

'Engines started, *The Road to Morocco*, which I sang as a little ritual every time we taxied out to take off was definitely not on the programme. We still expected a scrub in such awful conditions when incredulously, at ten sharp the first aircraft got a green light and lumbered off down the

---

14 *Final Flight* by J. Hartnell-Beavis (Privately Published 1985). By July 1943 Squadron Leader Hartnell-Beavis was nearing the end of his second tour, having flown twenty-five ops, five more than the required twenty for a second tour. On 25/26 July he and his crew were shot down by Major Werner Streib of I./NJG1 on Hamburg. He was taken prisoner. Five of his crew died and one evaded capture.

runway. I was number four for take-off and still hoping for the "scrub". I pointed "C-Charlie" into the black night and got the dreaded green light. I crossed my fingers and gingerly poured on the throttles; the strong wind lifted us off in no time. It was a struggle to keep the aircraft on an even keel. She was being bounced all over the sky. We entered cloud at 600 feet and the bouncing got worse, until at 6,000 feet she settled down to a slightly smoother ride. We left the English coast at 6,000 feet and she wasn't climbing very well. I knew what was happening, we were picking up ice. I felt sick. I really had to go on tonight after the last debacle.

'We struggled up to about 9,000 feet and had been flying for just over an hour. Suddenly, there was a big bang from the port inner engine and a great black mass sailed over the cockpit, striking the roof with a resounding clunk as it went. I thought we might have hit another aircraft. The port inner made a lot more noise and I was ready to feather it, but scanning all the instruments, I could see no malfunction and it still seemed to be turning. A check with the crew revealed no other problems.

'Peering out in the pitch-black night I couldn't exactly see what had happened, but it looked as though there was a big hole in the inner engine cowling. I still thought we might have clipped someone's tail wheel somehow. The port inner still sounded funny, noisy and rattling and still below 10,000 feet we weren't climbing much either. My thoughts ran riot. "Christ! What would they think? Two Berlin trips and we turned back on both. OK, we could do little else on the previous one. But problems with the aircraft again, who will believe it?" I gave it another ten minutes. We weren't climbing at all now and the engine still sounded very different, somehow it was all wrong. Sick at heart, I was forced to concede defeat and turn back for Linton. (The whole engine cowling had flown off. Passing over the aircraft, it hit the top of the fuselage and carried away all our aerials. It appeared that it had not been properly fastened.) When we called on the only communications we had left - the trailing aerial - we were No. 7 to land. Out of twenty-two Linton aircraft setting out, only five claimed to have reached Berlin. This made me feel a lot better.'

A 25-year-old Pilot Officer Alfred Ernest Fisher, and his crew of Lancaster 'Z-Zebra' on 57 Squadron probably felt a rush of excitement and trepidation in equal measure, as this was their first bombing operation. Fisher took off from Scampton at eleven minutes before 2200 hours and headed for the rendezvous point for the flight to Berlin.

Sergeant Tom Wingham was the bomb aimer on 'Q-Queenie' on 102 Squadron at Pocklington piloted by Sergeant Dave Hewlett. Wingham, a true cockney and the youngest of four children, wrote: 'We had visited Berlin two nights before and the word was that "Butch" Harris wanted one more crack at it before the lighter evenings made it too difficult. The weather forecast was appalling and unofficially our two met officers at Pocklington were backing a "scrub". At the original time of take-off at 1900 hours a postponement came through since there was an occlusion running north to south right through the Yorkshire and Lincolnshire bases. At the time it was pouring with rain with cloud up to 16,000 feet. The occlusion was moving more slowly than forecast and a further postponement was made as the new take-off time drew near, which is why we were taking off so late for a trip to Berlin. Having hung about the messes for nearly three hours awaiting a decision, no one really believed that we were going to face this weather and a great deal of incredulity was expressed when we finally found ourselves committed. One of the few nights I can remember when "Butch" Harris' parentage was in doubt!'

Ten Halifax bombers finally took off from Pocklington after the two postponements. 'Q-Queenie' took off at 2147 and from that moment they were in cloud. Dave Hewlett was unable to gain sufficient height and speed and by the time they reached the Flensburg area the Perspex in the windscreen and turrets was iced up. They jettisoned their bombs and turned back, returning to Pocklington at 0309. Two other aircraft on 102 Squadron had to turn back that night. After landing they found that one engine was leaking oil and another glycol. Halifax 'G-George' took off at 2158, but one minute later it was to crash into the West Green. All seven crew members were killed instantly. The story at the time was that 'G-George' broke cloud and there was another aircraft very close which made them take rapid evasive action and the aircraft stalled, or some such action occurred and they had not sufficient altitude to recover. The crew consisted of an American, a South African, a Scotsman, a Welshman and three Englishmen. From the prairies of North Dakota came the 27-year-old pilot, Flight Sergeant 'Bill' Comrie. In March 1941 he had crossed the Canadian border into neighbouring Manitoba to enlist in the Royal Canadian Air Force. He had got married a few weeks before the crash. His 32-year-old navigator, Flying Officer Douglas Harper, who came from the village of Oadby in Leicestershire, had been his best man. Twenty-year-old Sergeant Myles Squiers was the rear gunner. His father was an American diplomat working in South Africa. From the slip ways of the Clyde came the 23-year-old flight engineer Sergeant 'Jock' McGrath. The home of the 34-year-old bomb aimer, Pilot Officer 'Bill' Jenkins was in Birmingham, but he was born in Pembroke. Originally from the East End of London the 21-year-old mid-upper gunner, Sergeant John King had more recently been serving in the Hampshire Police Force. Sergeant 'Frank' Dorrington, the 23-year-old wireless operator, came from Brighton.

'We went straight in over Holland at 20,000 feet,' wrote Flying Officer 'Punch' Thompson on 106 Squadron, which dispatched a dozen Lancasters, three returning early due to severe icing. 'I did not fly straight and level until we reached Berlin and then only on the bomb run. The city was visible this time dead ahead of us as we neared our Estimated Time of Arrival. I was flying on a course slightly north of east when we entered upon the well-lit area of this large city. There was no cloud at all. I unfastened my shoulder harness and stood squatting on the pilot's seat, peering through the windshield, trying to see past the nose for a better view. I looked ahead at searchlights fingering their way through the black sky. There was a red glow below, not of fire, but red the colour of building bricks. Miles upon miles of streets were visible, miniscule ribbons from 20,000 feet, all showing light red in the haze and the searchlights. We continued on for what seemed a long time, carefully picking a path through the searchlights. Flak was exploding at our altitude. We were over the densely built up area of Berlin and the environment was hostile, but where did one bomb? Finally, my bomb aimer said, "Left-left-steady-steady-bombs gone." Then he added as an apparent afterthought, *"Rr-un for-r the shelter-rs you bastards."* [He would often roll his r's]. He had been engaged to a girl from Plymouth who had been killed in a German air raid.

'Flak and searchlights on the route out of Berlin were moderate and we saw no fighters. We returned to base without event, or so it seemed at the time. The next day the crew chief at the dispersal site of "K for King" showed me a small hole in the transparent plastic on the pilot's side of the cockpit. Strange, I thought, I hadn't heard any wind through the hole. Perhaps my helmet and the engine noise had obscured it. Then he pointed to a scratch on the armour plate behind my head and the flight engineer announced that his helmet had been cut. A piece of shrapnel had paid us a visit and had hit the armour plate behind my head, bounced off and cut the engineer's helmet. Three of our crews had returned early due to severe icing and we lost one aircraft, ED596, captained by Squadron Leader Eric Hayward DFC, who had needed only two more trips to complete his second tour. Hayward, a very tall man, left behind a large black Great Dane who appeared to mourn for several days before being adopted by a ground crew. It took a whole crew to feed him.'[15]

---

15  *Lancaster To Berlin* by Walter Thompson DFC and Bar.

Squadron Leader Eric Lewis Hayward DFC was shot down by Leutnant August 'Gustel' Geiger Staffelkapitän, 7./NJG1 flying a Bf 110G-4 and guided by 'Himmelbett' box 'Krote' ('Toad') over the Dutch-German border. All approaches to occupied Europe and Germany were divided into circular and partly overlapping areas, which took full advantage of Bomber Command's tactic in sending bombers singly and on a broad front and not in concentrated streams. Each 'Himmelbett' Räume ('four poster bed boxes') about twenty miles square with names like 'Hamster', 'Eisbär' ('Polar Bear') and 'Tiger', was a theoretical spot in the sky, in which one to three fighters orbited a radio beacon waiting for bombers to appear. Each box was a killing-zone in the path of hundreds of incoming prey. That night Geiger was the top-scoring pilot with five victories in two sorties. Over Schleswig-Holstein he intercepted Halifax 'K-King' (DT744) on 76 Squadron captained by 28-year-old Flight Lieutenant Jack Harold 'Shorty' Wetherly DFC MiD and shot it down. There were no survivors. On his second sortie at 0347 hours Geiger destroyed Halifax II 'Q-Queenie' (BE244) on 51 Squadron, which was returning from Berlin. It spun in at Vorden with the loss of Flying Officer Raymond George Harris' crew. These victories took Geiger's score to nineteen.[16]

The bombing force approached Berlin from the south-west and the Pathfinders established two separate marking areas, but both well short of the city. The marking for the raid appeared to be concentrated but in a position which was too far south and the Main Force arrived late. Largely as a result of the severe icing conditions only 213 aircraft bombed the target, most of the bombs falling in open country six miles south of the capital. The 'Oboe' Mosquitoes were unable to keep to their timetable; there were long gaps in the skymarking as a result and the raid was basically a failure.

'Analysis of bombing photographs after this raid,' wrote 'Punch' Thompson, 'showed that there had been poor concentration of bombs. There were lines of burning incendiaries from many bombers over a widespread area, but no large fires were started. Concentration of the attack, if accurate, was always desirable but it was not achieved this night.'[17]

A friend of Thompson's since they had met at the Conversion Unit at Swinderby, 26-year-old Flying Officer George Floyd Mabee RCAF on 49 Squadron had taken Lancaster III 'A-Apple' off from Fiskerton, five miles east of Lincoln at 2145 hours on the crew's first operation. Thompson

---

16  Hauptmann Geiger scored his fifty-first and final victory on 28 September 1943; he was killed the following night when he had to bail out of his Bf-110G but was drowned when his parachute dragged him under.

17  *Lancaster To Berlin* by Walter Thompson DFC and Bar.

learned from the intelligence office the following morning that his friend, who was from Toronto, had not returned. Mabee's Lancaster was shot down by Leutnant Hans Krause in I./NJG 3 for his third victory, the Lancaster crashing in flames at Eilvese near Wunstorf. Mabee and five crew perished. The rear gunner, Sergeant G.A. Jones, who was taken into captivity was repatriated in 1944. 'N-Nuts' on 49 Squadron, which Sergeant David W. Fyffe had taken off from Fiskerton at 2201 on the crew's first operation, was hit by flak over the target and some of the crew bailed out before control was regained. Shortly thereafter, the Lancaster was finished off by Hauptmann Herbert Lütje of III./NJG1 and it crashed at 0427 at Nieuw Heeten in Holland. Fyffe and three of his crew were taken prisoner. The other three crew members were killed on the aircraft.

Early in the morning of 30th March over Holland, Leutnant Werner Rapp and Unteroffizier Johan Ortmann, his bordschütze (gunner), found Pilot Officer Fisher's Lancaster and fired. None of the crew was able to bail out as 'Z-Zebra' fell to the ground near the Van Wick home at Waverveen, southeast of Amsterdam. Jan Treur their neighbour was in his barn feeding his cows when he heard the Lancaster scream overhead and slam into the soft earth behind the barn, six hours and twenty-two minutes after it had lifted off from Scampton. It was one of twenty-one aircraft - eleven Lancasters, seven Halifaxes and three Stirlings - that never returned from the raid on Berlin. As dawn broke the scene that greeted the farmers was horrific. There was little left of the Lancaster that was recognizable. The grim task of retrieving the remains of the crew began.[18]

Lancaster I 'S-Sugar' on 460 Squadron RAAF, flown by 28-year-old Flight Lieutenant Kenneth Hugh Grenfell RAAF, was shot down by Unteroffizier Christian Koltringer of 7/NJG1, an Austrian born in Salzburg, for his third and final Abschüsse. Grenfell was born on 23rd May 1914 on the tiny Ocean Island (Banaba), Gilbert Islands, where his parents were there working for the church. It is believed that the crew all bailed out over Sidculo in the

---

18  The remains of Alf Fisher and Sergeants (radio operator) 'Frank' Bandeen (flight engineer, 21), Harry Richardson (navigator, 22), Don Simmons (mid-upper gunner, 21), Roy Taylor (air bomber), Jack Westerdale (WOp/AG) and Alick Deane (rear gunner) were put in three wooden coffins which were placed in the back of a horse-drawn cart and Mr. Van Wick drove them to the Waverveen church for burial, escorted by several German soldiers marching behind. Following the funeral ceremony, the crew was buried in the church cemetery accompanied by a gun salute from the German soldiers. They joined 191 airmen that had died on that miserable night. After the war, they were moved to the war cemetery in Bergen op Zoom. I am grateful to Bob Van Wick and Andy Bird for sending me this story.

Netherlands but were too low and none of the parachutes opened. Only Flight Sergeant Phillip 'Pip' Wesley Dunn RAAF, the 22-year-old wireless operator was found when his body was discovered under the aircraft on 13th April. Flying Officer Stephen Falcon Scott McCullagh RAAF, the American navigator, who was born in Seattle; Sergeant Ronald Cordingley, bomb aimer; Sergeant George E. Lewis, flight engineer; Flight Sergeant Robert Lincoln Potter RAAF, air gunner and the 26-year-old rear turret gunner, Sergeant Sidney George Webb were the others killed on the crew. Koltringer and his bordfunker, Unteroffizier Willi Voght, were killed when the Bf 110F-4 was hit by fire from the rear turret and Sidney Webb at least had the satisfaction of sending the 110 down to crash at Kloosterhaar before he died.

On 12 Squadron at Wickenby anxious eyes scanned the horizon for the return of 'A-Apple', 24-year-old Sergeant 'Frank' Worley Pinkerton's Lancaster. Pinkerton arrived over the target five minutes ahead of time before the flares had gone down. The Lancaster was held by a Master searchlight, which suddenly exposed on the aircraft. Then a very large cone, estimated to be about forty searchlights, picked it up. The aircraft at this time was at 19,000 feet. Flak began coming up about one minute after the aircraft had been coned and Pinkerton believed that they were hit, probably in the wings. He then jettisoned his bombs, lost height in his attempt to get out of the searchlights and finally escaped from them at about 3,000 feet. The four engines were running well and there was no damage evident in the aircraft, but the Lancaster would not climb above 15,000 feet. Pinkerton found he could not get Sergeant George Charles William Warren, the 20-year-old rear gunner, on the intercom and sent Sergeant 'Frank' Morton the WOp to investigate. After quarter of an hour Morton returned saying that the rear gunner's microphone was u/s. Sergeant R.G. Irons, the flight engineer, gave Morton his helmet to take to the rear gunner. After quarter an hour Irons complained of lack of oxygen (they were at 15,000 feet) and about ten minutes later became unconscious.

They now ran into more searchlights and flak, possibly at Bremen. Pinkerton altered course in order to escape from this defended area. He also lost height to 3,000 feet to try and get Sergeant Irons round. Sergeant I.C. Clunas, the navigator and Sergeant N.H.S. Williams, the mid-upper gunner, went back to look for Morton and found him dead with a broken neck near the step. Forty minutes after leaving the area believed to be Bremen, Pinkerton changed course to due west. After a while both starboard engines cut due to lack of petrol, but the navigator turned on other tanks and they started up. About two hours after leaving Berlin the starboard inner engine failed, not due to lack of petrol, and the propeller was feathered. After a time they crossed a flak belt, which they believed to be at the Dutch coast. Irons now calculated that they had only twenty gallons of petrol left; only enough for one hour's flying. Just afterwards the starboard outer engine cut for lack of petrol. They were still at 3,000 feet. Pinkerton gave the order to bail out. Four crew members survived to be taken prisoner, but Sergeant Warren's parachute failed to deploy and he was killed. Pinkerton, who bailed out, landed three kilometres from Rotterdam. He managed to evade capture and with the help of the underground network, made his way through Holland and Belgium and into France and finally reached Spain. He believed that he should have had fuel for about ten hours and he thought that the flak hit over Berlin must have caused him to lose some petrol. When they bailed out they had been flying for seven to eight hours.[19]

After this second Berlin raid crews were given nine days' leave. At the start of the Battle of the Ruhr 'Bomber' Harris had been able to call upon almost 600 heavies for Main Force operations and at the pinnacle of the Battle, near the end of May, more than 800 aircraft took part. Innovations such as Pathfinders to find and mark targets with their TIs and wizardry such as 'Oboe', which enabled crews to find them, were instrumental in the mounting levels of death and destruction. Little it seemed could be done to assuage the bomber losses, which by the end of the campaign had reached high proportions. There was however, a simple but brilliant device, which at a stroke could render German radar defences almost ineffective.

On 24th/25th July, Harris launched the first of four raids, code-named 'Gomorrah', on the port of Hamburg. In his message of good luck to his crews Harris said that 'The Battle of Hamburg cannot be won in a single night. It is estimated that at least 10,000 tons of bombs will have to be dropped to complete the process of elimination. To achieve the maximum effect of air bombardment this city should be subjected to sustained attack. On the first attack a large number of incendiaries are to be carried in order to saturate the Fire Services.'

Led by $H_2S$ PFF aircraft, 740 out of 791 bombers dispatched rained down 2,284 tons of high explosive and incendiary bombs in two and a half hours. New British tactics combined the use of PFF, the massed bomber stream and new target finding equipment ($H_2S$). 'Window' - thin strips of aluminium

---

19  After the war Pinkerton joined British European Airways. He was killed in a crash on 19 August 1949 while flying a DC-3 from Belfast to Manchester Ringway with twenty-nine passengers.

which either appeared as a cluster of primary targets on radar screens or swamped the screen with multiple returns - paralyzed the Nachtjagd and the Flakwaffe who were unable to offer any significant resistance. Only twelve bombers, or just 1.5 per cent of the force, were lost in action. Harris was intent on sending his bombers back to Hamburg for another major strike. He said, 'I feel sure that a further two or three raids on Hamburg, then probably a further six raids on Berlin and the war will finish.'

General der Jagdflieger Adolph Galland commented: 'A wave of terror radiated from the suffering city and spread throughout Germany. Appalling details of the great fires were recounted and their glow could be seen for days from a distance of 120 miles. A stream of haggard, terrified refugees flowed into the neighbouring provinces. In every large town people said: "What happened to Hamburg yesterday can happen to us tomorrow." Berlin was evacuated with signs of panic. In spite of the strictest reticence in the official communiqués, the Terror of Hamburg spread rapidly to the remotest villages of the Reich. Psychologically the war at that moment had perhaps reached its most critical point. Stalingrad had been worse, but Hamburg was not hundreds of miles away on the Volga but on the Elbe, right in the heart of Germany. After Hamburg, in the wide circle of the political and military command could be heard the words: "The war is lost."'

In Berlin 27-year-old Marie (Illarionovna) Vassiltchikov sat down to write up her diary. 'Missie', as she was known, was a high-spirited, cosmopolitan member of European High Society and an anti-Nazi émigré from Russia who worked for the Information Department of the Foreign Ministry headed by her detestable superior, SS Brigadeführer Professor Doktor Franz Six. Through her contacts she had some advance warning of impending raids but having friends in high places did little to help her. On 1st August she wrote: 'The fate of Hamburg arouses great anxiety here, for last night Allied planes dropped leaflets that called upon all women and children in Berlin to leave at once, as they did before the raids on Hamburg began. This sounds ominous. Berlin may be next.

'Count Wolf-Heinrich von Helldorf [the Berlin Chief of Police] does not think that heavy raids on Berlin will start soon.'[20]

---

20  *The Berlin Diaries 1940-45* by Marie (Illarionovna) 'Missie' Vassiltchikov. (Chatto & Windus, 1985).

# Chapter 5

# Battleground Berlin

*'Berlin is an industrial centre, the second biggest inland harbour in Europe, the continent's greatest railway junction and the political centre of Europe... Any dislocation of its life would cause disorder and confusion throughout the whole of the Nazi empire. The battle of Berlin may well prove to be the decisive battle of the war.'*

**The Battle of Berlin, the Washington Post,**
**Tuesday, 10th August 1943.**

On landing from the pre-op air test on Sunday, 22nd August, Sergeant Thomas Chapman Edwards' crew on 158 Squadron at Lissett, six miles south of Bridlington near the Yorkshire coast, lingered, seeing the fuel bowser approaching. 'A squint at the driver's clipboard and we grimaced,' wrote Sergeant Dennis 'Sandy' Slack the bomb aimer. 'This was to be a long one. We trooped into briefing, into an atmosphere heavy with tension and cigarette smoke and heard just three words: "Ops are cancelled." We then joined in the unfettered cheering that drowned the permission to stand down.' In 1937, after leaving school at fourteen, 'Sandy' had begun training as a motor engineer with Westfield Transport in Mansfield. Seduced by postings urging 'Change your overalls for a flying suit' in August 1941 he volunteered for the RAF. Having hoped to be assigned to Lancasters he and his crew were 'miffed' to get Halifaxes and were not totally convinced when at the Halifax heavy Conversion Unit at Marston Moor, the already celebrated Leonard Cheshire said, 'I know how you feel but having flown all three heavies I regard the Halifax as the finest of the lot. Believe me; it will always look after you.'

With ops being cancelled, New Zealander, Sergeant Graham 'Mick' Cullen, the wireless operator on Flight Lieutenant Robert Richard Megginson's crew on XV Squadron at Mildenhall took his girlfriend,

Brenda Jaggard, to 'The Bird' at Beck Row for a drink to celebrate her birthday. The rest of the crew decided to go with him and they all spent the evening together. Megginson was a second tour man who had completed a period of instructing in Canada before joining XV Squadron. After closing time, Brenda invited them all back to her parents' home, where they were always made welcome. The rest of the evening was spent with Pilot Officer Desmond 'Mitch' Mitchell the rear gunner, seated at the piano playing the popular songs of the day, with 'Mick', Brenda and the others happily singing along. The evening came to an end with much laughter and happiness. Bomber crews lived for the moment because there was no telling when the 'Grim Reaper' might strike. On 4th August, the Reuters News Agency in London had reported, 'After the air raids on Hamburg, authoritative sources believe that other similar operations will be carried out, probably against Berlin. It has been noted that extensive preparations are already underway at a number of new airfields that are used exclusively by heavy four-engined RAF bombers. The predicted raids on Berlin will be mainly RAF night operations. The date of the raids will depend on the length of the nights, which now is increasing by half an hour per week. This means that each week the heavy bombers can penetrate fifty miles deeper into Germany. In two or three weeks the RAF will be able to reach Berlin just as easily as it can reach Hamburg, because Berlin is only 130 miles farther away. In several weeks' time the Americans may also begin daylight raids on Berlin. The 8th Air Force has already made daylight flights into Germany as far as Warnemünde, which is the same as the distance to Berlin.'

At airfields throughout Bomber Command on Monday, 23rd August it was prime summer weather and a rumour spread that the bombing of Berlin was on the cards. James Campbell, a Scot born in Inverness, who flew thirty-eight operations on Halifax bombers on 158 Squadron, which flew the most Halifax sorties in Bomber Command, describes the scene at Lissett at briefing time.[1] 'Eye catching Air Ministry contents bills with bold headlines screaming, *"Have You Done This?" "This is Important"*, *"Remember That?"* plastered the green painted walls of the main briefing room. Aircrews sprawled over the rough wooden forms and leaned inertly across the ink-stained tables. Others, who could not find seats, lounged along the walls in attitudes of complete and utter boredom. Through the blue-white haze of tobacco smoke a hundred and sixty voices rose in a

---

1   *Maximum Effort* (Futura 1957).

noisy babble. The older crews made pungent remarks, bitterly resenting that the early transport into town had been cancelled until the briefing was over. A shuffling of massed feet, punctuated by a few wooden forms crashing to the floor, greeted the wing commander [23-year-old Charles Cranston "Jock" Calder DFC] as he entered. He leapt lightly onto the raised dais in front of the huge wall map constructed from sections of Mercator charts. He searched the rows of white faces in front of him, contemplating for a full half minute the assortment of brevets and uniforms. "Sit down, gentlemen! Smoke, if you wish," he said crisply. The clamour of conversation had died down and the aircrews were seated quietly on the wooden forms in front of the plain tables. The wing commander toyed with a bright red pin. Attached to the pin was a long narrow red cord. He surveyed the room for a few moments... "Tonight - it's Berlin again!"'

'Our ground crew were prepping "A-Apple" rather than "F-Freddie",' recalled 'Sandy' Slack, 'but an aircraft change was not unusual. What was unusual was the timbre of the howl as the curtain came back at briefing. Berlin! Our first visit. And a rare enough target then, although some were to identify this very day as ushering in the "Battle of Berlin".'

'Jock' Calder waited until the low murmur of whispered comments died. He handed the red cord to the squadron navigation officer and watched him plunge the pin into the black square that was Lissett. Deftly the navigation officer placed another pin in a minute triangle over a DR position in the North Sea. Swiftly, from there, he laid off the legs to the enemy coast, then across Germany to Berlin.

'I don't put a great deal on what they think about you at Group. If you have had higher losses than other squadrons, then you're obviously not as efficient as they are... And if you go out thinking you won't come back,' thundered the wing commander, 'you give the "Hun" that psychological advantage which comes from your own inferiority.' A cathedral silence stifled the room. Someone at the back coughed. The sound reverberated sharply. 'For the benefit of the new crews, I must remind you that you do not divulge the target or anything which may identify it - not even to the rest of your crew. They will know soon enough at the main briefing at 1700 hours.'

When 'Jock' Calder completed his briefing of the pilots, the navigation officer took over. 'The flak defences,' the navigation leader announced, 'are thickest to the west of the city. To keep you clear, therefore, markers will be dropped even further west, beyond range of the guns. As you approach, you'll see reds to your left, greens to your right. Continue heading south, keeping between them.' His pointer travelled downwards, well to the south of the city, stopping where the red track-tape reversed direction to lead sharply upwards. 'At this point, gentlemen, turn north-east, bombing on that heading.'

'Sandy' Slack heard 'Tom' Edwards mutter in an uncomfortable sotto voce, 'Bloody tight turn, that'. But nobody else said anything audible.

Then came the bombing officer. Slowly and clearly they gave their instructions, repeating some points, stressing others. Two hours later, the main briefing hall was packed. This time the gunners, wireless operators and flight engineers were in the big room. The wing commander, a billiard cue in his right hand, traced on the map the course and heights they were to fly at, the estimated time of arrival at their turning points. He told them - and there was a sigh of relief at his words - that twenty minutes before they crossed the enemy coast twenty-two aircraft from the OTUs would make a dummy feint a hundred miles from their landfall.

The Bombing Leader said his piece, thankful he himself was not going out; he had an unpleasant memory of the last time he had gone to Berlin. He revealed that the Pathfinders would take as their aiming point the Unter den Linden. They would mark it with red indicators. The backers-up would aim at the reds with green markers in as tight a circle as the Mark 14 bombsight would allow. 'So your primary aiming points are the reds. If they are bombed out or otherwise obscured, bomb the greens.' He moved over to allow the Met Officer to be seen. Suddenly he hesitated; 'Remember,' he added sternly, 'Check your bombing stations for hang-ups.'

The Met Officer, a mild soft-spoken man with large horn-rimmed glasses, nervously unrolled his chart. He might as well keep it rolled, he thought. It was always the sign for a ripple of laughter to go round the room. He resented deeply this enforced role of briefing jester, for there were only two questions they ever wanted to know. The rest were phrased either to raise a laugh or make him look foolish. Glancing apprehensively at his weather chart, he was about to amplify a point he was making when a long-haired bomb aimer with a Cockney accent rose to his feet. 'Say, what's it like over the target? Is it likely to be clear?' He waited for a moment. He half turned to the wing commander and the group captain. They were smiling faintly, but still, they were smiling. The Met Officer spun round quickly, flushed and icily retorted; 'I was coming to that. Obviously, since you are to bomb visually, we expect fairly clear conditions.' A loud cheer burst from the centre of the hall as they applauded his retort. Finally, the wing commander stepped briskly forward, 'That's all then, except - Good Luck Gentlemen and Good Bombing.'

At Syerston, Flying Officer Geoffrey Willatt, bomb aimer/navigator on Pilot Officer Angus Alan 'Robbie' Robertson's crew on 106 Squadron recalled: 'On entering the Operations Room for the briefing, there was the large map plainly showing that Berlin was the target for 727 aircraft. We were all briefed by the chief navigator and then in their turn, Wing Commander R.E. Baxter DFC, our squadron commander and sometimes the station commander [37-year-old Group Captain Francis 'Frank' Hodder, who was killed later, on Mannheim on 6th September], the bombing officer and the intelligence officer.' Willatt was born in Nottingham in 1911, the second of three brothers. As a boy he showed an aptitude for sport and went on to captain the football team at his school, Repton. He played briefly for both Nottingham Forest and Ipswich just before the war and later played hockey and tennis at county level for Bedfordshire and Sussex, respectively. He volunteered for the RAF after the disaster at Dunkirk and on 14th April, had married Audrey, a teacher.

His crew came from very diverse backgrounds. 'Alan Angus Robertson was a 26-year-old Scot who had started his training as a barrister. "Frank" Cawley was a very friendly though rather shy Canadian navigator. Sergeant Arthur Edwin Taylor our American wireless operator [from Boise, Idaho] was older; perhaps about thirty. Moseley was the English flight engineer. Sergeant Freddy Tysall the mid-upper gunner was a chirpy Cockney and Merle Routson the rear gunner, a brash American from Bethlehem.'

Squadron Leader Waldo 'Wally' Harry Bentley Hiles DSO DFC, who had completed two tours on 218 Squadron before being posted as a staff officer to 3 Group HQ arrived at Downham Market from Exning Hall intending to fly on one of the station's Stirlings. Waldo was born on 1st September 1913 in Swansea, Wales. A brief move to India would see the family leave for Calcutta on 8th April 1921 aboard the liner *Sardinia*. Their stay however was brief, as they were back in Wales in May 1924. Waldo was now age ten. At Llandovery College he had a flair for hockey and was described as 'the best halve by far'. On leaving, Waldo started a career as a commercial traveller. It was during his second tour that he earned a reputation as a 'press-on type' with a penchant for attacking goods trains, which he seemed to excel at. Within months of starting his second tour the award of the DFC was announced on 15th December 1942. In June 1943 Waldo received the DSO, one of only four awarded to the squadron. The citation mentioned that he 'always presses home his attacks in the most determined manner, flying at low altitude regardless of enemy opposition'. He had only once attacked Berlin before, in September 1941. Undeterred, Waldo borrowed 'C-Charlie'

(EH925), a 623 Squadron Stirling and gathered together five inexperienced 218 Squadron aircrew and his ex-rear gunner, Flight Sergeant Desmond Michael De Silva DFM, who was from British Guiana. He had completed his operational tour and was kicking his heels awaiting posting.

At Chedburgh an airman on one of 214 Squadron's Stirlings recalled, 'Morale was so good despite our losses getting higher, that there was a great roar of joy at having a crack at the "Big City".'

On 115 Squadron Flight Lieutenant Aubrey Howell and his Lancaster crew on 'Y-Yorker' had just moved from East Wretham airfield to a new 'drome at Little Snoring near the Norfolk coast and found that it was 'a pleasant change to land on a concrete runway again after the completely grass covered field at East Wretham, which was also ringed "with damned great trees"'. 'How I missed those trees some nights I do not know,' wrote Howell. The crew's first two weeks at East Wretham had been spent on the Conversion Flight, familiarising themselves with the Lancaster and welding themselves into an efficient team, or so they thought. Howell wrote, 'Our ego was sadly deflated when we learned quite by accident that the instructors on the Conversion Flight had made an entry in their secret book that we were not expected to survive more than five operations; but it made us more determined to prove them wrong'. Their trips to Nuremberg, Milan and Turin were comparatively easy, although they were all long and tiring, but flying over the Alps to Italy in bright moonlight was quite a sight. Their fourth op would be a different proposition altogether. 'One glance at the route marked up on the big wall map at briefing told us it was Berlin, the "Big City",' wrote Howell. 'I think this one meant a bit extra to the mid-upper gunner "Tommy" Thomson and myself; both being Londoners, our families had had to put up with month after month of sleeping in air raid shelters, windows and doors being blown in and neighbours and friends killed by our German counterparts in the Luftwaffe.'

Seventeen Mosquitoes were being used to mark various points on the route in order to help keep the Main Force of 335 Lancasters, 251 Halifaxes and 124 Stirlings on the correct track. Despite reservations in some quarters who feared it might alert enemy night-fighters, at the Mosquito base at Marham in Norfolk three of 105 Squadron's 'Oboe' markers and five on 109 Squadron, so necessary for the Main Force to do their work, were to mark the bombers' route by dropping 'Red LB' TIs between the Dutch towns of Westerbork and Zweeloo and Green TIs just over the German border at Georgsdorf, 270 miles west of Berlin. The object was to keep the Main Force on the correct track and keep the bombers away from known flak areas and to achieve a heavy concentration of bombs at the target.

# THE BERLIN BLITZ BY THOSE WHO WERE THERE

Wing Commander 'Johnny' Fauquier DSO** DFC now commanding 405 Squadron RCAF - the first Canadian officer to lead a bomber squadron on operations overseas and the only Canadian airman to receive the DSO three times - was Master Bomber. For Operation 'Hydra' on 17th/18th August, the bombing raid on the German military research facility at Peenemünde, Fauquier acted as deputy master bomber to John Searby, who for his work in helping develop the 'Master Bomber' role that night was awarded an immediate DSO. Fauquier had made seventeen passes over the target. Later, he would step down from the prized rank of Air Commodore to take command of 617 Squadron from Wing Commander James 'Willie' Tait DSO* DFC.[2]

For Warrant Officer 'Eddie' Wheeler, WOp/AG on Flight Lieutenant Joseph Henry Jean Sauvage's crew on 97 Squadron at Bourn, the night of 23rd/24th August was his first trip to the 'Big One'. He had flown one tour of operations on Wellingtons without venturing to the 'Big City' once. Born on 5th November 1920, 'Eddie' would joke that surely fate had destined his entry into the world, for twenty years on he too was to be involved realistically and dangerously with fires, explosives and the burning of his fellow men. Life was not always so comical. Home was a three-roomed tenement in the North London Borough of Islington where he shared a bed with two of his brothers and was to succeed another brother and two sisters. Sleeping three to a bed was considered acceptable in the dominantly poorer families of that time, but life was miserable, so he decided to leave school at fourteen and the first chance he got, he enlisted in the RAF. It was then that he discovered that his real surname was not Wheeler but 'Scheidweiler' with a German heritage and a great-grandfather from Hanover!

'A trip to the "Big One" meant a long trip over heavily defended enemy territory and the Berlin defences were savage in the protection of the great city which the Nazis had sworn would never be subjected to air bombardment. What a long way I had come since those dark days in 1940[3] when there appeared to be no salvation from the gloom and here we were attacking the German capital in strength and talking more and more of an invasion of Europe. This was to be my fifty-seventh operation;

---

2  *Barnes Wallis' Bombs; Tallboy, Dambuster & Grand Slam* by Stephen Flower. (Tempus 2002)

3  'Eddie' flew in Fairey Battles on 150 Squadron in France and then flew ops on Wellingtons on 214 Squadron before re-joining 150 Squadron at Newton. Instructional duties followed. *Just To Get A Bed* by Alan Wheeler DFC.

could I survive to see that sixtieth operation? It did seem to be inviting the inevitable with each further raid. So many crews had not even reached double figures and with so many more aircraft involved, losses mounted so that the likelihood of aircrews surviving twelve raids was still minimal. For this trip, we had an additional crewmember - a Flight Sergeant Penny as second pilot for the experience.'

It was the custom for newly arrived pilots to begin by flying 'second dickie' or second pilot with an experienced pilot and crew. At Fiskerton, 20-year-old Sergeant Eric Jones on 49 Squadron would fly his second op as a 'second dickey' on an experienced crew, because on his first, on 22nd/23rd August to Leverkusen, very little had happened and so his flight commander detailed him for another 'second dickey'. The former builder's clerk from Newent in Gloucestershire and four of his crew had come together at 29 OTU at Bruntingthorpe near Leicester where they trained on the Wellington before transitioning onto the Lancaster at 1661 Lancaster Conversion Unit at Winthorpe near Nottingham. 'Some crew members had met on previous courses; some had met in the few days they had been on the station. I knew some of the pilots, we had trained together, but I didn't know any of the aircrew. Very cleverly the precise number of aircrew for the pilots available had been mustered into the room. I stood back, not knowing the abilities of any of the aircrew and also, I suspect, realising that friendship did not necessarily account for ability. I just let things happen; any positive choice I might have made might have been the wrong one. I was tall, very tall - 6 feet 5 inches - and also quite thin. My weight must have been around eleven stones and perhaps I did not look strong enough to handle a four-engined aircraft. On occasions like this I did not exactly ooze with confidence, so I suppose I was somewhat surprised that, before the room thinned out too much, I had started to collect my crew. Except for Steve, a bomb aimer, they all looked so very old. Ken Blackham, an ex-London policeman and my navigator-to-be was six years older. Herbert (call me "Peto") Whiteley, who would look after the rear turret was ten years older, red faced with a balding head. Clarence (call me that and I'll punch you on the nose, you call me "Pat") Peacock was a tough, square, smallish Canadian wireless operator, obviously older than myself. "Steve" Stevenson, who would look after the front turret and drop the bombs was a Londoner and had been in the Blitz and couldn't wait to get at the Germans. Steve was my age. Nineteen-year-old Ron Harris, the engineer, and a wee Scot, "Jock" Brown, joined the crew as the mid-upper gunner. Ron's task was to care of and nurse the engines, monitor the petrol supply from the various petrol tanks,

131

take stock of all the pressures etc and would be constantly at my right-hand side at all times in the air. He was the youngest member of the crew and I was second youngest and at first it sounded a little odd when they referred to me as "Skipper". I could not have wished for a better crew. Knowing the future that lay ahead of us and the absolute necessity of pulling together we all quickly became firm friends.'

On entering the Briefing Room the first thing Eric Jones noticed was the large map at the far end of the room and on it the route markers pointed straight to Berlin! His skipper for this second 'second dickie' trip was Flight Lieutenant Robert C. Munro, a New Zealander with the DFC who would fly twenty-three operations on the squadron before being posted that November. Although he felt a little minnow in the presence of such austere company Jones also thought, as he looked at him, 'This is experience and I am going to come back from this trip'.[4]

Another 'second dickie' that night was 20-year-old Flight Sergeant 'Tony' Bird, a newly arrived pilot on 61 Squadron in 5 Group at Syerston. He would make an eighth crewmember on the aircraft flown by Flight Sergeant Andrew Strange, a veteran of a dozen or so operations, instead of the usual seven. Strange would soon be listed among those who failed to return from operations, but not before his commission to pilot officer was confirmed. 'I was soon to get to know Berlin rather well, if only from the air,' wrote Bird, 'because of the length of the journey (almost eight hours return at an economical cruising speed of only 180 mph) and the fact that Berlin was so heavily defended, a groan went up from the waiting aircrew at briefing when the target was announced.'[5]

Soon after the briefing at Downham Market Flying Officer John Overton spoke to 'Wally' Hiles and tried to give him a friendly update on the current defences over Germany. Hiles response was not what Overton expected. It would prove to be a precursor to a tragic night.[6]

At all bases the bomber crews were driven out to their aircraft at remote dispersal sites on the airfields in Lincolnshire and Nottinghamshire and further afield. At Elsham Wolds 'Billie', on 103 Squadron, would be the first Lancaster in Bomber Command to achieve fifty ops if it returned

---

4  *Boots, Bikes & Bombers* by Eric Jones (Unpublished manuscript)

5  *A Bird Over Berlin: A World War II Lancaster Pilot's Story of Survival Against the Odds* by Pilot Officer Tony Bird DFC (Woodfield Publishing 2000).

6  Appreciation is due to Steve Smith, historian of No.218 (Gold Coast) **Squadron** for information on this story, which can be found on his website.

safely from the raid with Warrant Officer Clifford Annis and crew. But they almost did not make take-off. Each Lancaster had been fuelled and bombed up with a 4,000 'Cookie', 1,000 pounders and incendiaries and the crews were dropped off at their dispersals to complete their pre-flight checks and start engines. Flight Sergeant David Halstead Loop and crew and Flight Lieutenant Douglas William Finlay's crew were taken out to the northern side of the airfield to where Lancasters 'C-Charlie' and 'H-Harry' awaited them. The Annis crew ran up the engines, checked the aircraft generally, stopped engines and settled down to wait. 'There was not much conversation as the crew sat, or stood, on the grass near their Lancaster,' wrote 'Sandy' Rowe, the flight engineer on Annis' crew. 'The waiting before take-off was usually a bit trying; mostly thoughts of what lay ahead during the coming night. One of the reasons for the early check of the machine was to allow the engines to cool before their final start up, the Merlins being a bit difficult to start when hot. While waiting, we noticed activity around W4323. A petrol tanker was alongside and ground personnel were apparently doing some last minute work. We took no particular notice of this activity until a loud thump was heard from that direction. Within seconds a lot of people began running away from "C-Charlie", some in our direction. I forget whether a warning was shouted by the runners, but I remember that it looked ominous and we the crew began running also, although we were as yet unaware of the gravity of the situation. We all ran to what we considered a safe distance (it probably wasn't). I was then told that work was being carried out on "C-Charlie" with the bomb doors open. Somehow the bomb release electrical circuits had become energised and all the bombs had fallen out of the machine onto the ground, some of the incendiaries becoming ignited. A fitter unsuccessfully tried to remove the burning incendiaries from the jumbled heap under the machine before rapidly removing himself from the scene. Apart from someone ringing for the station fire brigade, nothing seemed to happen, our vision of "Charlie" being obstructed by the tanker alongside it.

'The Squadron CO [Wing Commander J.A. Slater DFC] was doing a circuit of the perimeter in his car, having his usual last check with his crews and happened to be near the scene. He asked Finlay to move "Billie" well out of the danger area in the event of an explosion. We rushed aboard, the ground crew also running to man the chocks and starting battery trolley. I commenced starting the engines. The port outer failed to start, the port inner started, the starboard inner failed to start, the starboard outer started. "Let's go," said Finlay, "two will be enough". This was easier said than done. I told him that the chocks were still in position and the battery trolley still connected. I could see some of the ground crew, but they were not looking in my direction, as they were watching and waiting for the other two engines to start. I could not communicate with them by shouting because of the engine noise. I opened up the throttle of one of the engines and gave them a blast of wind. Finlay by now was getting very impatient! This drew their attention to me and I was able to signal for the removal of chocks and trolley. As soon as the chocks were removed and trolley disconnected, the pilot, listening to my commentary, moved off rather quickly and struck the battery trolley with our tailplane. During all this time I could see nothing of what was happening to "C-Charlie".

'We moved out of our dispersal area and turned right. I looked ahead at this time and saw another aircraft getting away from the area, at right angles to us, moving to our left. It was travelling so fast that its tail was in the air and appeared to be approaching speed. This machine was piloted by Flying Officer Ready and was heading in the direction of the control tower on the opposite side of the airfield. The personnel in the tower were aware that something was happening at the far end of the airfield, probably because of the call for the fire engine, but knew no details. Their first intimation of trouble was to see Ready's machine fully bombed up, heading across the grass towards them at high speed. I believe they were very alarmed! We continued, in doing so getting nearer to "C-Charlie". I saw the fire engine stopped ahead of us as we were blocking its path, for which the fire brigade told us later they were grateful, having saved them from being blown up, because as we were passing at our closest point to "C-Charlie", it suddenly disappeared in a huge sheet of flame in which I thought I would be engulfed. I must have instinctively ducked, because the next day there was no Perspex in the window through which I had been looking. I never heard a sound. I was told later that the explosion was heard in Grimsby about twenty miles away. Presumably I was so close to the centre of the explosion, that all sound waves were travelling outwards from me. Our aircraft was struck by debris and it slewed around. Finlay shouted, "everybody out". I shut the throttles, opened and got out of the top escape hatch, followed by Finlay. I noticed one of our propellers still turning, leaned in the hatch, completely shut its throttle, got on to the port wing and jumped to the ground.

'By this time others had left the aircraft by other exits and joined the pilot and myself. Finlay said, "I should think the 4,000 pounder has not gone off, get moving," and in the same breath, "where is the wireless operator?" John McFarlane, the navigator, said, "in the aircraft". I rushed to the starboard side, jumped in the door and ran up through the fuselage. I saw "Harry"

Wheeler lying back against the main spar, put my arms around him and was lifting him over the spar when I looked at him closely and saw for the first time that he had been struck by something and was dead. I dropped him, left the aircraft and joined the others. We left the scene and walked across the airfield and runways to the main camp area.'

The only other casualty besides 'Harry' Wheeler was a civilian - Dr Woods - who was struck in a leg by a flying oxygen bottle as he was cycling nearby. Two of 'C-Charlie's' engines were found several hundred yards away. A third was found half a mile away. The tractor driver received the BEM. Pilot Officer Jack Birbeck the bomb aimer on 'Billie' recalled: 'We thought operations would be cancelled but the CO thought otherwise - he was keen to get us away so as to complete the record and we took off about an hour late.'

At Wyton, about two miles east of Huntingdon and a few miles west of Cambridge, deep in Pathfinder territory, 83 (PFF) Squadron once again helped to lead the attack. The ORB (Operations Record Book) for the night said: 'Ops laid on. Two areas given in morning but as one was Berlin the other was given very little thought. At briefing the crews showed great enthusiasm as this target had been expected daily and now was their chance to hit right at the nerve centre of Germany. The route chosen was not popular and the majority of [the sixteen] captains would have approved a much shorter route.' One of these captains was Flying Officer 'Punch' Thompson RCAF who had been posted from 106 Squadron to 83 when John Searby took command in May. 'One needn't have been clairvoyant to predict that the next target was Berlin,' wrote Thompson, 'or as my room-mate [Flying Officer Maurice Kendall Chick] loved to call it, "The Big City". He said to me after briefing, "Tommy, can you believe all those beautiful blonde Aryan popsies going for the chop? My God what a waste!" I realize how callous that sounds, but Chick was not then and is not now a callous man. It was his way of expressing regret at the carnage that was going on. He, even more than I, found it difficult not to fraternize with WAAFs; in fact he was on a campaign to fraternize with one of each rank of WAAF on the station and was already courting a senior NCO. On two occasions he had jumped on my bed when he came in late and found me asleep, to wake me up and give me a blow-by-blow description of the night's activities. He liked having a Canadian for a room-mate. Since I made twice as much as him, though we were both flying officers, he felt duty bound to borrow half the difference between my earnings and his. It got so that I was telling him to be careful - I didn't want him going missing when he owed me twenty pounds.

'On several occasions Chick and I and Flight Lieutenant Brian Slade DFC, who we called "The Boy Slade" because he was our youngest pilot, having just turned twenty-one, took the bus to Cambridge for an evening's pub crawl. Slade, a voluble Londoner, always sang the loudest, drank the most and told the funniest jokes on these nights out. I think too that he was loved by the most WAAFs, for he was another who refused to obey the non-fraternisation rule. Brian had joined the squadron in April and was one of our first trained "Y" crews with navigator, Flight Lieutenant Alexander Niven MacPherson DFM. The crew was without doubt one of our leading crews. Brian had set himself the goal of completing sixty trips. Having made fifty-eight trips; Berlin would be his fifty-ninth.

'We crossed the Dutch coast just south of Friesland and then flew eastward, south of Bremen and across the old Duchy of Brunswick-Lüneberg into Prussia. By 2345 we had reached a point about thirty miles south-east of Berlin where we turned on to a course of magnetic north for the target. An increasing number of Pathfinder aircraft had been equipped with $H_2S$ - its serviceability was better, and its operators were more experienced - and ninety-four aircraft were carrying $H_2S$. "T for Tommy's" job was to re-centre the attack.'[7]

When he had crossed the coast of Holland in his Stirling, Wing Commander Desmond McGlinn the 214 Squadron Commander said, 'it was not fully dark. It was a beautiful night; one could almost see Berlin from the coast.'[8]

'The alarm sounded at 11.40 on the night of Monday, 23rd August,' wrote German diarist Hans Georg von Studnitz, after driving with a companion through the devastated city the following evening: 'It was followed by a long pause, which is always a sinister sign. The flak opened up half an hour after midnight and things soon became so hot that we went down into the cellar. The firing continued till 1.45 am.'

'Missie' Vassiltchikov wrote that, 'There was a red haze over Berlin... and entire streets had collapsed.'

Hans Dieter Schafer was lying in a laundry basket. 'The sky cast a red light a long way down the corridor. In this red twilight my mother put her terrified face close to mine and when I was carried down to the cellar the rafters above me rose and swayed. The aircraft hovered above the city; it was an August evening and consequently the Müggelsee glowed with

---

7  *Lancaster To Berlin* by Walter Thompson DFC and Bar, Goodall 1985).
8  *Heroes of Bomber Command: Suffolk* by Graham Smith (Countryside Books, 2008).

crimson light while the Spree was already in darkness. The angel on the victory column seemed to move its heavy, cast-iron wings and look up at me with malicious curiosity; dusk was gathering beneath the television tower on Alexanderplatz, the shop display windows gave off an eerie glare and the gloom sank slowly over the west and away to Charlottenburg, while the water of the lakes shone mildly in our eyes; the closer we came to land, the more frantically did endless streams of traffic race around; I turned to my other side and saw ducks flying in a kind of plough formation over the Zoo. A little later I was standing at its entrance, as if lost. Elephants tugged at their iron chains beneath sombre trees and over in the darkness ears were pricked and heard me coming.'[9]

At Parchim airfield about ten kilometres north of the Hamburg to Berlin road, Oberleutnant Wilhelm Johnen of 5./NJG 5, his bordfunker Facius and bordmechaniker Paul Mahle and their fellow crews rushed to their Bf 110s at 2306 hours, took off and headed towards Berlin. Born 9th October 1921, Johnen joined the Luftwaffe in 1939. In 1941 he joined the Nachtjagd and took part in the Defence of the Reich campaign. He achieved his first success on 26th March 1942. Johnen became a night-fighter ace on 25th June 1943 after achieving his fifth victory. 'Night after night we sat at readiness in our machines and then when the first bombs fell on our brightly lit airfield and fast British bombers strafed our installations with cannon and machine guns, we knew that in Germany there was now no safe rear line position. With round the clock bombing by the Allied bomber streams, the Reich itself had become a gigantic battlefield. According to a predetermined plan of attack Berlin was sinking into dust and ashes. On their nightly forays the Allies no longer needed to search for the capital, for the huge fires of the previous night were still blazing and lighting up the darkness. A blood-red glow lay over Berlin for weeks and months on end.'[10] The night was bright and at 18,000 feet over Hanover Johnen could see for 350 miles, he could see the Hamburg flak in action and bombs dropping on Berlin, fires in Leipzig and incendiaries falling on Cologne. Shortly before the raid the Jagddivision ordered its night-fighters to pursue the enemy to the capital and to ignore their own flak, which had permission to fire as high as 24,000 feet. If Johnen's bordmechaniker was worried, he had every right to be. Mahle's wife lived in Berlin.

At Parchim also, Leutnant Peter Spoden of 5./NJG 5 in a Bf 110 was ordered to take off on his first 'Wild Boar' sortie west of the capital...

---

9  *On The Natural History of Destruction* by W.G. Sebald.
10  *Duel Under The Stars* by Wilhelm Johnen.

'It was one of these nights you never forget your whole life,' he wrote later. 'There was a terrible turmoil over Berlin. On the ground in the "Great City" fierce fires were blazing: first of all the high-explosive bombs and then the phosphorous incendiary dropped into the shattered ruins of the buildings. It was an inferno without equal. Hundreds of searchlights rose up towards us, sweeping the heavens like the fingers or corpses and the hands of ghosts, dazzling friend and foe alike. The anti-aircraft guns fired a furious barrage up to 10,000 feet and above that were the "Wilde Sau" ["Wild Boars"] and the "Zähme Sau" ["Tame Boars"]. At times I could see between thirty and forty aircraft at once milling around. Tracer cannon and bullets, cascades of flares of every colour, night-fighters' recognition signals when the flak had fired on one of them. Huge clouds of smoke, garishly illuminated, rising into the sky. White condensation trails everywhere and down below fearful explosions. A Lancaster attempting to escape from a cone of searchlights did a full loop. I got the impression that everyone was firing at everyone else. And I was in the very middle of it all. It was hell – Dante's Inferno!'

The 'Wild Boars' and the 'Tame Boars' that Spoden described were the creation of Ritterkreuzträger Oberst Hans-Joachim 'Hajo' Herrmann, an extremely bright, single-minded officer with stern Aryan good looks and piercing blue eyes. Originally a bomber pilot and one of the foremost blind flying experts in the Luftwaffe, Herrmann had agitated for a long time without success for permission to practice freelance single-engined night fighting. He had reasoned that by the light of the massed searchlights, Pathfinder flares and the flames of the burning target below the freelance, single-engined 'Wilde Sau' ('Wild Boar') fighter pilots could easily identify enemy bombers over a German city. By putting a mass concentration of mainly single-engined fighters over the target, his pilots could, without need of ground control, but assisted by a running commentary, visually identify the bombers and shoot them down. It was not until the night of 3rd/4th July 1943 that freelance single-engined night-fighting was hastily introduced in an effort to try to overcome the crisis caused by 'Window', which threatened to paralyse the Nachtjagd and the Flakwaffe, which relied heavily on radar. When 653 bombers were dispatched to bomb Cologne and thirty-one bombers failed to return, a dozen of them were claimed by 'Geschwader Herrmann', whose freelancing fighters were allowed to operate over a burning city above the height at which the flak guns reached. Now, on the night of 23rd/24th August, Herrmann took off from Bonn/Hangelar in his Bf 109 to test his theory further.

'The running commentary gave a constant easterly course for the bombers and I never thought of any other target; I was totally fixed on Berlin. As I approached the bombers' route, I saw some of the "torches" going down, bombers crashing; they were my "pathfinders" so to speak. On the frequency of my own unit I heard Müller [Oberleutnant Friedrich Karl Felix Müller, a pre-war Lufthansa captain and now Herrmann's Operations Officer] reporting that he had found a bomber about 100 kilometres west of Berlin and another of my pilots reported the course was still due east. I heard the ground control order them not to attack but to fly with the bombers and plot the exact course of the bomber stream. We kept being told that the Spitze - the vanguard of the stream - had reached a certain point. Then suddenly I felt the turbulence of the bombers' slipstream and I knew that I had arrived.

'They seemed to turn at Potsdam and go straight into Berlin from the south-west. I think I arrived a bit later than the others. I did not need the glare from the target; it was searchlight fighting that night. It was clear, no moon, and the searchlights were doing a good job. I tried for one bomber, but I was too fast and went past him without firing; I was still a beginner as a fighter pilot.

'I came up to the next one more slowly, level, from the rear, but before I could open fire another chap coming down from above me attacked the bomber and set it on fire. I do not know what type of fighter it was; I only saw the tracer.

'I circled back over the target and had no difficulty in finding a third bomber. Normally, if a fighter wanted to attack a bomber in the searchlights, we should have fired a flare, so that the flak would cease fire, but we "Wild Boar" men rarely bothered to do this. We usually waited until the bomber weaved or dived out of the searchlights and then attacked it. I shot that third bomber down.'[11]

Herrmann's pilots were a motley collection, loosely organized and rather like guerrilla bands in their attitude to authority, composed as they were by volunteers drawn from all sections of the Luftwaffe, including highly qualified ex-bomber pilots and even pilots in disgrace seeking reinstatement, but of the record 290 Nachtjagd victories achieved that August, 80 per cent were credited to the 'Wild Boar' units and to twin-engined crews operating in 'Tame Boar' fashion (the tactic of feeding them into the bomber stream by ground broadcast running commentary). Herrmann would claim nine

---

11   'Hajo' Herrmann, *Eagle's Wings; the autobiography of a Luftwaffe pilot.*

RAF bombers shot down in fifty sorties. By early March 1944 the 'Wild Boars' had claimed 330 bombers destroyed at night.

As 'Tony' Bird approached the target, he could see what appeared to be a solid wall of bursting flak shells immediately ahead. 'It seemed like suicide to attempt to continue onwards and it was with great relief that I discovered as we flew right through the puffs of black smoke that they were from shells that had already exploded and apart from turbulence from the swirling smoke, were quite harmless. The thing to worry about was from shells about to burst in the vicinity - but there was no way of knowing of them until too late. We were fortunate, however, and were able to avoid the dreaded searchlight fingers probing the sky all around us, our only damage being slight peppering from the shrapnel of shells that had burst some distance from us.'

'Our route took us straight through the middle of Germany,' recalled Flight Lieutenant Aubrey Howell. 'We were in the first wave of the attack meeting very heavy defences of searchlights and flak, but fortunately we got in and out again before the night-fighters got up in force. It was the later waves of bombers that were intercepted and caught it very badly as they were silhouetted against the glare of the fires in the city and the PFF (Pathfinder Force) marker flares still falling.'

Geoffrey Willatt on Pilot Officer 'Robbie' Robertson's crew would agree. 'We approached Berlin through a vast number of searchlights, with flak bursts all around. There were dark silhouettes of other bombers and night-fighters passing and re-passing in front and around. We saw one bomber in front being hit and bursting into flames. One parachute was seen to open but the rest of the crew "bought it". We successfully ran the gauntlet and dropped our bombs over the biggest and widest conflagration of fires, flashes and columns of smoke. We came in after the blind markers on this occasion and dropped four Green TIs in addition to a 4,000 pounder and three 1,000 pounders. Our drop time was 0003 hours; altitude was 19,500 feet and the speed was 155 knots indicated. The first greens seemed well placed around the reds and all of them were well concentrated. We saw many fires starting up and observed two large explosions. Some of the red flares only burned red for a few seconds then became yellowish, which caused a little confusion. Some crews thought them to be dummies, but this seemed unlikely. Probably a batch of inferior flares. There seemed to be no shortage of flak or fighters in the Berlin area. As we headed north-west from Berlin to the Baltic I saw a Lancaster on fire close by, on our port quarter... The target was so large that all that could be seen by the H$_2$S operators was a blaze of light indicating solid built-up areas and the searchlights were so dangerous that one simply could not map-read properly. This, combined with sometimes intense flak, made it almost impossible for a crew to say that they had visually identified the aiming point. Nevertheless, Berlin was well and truly bombed. The success of the raid was not due to our accurate bombing but to the Germans for building so large a city.'

'S for Sugar', a 7 Squadron Blind Marker Lancaster flown by Squadron Leader Charles J. Lofthouse OBE DFC was probably the first Lancaster to go down. It carried the 38-year-old Oakington Station Commander, Group Captain Alfred Henry Willetts DSO, who Lofthouse had welcomed aboard with a jaunty, 'Don't forget to bring your sandwiches for the trip home, sir'. Lofthouse, born on 26th September 1921 at Mountain Ash, Glamorgan, had already survived thirty-seven bombing raids and been awarded the DFC when in November 1942 he rescued five aircrew from a Stirling which crashed on the airfield at Waterbeach in Cambridgeshire. Lofthouse was appointed OBE (military). In June 1943 he resumed operational flying and was posted to 7 Squadron in the Pathfinder Force, as a replacement skipper; the squadron having lost seven crews in two nights.

Lofthouse recalled: 'We had arrived over Berlin a little early and were losing a couple of minutes in a turn, when the sky lit up with tracer.' They had been hit by a night-fighter near Oranienburg. 'I looked across to the port engines and saw the outer brewing up. A deep blue flame was growing from the fuel tank which spread rapidly, producing a huge, bright yellow flame streaming behind the aircraft, which was becoming uncontrollable.'

While the flight engineer frantically tried to extinguish the fires, the navigator, Flight Lieutenant Berkeley Denis Cayford DFC bravely volunteered to try crawling out onto the wing to attempt to put out the flames but Lofthouse said no. He said, 'I think it's time we got out' - at which point Willetts was out through the nose escape hatch like a rat out of a trap and the rest of the crew quickly followed.

'The flames were very fierce by now, stretching back from each engine, and there was a large hole in the wing between the two nacelles, with flames coming out of it, being beaten back by the airflow. The flight engineer put my parachute ready beside me. The wireless op came forward and gave me a thumbs-up to indicate that the boys at the back had gone. Cayford came back at that stage, went back to his "office" and then went forward and out. He told me later that he had come back for a gold signet ring from his girlfriend, which he always took off when flying because it got so cold. That horrified me because I was fighting the controls hard by then, but I managed to get out.'

All on board were destined for prisoner of war camps. Lofthouse, when he bailed out, came down in a tree near a hut used by a Concentration Camp outside working party, dislocating a shoulder and breaking an arm. He was later lodged in Stalag Luft III. Employing his skills as a draughtsman Lofthouse became a member of the team which produced maps and forged documents to assist the escapees - although he himself was in hospital when the 'Great Escape' took place. Cayford, who was born in 1918 and grew up in Wolverhampton, was educated at a local grammar school where he excelled academically and at sport. He was a county swimmer and travelled with the British swimming team to the Berlin Olympics in 1936. The experience convinced him war was inevitable and although he had taken articles with a local firm of solicitors he signed up to the RAF in 1938, neither wishing to spend a war in the trenches, nor at sea.

Cayford parachuted onto a church roof and was hurriedly cut down by a German civil guard before being dragged into an air raid shelter. Sent to Stalag Luft III, Cayford served as a 'penguin' for the disposal of soil from 'Tom', 'Dick' and 'Harry', the tunnels used in the Great Escape. Cayford volunteered for the breakout: his plan was to travel across Germany as a Bulgarian labourer returning home (he spoke neither German nor Bulgarian) and he was allocated number 82 in the line of escapers. The tunnel proved to be fifteen feet short of the intended exit and it was not until 4.50 am on 25th March 1944 that Cayford reached the final ladder - at which moment the tunnel was discovered.

Flight Lieutenant Munro and his 'second dickie', Sergeant Eric Jones were on the very first Lancaster to get airborne in the Battle of Berlin. Jones wrote: 'The weathermen turned out to be correct; there was a clear sky over the target with no cloud! The trip I had made the previous night bore no comparison to this one. The "flak", the marker flares on the ground, the fires, the bombs bursting, the searchlights and the fighter flares all contributing to a scene I had never thought possible. As we left the target area I reflected with amazement on our survival and thought of the remainder of the tour which I had to complete with my crew.'

'C-Charlie' on 100 Squadron had crashed on take-off from Grimsby and four more of the squadron's Lancasters were lost on the operation. 'X-X Ray' on 97 Squadron at Bourn was shot down near Döberitz. Another of the Lancaster losses was 'S-Sugar' on 101 Squadron at Ludford Magna, or 'Mudford Magna' as it was known because it was still marshy although built on one of the highest stretches of the Lincolnshire Wolds. Home to special Lancasters, 101 was a three flight squadron, flying up to twenty-four Lancasters in the bomber stream, armed and loaded with bombs just like the other heavy bombers but with an extra crew member in each squadron aircraft to jam enemy radio transmissions. 'ABC' or 'Airborne Cigar' night-fighter communications was a massive piece of equipment consisting of four VHF wireless sets. One scanned up and down the airwaves, seeking transmissions from enemy fighters. When a blip showed on the operator's CRT scope a German-speaking special operator positioned halfway down the fuselage between the main spar and the mid-upper turret, tuned one of the other sets to that frequency and listened in. If the speaker was a Jägerleitoffizier (JLO, or GCI-controller) the special operator would flood the enemy controller's instructions with interference.

Twenty-three-year-old Flight Sergeant Robert Clarence Naffin RAAF and his crew on 'S-Sugar' all died. Sergeant John Henry Phillips the 19-year-old mid-upper gunner had walked twenty miles from Crewe to Stoke with his friends to sign up when he was told his apprenticeship would exclude him from being called up. He had trained as a pilot in Winnipeg but lost his wings after a brawl and ended up as an air gunner. He had flown over twenty ops. It appears that 'Sugar' was attacked by two or three night-fighters and it exploded in mid-air scattering the crew and the Lancaster over a one kilometre area. The Abschuss was claimed by 23-year-old Oberleutnant Werner Husemann of Stab[12]/NJG 1 at 0050 hours for his ninth victory. Naffin and crew were buried with full military honours in the local cemetery in Beisenthal and were re-interred at the Berlin 1939-1945 War Cemetery. By the war's end Husemann had scored thirty-four Abschüsse in over 250 night combat sorties.

'The fighter flares floated down when eight minutes from the city,' wrote James Campbell on 158 Squadron, 'and burst in brilliant pools of light on each side of the bomber stream. And they burned lazily as they lit up the broad avenue to Berlin. As first they drifted in strings of twos and threes. Then rapidly they fell, wiping away the cover of darkness shielding the bombers. The first combats were on. An orange glow splashed the darkness below and I caught the fiery outline of a Lancaster plunging earthwards, tracer streaming from her rear turret.' Campbell pulled off his leather gauntlets and dragged a pair of newly washed white silk gloves from his pocket. He thrust his hands into them and screwed and twisted the silk until his fingers fitted smoothly into the sockets. The heavy flying gloves were too bulky for him to feel sensitively in the blacked-out nose for the delicate

---

12   Staff flight.

143

switches on the bomb panel. 'White gloves,' wrote Campbell, 'brought to mind the executioners of old, masked men in hooded headgear, bending slightly as they leaned on their axes.' He smiled into his oxygen mask and looked out of the transparent nose. The smile died on his lips. A searchlight flashed on, dead, straight and blinding. As rapidly as it appeared it went out. Suddenly, it was there again, slowly toppling backwards as if pointing their course to the fighters hurtling through the night to the defence of Berlin. Within seconds the darkness was pierced by hundreds of other groping beams. Must have been one of the master searchlights.

'Another batch of flares burst above and ahead. Specially converted Ju 88s were, beyond any doubt, flying along the bomber's track, releasing them at timed intervals, making it easier for the fighters to select their "kills". The flares threw the black floating puffs left by the spent AA shells into sharp terrifying relief.' Campbell was grateful that he could not hear the mass thunder of the barrage below, above the roar of the bomber's four engines. The spine-tingling crump of the shells as they burst uncomfortably close spewing out their shrapnel jarred his tensed nerves.

'The petrified sky was getting brighter.' Campbell looked up sharply and saw the dim silhouette of a Halifax below his port quarter 'stuck in long lines of tracer and burst into a rich deep glow'. The exploding bomber cart-wheeled slowly and illuminated a Lancaster on its starboard bow. The Lancaster pilot corkscrewed violently away from the stricken bomber, to be caught relentlessly by a searchlight. Bombers were exploding ahead, below and on each side, sky-writing their death trails in spirals of black smoke. The red target indicators sailed down, plump in the middle of the forest of searchlights, trailing through the flak in a leisurely fall of fiery bells of colour. They splashed lazily over the ground, beckoning impatiently to the armada above, gurgling voraciously as they waited to receive the bombs. After them came the secondary markers, equally vivid clusters of bewitching greens. The bomb aimer pressed the bomb release button as the red TIs crawled over the cross hilt in the graticule sight. 'Bombs Gone!' At the same time his right hand flicked down the four switches controlling the bomb stations he had purposely left unselected. Then he shot across the jettison bars. That lot should fall clear of the markers to burst, he hoped, in the suburbs.[13]

'There was always tension going into Berlin,' wrote George Mackie on 115 Squadron. 'I always tried to get in early. I tried to get in with the

---

13    Adapted from *Maximum Effort* (Futura 1957)

Pathfinders when I could, because I fancied that I was as good as any Pathfinder. When you went in all hell let loose. They had extraordinary devices that exploded with a tremendous bang and lit up the whole sky to frighten you. The Pathfinders were remarkably good. You saw the flares and incendiaries go down. Then 600 bombers were all around you. The risk of collision was very great. Looking down you gradually saw the city explode with bombs dropping and with incendiaries. Looking back you saw Berlin burning. This was the turning point at which extreme caution had to be exercised. If everyone did not turn at the same time the risk of collision was very great. On one particular night two Lancasters collided in front of us and one of them exploded and went straight down. The other did two upward rolls with all four engines burning and exploded right in front of us, a hundred yards away. The pilot shouted to the gunners to turn away so that their night vision would not be impaired. One gunner asked why and when he was told his knees shook. Quite an extraordinary scene.'

Thirty-one bombers fell victim to fighters in the target area with another seven crashing on the way home as a result of fighter attacks over Berlin. 'Punch' Thompson on 83 Squadron had a close-up view of a Focke Wulf 190 'Wild Boar' over the target in the dark red from the glow of searchlights and incendiaries and lived to tell the tale, but two other crews on the squadron did not make it back. Thompson wrote later. 'We had the sad misfortune to lose two very fine crews; Pilot Officer John Alexander Reid's on "O-Oboe" and Flight Lieutenant Brian Slade's DFC on "A-Apple". Having set himself the target of completing sixty trips, he was killed on his fifty-ninth. It was probably Slade whom we saw hit as we entered Berlin, because we saw an aircraft far to the north of us, coned in searchlights; it blew up in a shower of red Target Indicators before we reached the bomb-run. Brian was a good friend and I felt his loss keenly. We certainly suffered a severe loss, including Flight Lieutenant Turner, gunnery leader of "A" Flight and Flight Sergeant Vernon Charles Lewis the flight engineer and one of the squadron's oldest members.'[14]

In total, ten of the $H_2S$ carrying aircraft failed to return and ten more made abortive sorties, but sixty-four of the remaining seventy-four $H_2S$ crews

---

14    Pilot Officer John Alexander Reid who was on his tenth trip with PFF was the captain of the other crew who were killed. *Lancaster To Berlin* by Walter Thompson DFC and Bar. Flight Lieutenant R.F.W. Turner was the only survivor on Slade's crew. He was taken prisoner. Flight Lieutenant Vernon Charles Lewis was the son of Hubert William Lewis who was awarded the VC in WW1 and his Christian names were likely chosen as a result of the award of the Victoria Cross.

found that the equipment functioned well throughout.[15] The Pathfinders were unable to identify the centre of the city by $H_2S$ and had marked an area approximately six miles west of actual aiming point in the southern outskirts of the city. Crews spoke highly of the punctual and efficient way the Pathfinder Force marked the route and the target. A very concentrated attack quickly developed round the markers, causing large fires and a series of very heavy explosions which lit up the sky and from which flames appeared to leap to a great height. Smoke from the fires billowed up over 15,000 feet. In the final analysis the Main Force had arrived late and many bombers cut a corner and approached from the south-west instead of using the planned south-south-east approach. This resulted in most of the 1,700 tons of bombs that were dropped in the space of fifty minutes falling in the sparsely populated southern suburbs of Berlin and in open country than would otherwise have been the case and twenty-five villages reported bombs. Even so, it was the 'Big City's' most serious bombing raid of the war so far with a wide range of industrial, housing and public properties being hit and over 2,600 individual buildings destroyed or seriously damaged. Some crews claimed to have identified ground detail in the Tiergarten area in the light of the fires and bomb bursts and it was evident from the pilots' reports that the main weight of the attack fell to the west and south-west of the city.

Bomber Command had suffered its greatest loss of aircraft in one night in the war so far. The flak and night-fighter defences were extremely fierce and sixty-three aircraft, twenty-seven of them Halifaxes, seventeen Lancasters and sixteen Stirlings were lost or written off; a 12.9 per cent loss rate. Additionally, a Stirling on ASR duty was ditched off Esbjerg and all the crew were taken into captivity. 'M-Mother' the Stirling flown by Pilot Officer Ray Hartwell on 214 Squadron at Chedburgh went down after attacks by a night-fighter and all seven crew were taken prisoner. Another Chedburgh Stirling, 'X-X ray' on 620 Squadron flown by Sergeant George W.M. MacDonald, a former Glasgow policeman, who was on his thirtieth operation, was shot down by a Ju 88. The regular rear gunner was sick with flu and was replaced by a gunner straight from training school who froze when the night-fighter attacked. He was killed by a cannon shell. MacDonald told the crew, 'For Christ's sakes get out.' Flying Officer E. Walker, the

---

15  From the late summer of 1943 British bombers could be 'homed in' on their $H_2S$ set by the Naxos 7 (FuG 350) 'homers' fitted to German night fighters and Flensburg (FuG 227/1) could home in on the 'Monica' tail-warning device.

bomb aimer and Flying Officer J.D. Sutton, the navigator, left the aircraft just as the port wing dropped off. The only other survivor was Squadron Leader A.P. Philipsen who was on an acclimatisation flight with the crew.

At Lakenheath no word was received from four Stirlings. On 149 Squadron, 'P-Peter' flown by Squadron Leader J.J.E. Mahoney crashed near Hanover and 'R-Robert', captained by 24-year-old Flight Sergeant Arthur Ernest May was abandoned in the target area. Mahoney and four crew survived and were taken prisoner, one was killed and the other evaded. May and five crew were killed, only the flight engineer surviving to be taken into captivity. On 199 Squadron 'E-Easy', piloted by 22-year-old Pilot Officer Ronald James Widdecombe from London, was shot down shortly after completing its bomb run and crashed near Döberitz. Sergeant A.N. Nixon, the rear gunner, was the only survivor. He recalled: 'We had bombed and had nearly got to the edge of the searchlight area. We thought we were over the worst. Then it was as though a giant hand took hold of us and there was a huge shuddering and shaking sensation, just like a massive dog shaking a rat... The next thing I knew was that I was coming down on the end of a parachute.'[16] He was taken prisoner. 'K-King' flown by 29-year-old Pilot Officer Russell Gardiner Fisher RAAF of West Brunswick, Victoria, was probably shot down by Feldwebel Günther Bahr of 3./NJG6 south-west of Berlin. The Stirling crashed at Ruhlsdorf, north-north-east of Berlin with no survivors. A few miles from Lakenheath, at Mildenhall, two more Stirlings were missing. 'S-Sugar' on 15 Squadron flown by Pilot Officer Eric Raymond Ivan Cornell had crashed in the vicinity of Döberitz and 31-year-old Flight Sergeant Noel Charles Rollett RNZAF and crew on 'H-Harry' on 622 Squadron went down in the same area. There were no survivors on either aircraft. Rollett had previously survived being torpedoed and wounded in the head while crossing the Atlantic in the *Waiwera* en route to Britain on 29th June 1942.

Stirling 'B-Baker' on 622 Squadron, skippered by Flight Sergeant 'Gil' Marsh, had a narrow escape after being coned by searchlights over Berlin and a 'Wild Boar' night-fighter homed in. They had taken off from Mildenhall at 2035 hours and bombed the target from 14,000 feet. As Marsh came to the turning point the Pathfinders markers went down and immediately hundreds of searchlights came on, forming a circle of ten miles or so. It was described by Marsh as, 'like a huge circus cage. The whole sky over Berlin was as light as day and fighters were seen roaming round looking for their prey.'

---

16 *Heroes of Bomber Command: Suffolk* by Graham Smith (Countryside Books, 2008).

They bombed at 1207 hours and just after the 'Bombs Gone' call came over the intercom from the Canadian bomb aimer, Sergeant John Calder Bailey, born 1920 in Saskatoon, Saskatchewan, a Ju 88 approached and opened fire from 500 yards. The rear gunner, Flight Lieutenant Berry the squadron's Gunnery Leader and the mid-upper, Sergeant Hynham, opened fire as Marsh took evasive action. The fighter was hit and claimed as a 'probable'. Then another fighter attacked. A cannon shell exploded in the cockpit, tearing a hole in Marsh's right thigh, shattering his right hip and cutting his sciatic nerve. His hands were covered in green luminous phosphorous. He lost consciousness. When he came to the Stirling was in a dive and it plummeted from 12,000 to 1,500 feet. Marsh managed to pull it out and climb back to 4,000 feet but the tailplane and elevators had all been damaged in the attack and he could not go any higher. He managed to evade the fighter by diving steeply but the hydraulics to the rear gun turret was cut and one engine was on fire. He called to 'Jack' Bailey for help, but the bomb aimer had been temporarily knocked out as he had not been strapped in when they had taken evasive action. Marsh then told Pilot Officer Richards the navigator to get into the second seat and between them they managed to set a course for the Baltic, still flying at 4,000 feet. The flight engineer called up to inform Marsh that the port engine pressure had gone, the engines were overheating and there was an imminent chance of a fire. Marsh mistakenly feathered the propeller on the port inner engine and when an attempt was made to restart it, it threw out a large sheet of red and orange flame, so he shut it down again and they flew on with three engines. Pain, loss of blood and bouts of unconsciousness affected the pilot, but the aircraft was kept under control by the navigator and the bomb aimer. Eventually, Marsh had to be removed from his seat and 'Jack' Bailey flew the Stirling back to Mildenhall where he made a perfect landing. He was helped by the fact that he had nearly completed pilot training but had failed his exams before being transferred to bomb aiming duties. Richards too had failed a similar course. Bailey was awarded the Conspicuous Gallantry Medal and immediate commission for his actions. Later inspection revealed that only seventy-five gallons of fuel remained in the tanks.

Two other airmen on Stirlings were awarded Conspicuous Gallantry Medals this night. Sergeant Bertram Gordon Bennett, wireless operator on Flying Officer Overton's crew on 623 Squadron at Downham Market was wounded in the back during an attack by a Bf 110 and he tackled a fire in the aircraft with his bare hands until Sergeant Aubrey the flight engineer put the flames out with a fire extinguisher. Sergeant Dallman, the rear gunner, was wounded in the leg and the mid-upper turret was damaged. The Stirling had been holed in the flaps, the fuel tanks hit and the rear fuselage damaged, but Overton managed to get the aircraft back to Downham Market and Bennett and Dallman were taken to Ely Hospital for treatment. Bennett was recommended for the award of the Conspicuous Gallantry Medal.

At Mepal, 75 Squadron RNZAF, which had despatched twenty-three Stirlings were missing three Stirlings and it could have been four. 'W-William' captained by 20-year-old Pilot Officer Alan Joseph Lyle Sedunary DFC RAAF is thought to have been shot down by Oberleutnant Heinz Ferger of 3./NJG3 at 0051 hours south-west of Berlin at 3000 metres. All eight crew were killed. Ferger had twenty-three confirmed Abschüsse and three probables by the time he was killed on 13th/14th April 1945 when he was shot down by a Mosquito whilst on finals to Lübeck airfield. The rear gunner was the only man to survive on 'K-King' flown by Pilot Officer A. Rankin. There were no survivors on 'X-X-ray' piloted by Warrant Officer Trevor Fear which crashed at Mahlsdorf, twelve kilometres east-south-east of Berlin. Whilst approaching the target area the aircraft captained by Flight Sergeant Osric Hartnell White DFM*, a former salesman of Christchurch, New Zealand, who was on his twelfth operation, was coned by searchlights and repeatedly hit by heavy AA fire, sustaining considerable damage to the port mainplane. He continued towards the target though still coned by searchlights and was then attacked by a Ju 88, sustaining hits in the rear of the fuselage which shattered the rear turret and killed the rear gunner, Sergeant Jack Poole. The Stirling was forced into an uncontrollable dive and White warned his crew, 'Prepare to abandon the aircraft'. Unfortunately, in the middle of this order the intercom failed and unable to contact their captain, the navigator, air bomber and wireless operator abandoned the aircraft. Flight Sergeant White jettisoned his bomb load whilst in the dive directly over the target area and managed to regain control of the aircraft when height had been lost down to 6,000 feet. The captain and two remaining members of the crew, after taking stock of the damage, decided to attempt the long and hazardous return journey to base. This they did successfully with White using his pre-war experience as a yachtsman, which helped him navigate by the stars and he made a perfect crash landing at Mepal without lights, flaps or undercarriage, as the electrical leads were shot away. White would receive a commission and the CGM and the two other crew members were awarded DFMS.

At Wratting Common (West Wickham) in Cambridgeshire three Stirlings on 90 Squadron were missing. 'S-Sugar' skippered by 25-year-old

Flight Sergeant Kenneth William Longmore RAAF crashed in the Ijsselmeer with no survivors. 'L-Leather' piloted by Sergeant 'Frank' W. Mulvey, a big Canadian, crashed in the North Sea ninety miles from Denmark and sixty miles from Germany and went down 'like a steam-roller' with four of the crew. Sergeant J.R. Laing the wireless operator who continued to send out distress signals was probably killed when he was thrown against his set as they hit the sea. Pilot Officer William Hector John Yeo the mid-upper gunner was killed when he was thrown through the door of the wooden bulkhead and right up the fuselage. Sergeant John Francis Quickfall the bomb aimer was stood behind the pilot's seat trying to help and he died also. Mulvey, who was concussed, had managed to scramble out while the cockpit was under water and had come up from below. Sergeant Jack Burland the flight engineer of Huddersfield, Yorkshire and Sergeant J.A. Pighills the rear gunner, got him into the dinghy. Pilot Officer Lloyd Elmer Sibbald RCAF, the navigator, also died. Mulvey recovered from his concussion and when the dinghy got toppled over during a storm, he turned it over again by brute strength. They were rescued by a German minesweeper after precisely seven days, sixteen hours and ten minutes adrift, after being spotted by Ju 52s with degaussing rings for clearing minefields. The minesweeper took them to Cuxhaven where they recovered fast on 'a copious provision of lemon barley water' and spent the rest of the war in a prison camp.

'R-Roger' skippered by Flying Officer William Selfridge Day was badly damaged in an attack by an FW 190. Born on 17th February 1921 in Nova Scotia, Canada, after enrolling in the RCAF Reserve in July 1940 and attaining his wings, Pilot Officer 'Bill' Day was appointed instructor at Brandon, Manitoba, until his transfer overseas in December 1942. Berlin was their thirteenth trip. 'R-Robert' limped home and put down at Bodney, Norfolk; only taken over that day by a Thunderbolt squadron of the 352nd Fighter Group USAAF. 'Bill' Day received an immediate award of the DFC and Sergeant Colin 'Mitch' Mitchinson, the Australian rear gunner, the DFM for shooting down the FW 190. 'Bill' Day's crew would finish their tour late in November. Sergeant Ron James, the crew's mid-upper gunner, said that they were loath to leave. 'After losing a total of forty-three aircraft in six months, or to put it another way, two complete squadrons, to say that we enjoyed our stay seems rather paradoxical, but it was true.' By the end of July 1944 this crew had completed their second operational tour with twenty-seven sorties, seven of which were on 214 Squadron on Fortresses.

At Downham Market two Stirlings on 218 Squadron were missing. Flight Sergeant William Martin RCAF and crew on 'N-Nuts', which is believed to have been shot down by Oberleutnant Hermann Müller of 10./NJG3 crashed off the coast of Denmark. A Stirling on 149 Squadron at Lakenheath took off on a sea search at 0930 and they and another Stirling located the dinghy 160 miles north-west of Heligoland. Two hours after transmitting a request for assistance two Hudsons on 279 Squadron at Bircham Newton arrived in the search area. One of the Hudsons dropped its lifeboat and all five survivors clambered aboard but they must have been killed shortly after when two Bf 110s strafed the boat and shot down one of the Hudsons.[17] 'X-X-ray' skippered by Flight Sergeant Walter Stanley Williams crashed at Tempelhof Flugplatz, killing Williams and four of his crew. The flight engineer and the bomb aimer were taken prisoner. A third loss on the base was 'C-Charlie', the 623 Squadron aircraft which had been borrowed by Squadron Leader 'Wally' Hiles who had taken off at 2052 hours with a full incendiary load. Their route had taken them over Cromer on the Norfolk Coast and across the North Sea. Landfall was near Egmond on the Dutch Coast from where it was almost a straight route to just south of Berlin. On the run into the target the crew was shot down by a night-fighter and the Stirling crashed near Zossen, about twenty miles south of Berlin. All seven crew were lost without trace. On 20th February 1945 'Wally's' widow Elizabeth collected his DSO from the King at Buckingham Palace.

After being in the air for around one hour, Leutnant Peter Spoden saw a Viermot with two tail fins which was illuminated by searchlights. 'I fired several bursts from a distance of 200 metres and as a result the aircraft plunged down in flames. I next engaged an enemy aircraft over the city at a height of 4000 metres [13,000 feet]. The results of my bursts of fire however could not be observed. The last enemy aircraft I could determine was a Short Stirling, which turned into me and so I was forced to attack it from head-on. My bursts of fire were aimed so well that the aircraft dived down steeply and approached the ground fast. In the meantime, the enemy rear gunner fired at my own aircraft and inflicted a number of clearly audible hits in the fuselage, so that it started to burn.' Spoden was hit in the upper left leg and he immediately checked if his crew were all right but received no reply. When the heat from underneath him became unbearable, he loudly and clearly ordered them to bail out four or five times. After some more time had expired, he jettisoned the cockpit canopy and got out. He hit the

---

17   See *3 Group Bomber Command* by Chris Ward.

tailplane and whilst exerting all his strength, being hampered by his injured upper thigh and the speed of the aircraft pinning him for some time, he eventually broke free and pulled the ripcord at a height of 1000 metres [3,250 feet]. Spoden lost consciousness and came to in an air-raid shelter at Grunewalddamm 69 where German civilians, thinking that he was an RAF airman, attacked him. But when he spoke to them in German they stopped. His bordfunker, Unteroffizier Rüdke, survived, but Unteroffizier Franz Ballweg his bordmechaniker was killed. The bullet which had hit Spoden in the left leg shattered his femur and he underwent surgery in hospital.[18]

Over north-west Berlin Wilhelm Johnen loaded his guns, but just as he was about to go into the attack, his bordfunker reported that his SN-2 was out of action. 'The only solution,' wrote Johnen, 'was to fly with the bomber stream over the city and try to spot the 'furniture vans' [bombers] with our naked eyes.' No one lacked a target. Red, yellow and green tracers tore through the air past Johnen's cockpit. Shortly after 0100 hours a Halifax crossed Johnen's path. He attacked immediately with no fear for the defence and fired at the bomber's petrol tanks in the wings. The Viermot (four motor bomber or '4-mot') exploded and fell to earth in a host of burning fragments. It was 0103. Five minutes later he saw a Stirling. The huge Viermot grew larger in his sights and he sprayed the rear gunner with his guns and silenced them just as they opened fire. 'The rest was merely a matter of seconds. At 0108 the Stirling fell like a stone out of the sky and exploded on the ground... The nightmare came to an end. The Britishers were on the way home. I circled over the burning city waiting for stragglers. The flak guns fell silent. Huge fires lit up the night. The crew was silent. We could not get it into our heads that our capital - Berlin - was doomed.'[19]

The Stirling losses were bad enough, but the Halifax losses were even worse, and three squadrons in particular were badly mauled. On 35 Squadron, 'R for Robert' piloted by 29-year-old Flight Lieutenant 'Harry' Webster DFC went down with 31-year-old Group Captain Basil Vernon Robinson DSO DFC* AFC, the Graveley Station Commander, who was from Carlisle, was one of four machines lost. Everyone on board was killed. Nothing was heard from 'H-Harry' piloted by Flight Sergeant J.J. Williams after take-off. Williams and J. Colgan the flight engineer initially evaded capture, but

---

18  *'Enemy in the Dark, The story of a Luftwaffe Night Fighter Pilot'* by Peter Spoden (Cerberus Publishing Ltd).
19  *Duel Under The Stars* by Wilhelm Johnen.

Williams was caught at Frankfurt on 27th August and Colgan went 'into the bag' after being captured north of Nuremburg on 31st August. They joined three others on the crew behind the wire. The two other crew members were killed. 'A-Apple' skippered by 22-year-old Pilot Officer Lawrence Edward Nicklan Lahey RAAF was claimed shot down while at 17,000 feet by Hauptmann Prinz zu Sayn-Wittgenstein of Stab II./NJG 3 while outbound, 200 kilometres short of the target and crashed about twenty miles from Brandenburg. The damage caused a breakdown in the hydraulics and set fire to the starboard wing. After applying fire extinguishers to the starboard inner engine without avail, Lahey, who was on his twenty-second operation, ordered the crew to bail out. The mid-upper gunner was slightly wounded in the legs and Lahey had a slight head wound but landed safely. The crew was taken prisoner. Flight Sergeant Dave 'Shag' Cleary, Lahey's 22-year-old wireless operator, was only seventeen when he flew the first of his thirty operations. Cleary had an odd superstition. He always flew on operations with a pair of his girlfriend's knickers in his pocket. It was the only comfort in the Halifax during the cold black hours before they reached the target. He was fiercely misogynistic and considered women in Pathfinder Force were a jinx. 'Flight Lieutenant Annetts our flight engineer got married. That's why we went down,' he said later. Cleary was captured outside Genthin near Berlin and imprisoned at Stalag IVB Mühlburg where the knickers which accompanied Cleary on his last trip were decorated by a fellow prisoner of war. 'Jimmy' Hughes, who once flew with Cleary, knew someone who always flew in his pyjamas under his flying clothes. '"Pyjama Joe" we used to call him.'

Five Halifax IIs on 78 Squadron failed to make it back to Breighton. 'C-Charlie' piloted by Flying Officer John Austin was very badly shot about by night-fighters and he tried gallantly to reach Breighton but the Halifax crashed into the North Sea. Austin, his flight engineer and the mid-upper gunner, were unable to escape before the aircraft sank beneath the waves. An empty fuel tank broke free, onto which Sergeant G.E. Russell, the rear gunner, helped the injured navigator and wireless operator. Pilot Officer Ronald Arthur Winn the bomb aimer also climbed onto the tank, but in the sixteen hours before help arrived he fell into the sea and drowned. The navigator and wireless operator died from their injuries soon after being taken aboard the ASR launch. Russell was awarded a DFM for his brave attempt to save his fellow crew members.

'K-King' and 'E-Edward' were instructed to divert to Leconfield. While circling this aerodrome in readiness for landing a collision occurred and both aircraft were destroyed in crashes near Beverley. Sergeant John Greet the mid-upper gunner on 'E-Edward' was the only man to survive the collision. He woke up two weeks later in Beverley Hospital, suffering from fractures to the base of his skull and right femur. So serious were these injuries that almost five years were to elapse before he was fully recovered.

At Lissett five Halifaxes on 158 Squadron were missing. For six operations 21-year-old Flight Lieutenant Harold Kevin Hornibrook RAAF, who was from Brisbane, had managed to evade enemy night-fighters and escape the searchlights, but over Berlin he was a sitting duck. Despite repeated corkscrewing the searchlights held 'L-Leather' in their grip and then a night-fighter pounced, firing a fusillade of incendiary shells into the Halifax until ten fires were burning fiercely. Flight Sergeant Graham Albert George McLeod RAAF the 20-year-old rear gunner, a former insurance clerk from Hawthorn East, Victoria, and Sergeant Lawrence George Chesson the 21-year-old mid-upper gunner were killed. Three crew members bailed out in quick order leaving just Hornibrook and Pilot Officer Alan E. Bryett, the 21-year-old bomb aimer, alone in the aircraft, which was now rapidly spiralling down from 20,000 feet. Bryett had taken the precaution of putting his parachute on and he got to the escape hatch but he could not get it open. It was jammed. Hornibrook came down from his controls, got the escape hatch opened and pushed Bryett out saying, 'I'm coming.' Once out of the burning Halifax Bryett pulled his D-ring and his parachute opened and he landed in something soft, which seemed like bushes. He was still blinded by the searchlights. When his sight returned after about twenty minutes, to his horror he discovered that he was in a forest about 80 feet up a tree and the Halifax had crashed nearby. Eventually, Bryett, who was badly covered in blood, got down to the ground with some difficulty. Kevin Hornibrook had saved the bomb aimer's life, probably at the cost of his own. 'The pilot couldn't get out; he couldn't pull his parachute and he couldn't save his life and he gave his life for me. It was something I would think about every day. In that one moment of time, when he did what all captains of aircraft would do, he saved his crew but he lost his own life.'

Pilot Officer H.B. Frisby RAAF the pilot of 'C for Charlie' bailed out safely and he and five other members of his crew, who also survived, were taken prisoner. (Later, in Stalag Luft III at Sagan, Frisby earned a reputation as a very skilful forger and map maker and his efforts were rewarded when in March 1944 his fake identity cards and maps were used by the escapers after the Great Escape.) 'K-King', piloted by Flying Officer Frederick Albert Unwin, crashed in Schulzendorfer Strasse,

Heiligensee in the north-western suburbs of Berlin. Six of the seven-crew survived and they were captured, although Sergeant E.F. Wood RCAF, the rear gunner, died in captivity on 2ⁿᵈ August 1944. 'E-Edward', which had arrived on 158 Squadron on 3ʳᵈ August, was on its inaugural trip in the hands of 21-year-old Flight Sergeant William Arnold 'Bill' Burgum RAAF of Maryborough, Queensland, whose crew had flown their first op on Peenemünde on 17ᵗʰ/18ᵗʰ August. That had been bad enough but now, flying at 3,000 feet, at 2200 hours 'E-Edward' was attacked just north of Berlin by Oberleutnant Rudolf 'Rudi' Altendorf of 2./NJG4. For fifteen minutes Burgum managed to keep the burning Halifax airborne but part of the wing broke off on the approach as he circled what looked like an open field not far from Hermann Goring's estate at Karinhall and 'E-Edward' crashed into a swampy area. Only Flight Sergeant Harley Cecil 'Happy' Harber RAAF the 27-year-old rear-gunner and the wireless operator, Sergeant Arthur Cox RAFVR could be identified. Burgum; his flight engineer, 32-year-old Sergeant Roland Hill; navigator, 20-year-old Sergeant Peter Leighton Buck; air bomber, 21-year-old Sergeant Donald Roy Hempstock RAFVR and the 22-year-old mid-upper-gunner, Flight Sergeant Gordon Rudolph Harrison RCAF are listed as 'missing'.[20]

'Sandy' Slack on 'A-Apple' flown by Sergeant 'Tom' Edwards wrote: 'The city's opposition was formidable, but in the early minutes George Chapman's advisory from the rear turret was quietly controlled, "Plane going down to starboard, Skipper." The next casualty report, just moments later, came from the mid-upper. Then as more and more reports filled the intercom, "Tom" called a halt. "Note 'em, lads, but keep a sharp lookout for fighters."

'The routing markers floated by as we dutifully continued south. Then came the turn! "Tom" made it all right, but only by excessive banking. At which point "Freddie" Fields handed the navigation to me. With the bomb doors open, I threw my switches. Then, flat on my tummy, concentrated on the aiming point.

'George spoke swiftly, not wishing to balk my commentary. "It's that turn, Skipper, the fighters are swarming." His microphone clicked off.

'"Steady," I mouthed, "steady ... Left, lef..."

'Two streaks of light broke my concentration, peripherally demanding attention and only feet away. Christ - tracer! A fighter!

---

20   See John Williams' article in *After the Battle Magazine* (No.131, 2006).

'"Corkscrew, starboard... go!" I yelled. Instantly, "Tom" banked and shoved. A moment later though, bullets began rapping at the bulkhead behind me. Then fragments were flying everywhere, the sounds-off including an ugly crackling.

'"Sorry, lads," "Tom's" voice was terse. "We'll have to bail out."

'I craned up, to see "Freddie" busy unshipping the escape hatch beneath his seat. He gave a hurried thumbs-up, then disappeared, "Dick" Goddard, the flight engineer, followed suit.

'Getting to my knees I saw the mid-upper reach the hatch. I realised too that "Ernie" Whitfield was still stuffing leaflets down the chute! Then, as more bullets rattled in, the mid-upper was nowhere to be seen, while "Ernie" was a bloodied heap.

'Scrambling upright, I seized "Tom's" chest parachute, placed it next to him and then clipped on my own. "Tom" had no time to look around, merely gritting, "'Sandy', get out."

'I sized up the situation. Beyond him, the port wing was a fiery mass. By lingering I could only hamper his escape. *His escape*! A fiction. I knew it even then. But I had no option. Indeed, even as night and the air-rush embraced me, so the port wing folded upwards, sending "A-Apple" into an ever steepening spiral. Just one of the fifty-one bombers lost that night, including five from 158 Squadron.'[21]

'On the way home and well clear of the target,' wrote Geoffrey Willatt, '"Robbie" was taken short. He put the plane on automatic pilot and went back to the Elsan closet in the rear. Just as he'd lowered his trousers and sat down, there was a sudden fault in the automatic pilot, causing the nose to lift in an alarming way and bringing the 'plane near to stalling. The flight engineer disconnected it and the pilot ran forward, pulling up his trousers to take manual charge again. I was supposed to be the emergency pilot but he arrived back, thank goodness, before I had time to climb up from my position in the nose.'

Pilot Officer John McIntosh on 207 Squadron, a veteran of the earlier Berlin raids only just made it back. An hour's flying time from the target McIntosh's Lancaster 'M-Mother' was attacked by a Ju 88 night-fighter. The rear gunner, Sergeant R. Middleton from Leeds and the Junkers' gunner

---

21   *Corkscrew, Starboard...Go!* by Warrant Officer Dennis Slack writing in *Bomb On The Red Markers* by Pat Cunningham. The Halifax crashed near Döberitz where the pilot's body and that of Sergeants Frederick George Chapman and Ernest Whitfield were recovered from the wreckage. The survivors were rounded up and taken prisoner.

exchanged fire. A red glow appeared in the cockpit of the enemy night-fighter and it disappeared below, but the starboard fuel tank of the Lancaster, then more than half full, had taken hits and was set on fire. McIntosh jettisoned the bombs and turned for home. Three times he dived in an effort to blow the flames out, but each time the flames spurted when the bomber levelled out. Luckily all four engines were still working and McIntosh gave them full throttle to cut time to the coast. The flight engineer unsuccessfully hacked at the fuselage to try to make a hole to get an extinguisher into the flames. As the coast of England came into view the port inner engine stopped and an emergency landing was made at the first airfield they saw. With the port wing framework red-hot the Lancaster landed and the station fire-fighting personnel soon had the fire out. Another five minutes flying and the metal would have been completely burned through.

Pilot Officer Wilfred Eric Elder RNZAF and one crew member were injured on Halifax 'Q for Queenie' on 76 Squadron when it crashed at Holme on Spalding Moor. Pilot Officer William Alexander Wilkie Wanless DFM RCAF the rear gunner and the four others on the crew walked away unharmed. Elder and Wanless had each survived earlier crashes on 3rd/4th October, but the Canadian rear gunner's luck finally ran out on his twenty-fourth operation when 'P-Peter', flown by Pilot Officer Arthur Thorp, was shot down on Kassel. Wanless was taken prisoner. His skipper and the top turret gunner were killed.

Near Shouldham in Norfolk, Lancaster 'Q-Queenie' on 97 Squadron at Coningsby, flown by Sergeant Clifford Stanley Chatten, was attacked by Oberleutnant Wilhelm Schmitter, Staffelkapitän of 15/KG2 flying an Me 410A-1 intruder. Unnoticed by the crew of the Lancaster, Schmitter closed in on his target and his Bordfunker opened fire with the twin 13mm remotely controlled MG 131 guns fitted in the fuselage barbettes and controlled from the cockpit. Shells exploded in the Lancaster's fuselage and starboard wing. Flight Sergeant John Robert Kraemer RAAF the 23-year-old mid-upper gunner was killed and Chatten was wounded in the leg and ribs. He ordered the rest of the crew to bail out and left it late to get out. As he came down in his parachute he was injured when the Lancaster exploded below him and was taken to Ely Hospital. After this experience three of the crew refused to fly again but Chatten, a confirmed teetotaller, recovered to fly a full tour of operations. On 22nd/23rd May 1944 his Lancaster was intercepted by a night-fighter, but it was cleverly evaded. When nearing the target area he was coned over the target at Brunswick and another fighter was encountered. As a result, his Lancaster was severely damaged. The nose part was smashed and the air pressure thus caused blew out the windows at the side and most of the windscreen around the pilot's cupola. Despite the loss of his instruments Chatten got the bomber back to England and he circled the Wash until it was light enough for a crash-landing. Everyone walked away. 'Cliff' Chatten was awarded an immediate DSO and resumed his tour ten weeks later after recovering from his injuries. He also decided that he no longer wished to remain teetotal!

For the lucky ones the return from Berlin was a welcome homecoming. A relieved Warrant Officer 'Eddie' Wheeler wrote: 'Apart from the heavy flak and searchlight activity, the flight was uneventful, far less frightening than any trip to the Ruhr and after bombing from 18,000 feet we were back at Bourn in six hours thirty-five minutes.' On 22nd/23rd September 1943, 'Eddie' Wheeler would fly his sixty-third operation of the war, on Hanover, the birthplace of his great-grandfather and then endure a few more equally punishing trips to Mannheim (twice), Brunswick and Munich; the last on the night of 2nd/3rd October. When he and three other members on 'Johnny' Sauvage's crew were 'tour expired'. Flight Sergeant William 'Bill' George Waller the flight engineer, Pilot Officer 'Frank' Peter Burbridge the bomb aimer and Flight Sergeant 'Geoffrey' Walter Wood DFM the rear gunner had no option but to continue. 'Geoff' Wood's luck would finally run out on 21st February 1944 when he was killed on the raid on Stuttgart.

'Punch' Thompson on 83 Squadron landed back at Wyton at 0342, having been in the air seven hours and twelve minutes. They had crossed the Baltic coast near Rostock and then flown south of the large Danish islands and crossed Denmark near the border of Germany. 'Nearby, to the south at Flensburg, the usual display of fierce flak blossomed in anger,' wrote Thompson. 'After keeping well away from Sylt and its flak, at last we were out over the North Sea, north of the Frisian Islands and we headed for home.'[22]

Sergeant Eric Jones on 49 Squadron faced a barrage of questions from the crew at Fiskerton when he returned from his 'second dickie' trip.

'Well, what was it like?'

'Was the flak heavy?'

'Did you see any fighters?' etc, etc.

'How could I adequately describe the scene over the target? They would have to wait and see for themselves.'

---

22  *Lancaster To Berlin* by Walter Thompson DFC and Bar.

'Tony' Bird, another 'second dickey', who had been airborne for almost eight hours, wrote, 'after debriefing and the usual bacon and eggs early breakfast I related the experience to my crew who had waited up for my return. The conversation rarely strayed from details of our flight. In common with other returning crews, we had witnessed several of our aircraft going down in flames - a sad and frightening sight, visible for several miles on a clear night. We did not see any escapes by parachute, but it was no easy matter to exit a steeply diving burning bomber. At our operational altitude of about 20,000 feet, nearly four miles high, any physical activity became difficult in our unpressurised aircraft once the oxygen supply was disconnected, especially with our heavy flying clothes to hamper any movement. Portable oxygen bottles, suitable for short periods were available, but connecting them in emergency wasted precious seconds, which could make the difference between life and death for us.'

On return to Mildenhall Flight Lieutenant Robert Megginson's crew were given a few days' leave but 'Mitch' Mitchell the rear gunner was not with them. Megginson had taken 'O-Orange' off the runway at Mildenhall at 2040 hours and struggled into the air, crossing the Norfolk coast at Cromer and heading east. The weather was clear and visibility excellent; it was obvious that the enemy night-fighters would be active. Megginson's wireless operator, Sergeant 'Mick' Cullen recalls: 'Having reached the turning point thirty miles south of Berlin, our navigator, Pilot Officer Burrows, gave Megginson the new course. We carried out our bomb run without any problems and when "Andy" Haydon called "bombs gone" Megginson turned onto the course for home. It was at this point we were attacked by a night-fighter, which fired aggressively before losing us. The Skipper called for a damage report and one by one the crew responded from their respective stations that all was well. That is except for "Mitch". There being no reply, Megginson instructed me to investigate. I made my way down the fuselage towards the rear turret, feeling slightly apprehensive. The turret was jammed but with the aid of an axe I managed to break open the doors. The night-fighter had turned the turret into a twisted mass of tangled steel and shattered Perspex and there, slumped over the gun butts, lay "Mitch". I gently eased him back and found he had been killed by a solitary bullet through his left eye. I informed the Skipper of the situation and then proceeded to remove Mitch's body from the turret. I struggled for a few minutes and then called Andy Haydon on the intercom to come down and assist me and between us we managed to extricate "Mitch" from the wreckage. Although the guns were useless, Megginson requested me to occupy the shattered turret to watch for night-fighters on the homeward journey. With no heating it was a cold, uncomfortable and unenviable trip. We all travelled to Rugby to attend "Mitch's" funeral.'

At Elsham Wolds, personnel on the base, as usual, waited for as many crews as possible to return. The gunner on one of 103 Squadron's badly riddled Lancasters poured out his story of how they were attacked by six Bf 109 'Wild Boar' fighters that approached in pairs, but the biggest story of the day was reserved for Warrant Officer Clifford Annis' crew when they returned safely on 'Billie', which was now the first Lancaster in Bomber Command to achieve fifty ops. But they too had had a close shave, as Jack Birbeck recalled. 'I think we were about last over the target and consequently had a rough time, getting coned in searchlights etc. However, we survived and returned to base unaware of our landmark trip until next day when we were ordered to report to flights for a photo.' Station Commander Group Captain L.W. Dickens DFC AFC, rivet gun in hand, fixed a dummy DFC to 'Billie's' nose. 'Doug' Finlay's crew for one missed the celebrations having spent some time in the Sergeants Mess drinking beer after their brush with death when 'C-Charlie' had blown up at dispersal before the raid. 'Doc' Henderson had located them to check them out and had given them all a couple of tablets each. 'Sandy' Rowe wrote: 'By midnight I was ill - presumably "Doc" thought we were going to bed and failed to tell us that his tablets and beer did not mix.'

Four nights later 'Billie' and Cliff Annis' crew were lost when the aircraft was shot down by a night-fighter on Nuremberg. The WOp/AG, the two gunners and the Canadian navigator were killed. Annis sustained serious back injuries and after hospitalisation, was repatriated in September 1944.

Meanwhile, morale on 'Doug' Finlay's crew had plummeted as they were forced to 'loaf around' for a month because of the damage their aircraft had sustained in the explosion of 'C-Charlie'. Having to attend 'Harry' Wheeler's funeral at the South London Tabernacle, Peckham Road, Camberwell had done nothing to lift spirits either as 'Sandy' Rowe recalled: 'He was an only son. I felt particularly upset as I was the only one of the crew who had previously met his parents. A few weeks before I had spent a few hours with them and 'Harry' while going on leave to Cornwall - having to wait some hours for the appropriate train from Paddington. I was further distressed at the cemetery by the small number of mourners, it was as if we were in this large teeming city and no one cared. It was suggested to me that others who would have attended the funeral were working!'[23]

---

23   WW2 People's War website.

'Doug' Finlay's crew finally resumed operations on the night of 22ⁿᵈ/23ʳᵈ September, successfully taking part in an attack on Hanover, but they were destined never to visit Berlin because the next night on Mannheim they were shot down by Oberleutnant Lenz Finster and his bordfunker Feldwebel Siegfried Buegel of 4./NJG 1 flying a Bf 110G-4 night-fighter. Finlay and four of his crew were taken prisoner. Thirty-six-year-old Flight Sergeant William Henry MacDonald the replacement wireless operator, who was married and came from East Croydon and Pilot Officer Robert James Francis Vivers RAAF were killed.[24]

In Berlin on 24ᵗʰ August, 'the "all clear" was not given till 2.30,' wrote Hans Georg von Studnitz. 'Once, someone shouted: "The house is on fire!" Armed with a regulation stirrup pump we rushed upstairs but could see no sign of conflagration. Later we found out that a flare had dropped in the courtyard and had illuminated the whole place. In the Kaiserallee the Bulgarian Legation in the vicinity had been reduced to powder by an air-mine. In Steglitz, Friedenau, Lichterfelde and Marienfelde, places [were] impossible to pass by car. Craters filled with water, heaps of rubble, fire-hoses, pioneers, firemen and convoys of lorries blocked the streets where thousands of those rendered homeless were searching the ruins, trying to rescue some of their possessions, or were squatting on the pavements and being fed from field-kitchens. Although eighteen hours had passed since the attack, fires were still burning everywhere. The tramway lines had been destroyed. Burnt-out buses jammed the streets. Hundreds of trees had been shattered or bereft of their branches and foliage. Of one block of single-family houses all that remained was one solitary chimney. Notices everywhere gave warning of unexploded bombs. In the pale, dust-laden sky the red, fiery ball of the evening sun glowed like the harbinger of the Day of Judgment. On the edge of the city herds of cattle wandered untended among the ruins. Then suddenly, beyond the town, destruction ceased. The first village, Grossbeeren, which is six kilometres from Berlin, remained unscathed. What a contrast between the torn and twisted profile of the giant metropolis and this countryside, dozing in the peaceful evening sunshine! The next morning we passed by the burnt-out works of Henschel and Siemens in Tempelhof. The attack had been plunged into the heart of Berlin,

---

24 On 23/24 December 1943 Finster was killed, his wounded bordfunker and his bordshütze bailed out safely when they were shot down by a Mosquito night-fighter. 'Doug' Finlay was killed in 1947 whilst flying a Tiger Moth trainer of the Cambridge University Air Squadron. Warrant Officer David Halstead Loop was KIA on 18 October 1943.

like a knife into a cake and had sliced out a great triangle, the apex of which stretched as far as the Bahn Zoo railway station. There the last bomb fell in the Hardenbergstrasse, destroying the local military headquarters, blowing the roof off the High School of Music and smashing every window in the vicinity.'

A photo-reconnaissance pilot who was over Berlin the following afternoon reported dense columns of smoke rising to 20,000 feet: Preliminary examination of the film revealed that the smoke completely obliterated the whole of Berlin south-east of a diagonal line running from south-west to north-east of the city. The Charlottenburg district suffered greatly from fires. A chain of about eighty fires was seen on the western fringe of the dense smoke. The fires appeared to be burning in the top storeys of residential buildings, starting from Bismarckstrasse in the north of the Charlottenburg district to Bahnhof Steglitz in the south. In all, about 100 fires were seen. Despite the devastation, as far as the RAF was concerned, the raid was only partially successful. There was little fresh damage in the central city area or the north of Berlin. Casualties were heavy considering the relatively inaccurate bombing and 854 people were killed and eighty-three more civilians were listed as missing. The death toll was caused by an unusually high proportion of people not having sought shelter in their allocated air-raid shelters as they were ordered to do.

'In the areas which had been stricken twenty-four hours earlier,' wrote Hans Georg von Studnitz, 'thousands were still wandering about the streets, because no transport was available to take them away. On the faces of the poorest among them was written clearly the fear of another night, which, helpless and homeless, they would have to face. The official figures speak of 245 dead, 2,000 injured and 35,000 rendered homeless. The question on everybody's mind is - was Monday's attack the beginning of the end, or was it merely a warning shot, designed to bring home to the Berliners the might of the Royal Air Force?'[25]

---

25  *While Berlin Burns: The Diary of Hans Georg von Studnitz, 1943-1945*, (Frontline Books, 2011).

Squadron Leader John Searby commanding 405 'Vancouver' Squadron who would become legendary in the annals of the Pathfinder Force.

F/Sgt 'Stan' Mason, skipper of Stirling EH906/T on 90 Squadron at Wratting Common had come of age over Berlin at midnight, 23/24 August 1943, a strange way to spend the first hours of one's 21st, with the crew toasting him with orange juice. As soon as they were clear of Berlin's defences the crew had united to croon into the intercom 'happy birthday to you'. Stan's only comment was that 'a lot of German night fighters tried to gatecrash his birthday party'.

'S for Sugar', a 7 Squadron Blind Marker Lancaster flown by Squadron Leader Charles J. Lofthouse OBE DFC (pictured) was probably the first Lancaster to go down on 23/24 August 1943. All including the Oakington Station Commander, Group Captain Alfred Henry Willetts DSO were taken into captivity.

Squadron Leader Charles Lofthouse's navigator Berkeley Denis Cayford (2nd from left) seen here returning from a reconnaissance and leaflet dropping trip with 'Hamish' Mahaddie (Second from right). Tension and fatigue but also the relief to be home safely is visible on the crewmembers' faces.

Briefing at Elvington in August 1943. On the front row is Sgt Alan Baxter's crew that was lost on Halifax 'C-Charlie' on 23/24 August on Berlin. Far right is Sgt Arthur Leslie 'Bill' Thomas the flight engineer (KIA). There were only two survivors, Sgt E.G. Classen, WOp/AG and Sgt A. Lane, air gunner.

Flt Lt John Arthur Ingham DFC and crew on 44 Squadron just returned from bombing Berlin on 23/24 August 1943. Born in 1912 at Bolton, the son of a northern wool-merchant's family, Ingham's DFC was awarded on 14 May 1943 when he had flown 21 sorties. Wing Commander Ingham DSO DFC AFC completed fifty sorties, among them five to Berlin. During his second tour he commanded a Pathfinder Force squadron with outstanding success.

Stirling with bomb racks open ready for 'bombing up' is refuelled at dispersal.

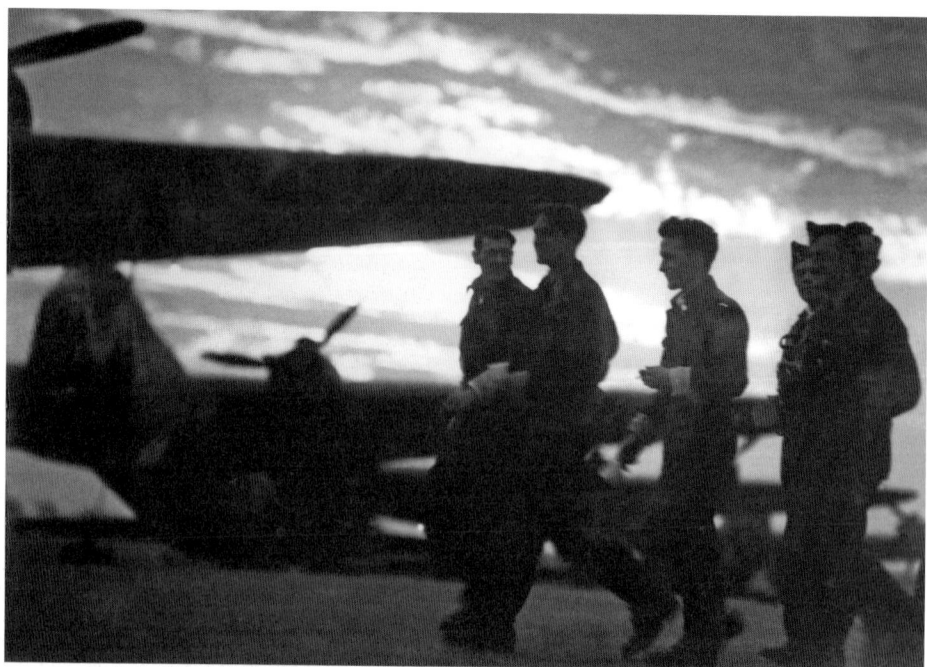

Stirlings on 90 Squadron lined up on the perimeter track at Wratting Common on 31 August/1 September 1943 waiting to take-off for Berlin.

De-briefing a Stirling crew on 90 Squadron after the raid on Berlin. Of the 622 bombers dispatched by Bomber Command that night 106 were Stirlings, of which seventeen were lost. 90 Squadron detailed twenty Stirlings for this raid and one failed to return.

Sgt 'Chris' Chatten in the cockpit of his Lancaster on 97 Squadron at Coningsby in 1943. On 23/24 August Chatten's Lancaster was shot down over eastern England by Oberleutnant Wilhelm Schmitter, Staffelkapitän of 15/KG2 flying an Me 410A-1 intruder.

Digging trenches in Berlin in August 1943.

PM-H on 103 Squadron at Elsham Wolds which was badly damaged on the 23/24 August raid on Berlin and was later repaired and transferred to 576 Squadron, completing more than 50 trips before the end of the war. Those in the photo include Doug Finlay (top), Jim Wivers (KIA 9.43), Sandy Rowe, Sgt Harry Wheeler (who was killed on 23 August when Lancaster W4323 PM-C was destroyed by fire at Elsham; middle, hand on knee), Bill Gillespie, Sgt Steel, Ian Fletcher, John McFarlane and the MT driver, Peggy Forster (centre, below ladder).

Halifax JD379/M on 77 Squadron at Elvington, flown by F/Sgt Alexander Massie and crew was one of the 56 Bomber Command aircraft that failed to return from Berlin on 23/24 August 1943. Hit by flak, the bomber came down at Quelch, north of Celle. Massie and two crew were killed; the rest were taken prisoner.

F/Sgt Bertram Raymond Jones' crew on 'M-Mother' (ED547) on 467 Squadron RAAF at Bottesford, Leicestershire prepares to set off for Berlin on the evening of 31 August 1943. Left to right: F/Sgt John Warrington Scott; F/Sgt's George Edward Erickson and Albert Reginald Thomas Boys; Sgt Charles Edward Adair; F/Sgt's Bertram Raymond Jones and John Hudson Wilkinson, (bending down) (lost on operations on 83 Squadron on 30 August 1944); and Sgt E. L. Tull, the only Englishman on the crew. Adair was killed on 23/24 September, flying as rear gunner on DV233 on the Mannheim operation. 'M-Mother' was shot down on the night of 29/30 December, during another operation to Berlin. All on the crew skippered by P/O Bruce Alexander Tait RAAF were killed. The emblem on 'M-Mother' was originally 'U-Uncle', hence the pawnshop or 'uncles' sign. Quite appropriate is the note 'we take anything' for the former captain, P/O J.H. Whiting, Adelaide, Southern Australia. The forty bombs represent raids over enemy territory and the inverted swastika, a night fighter which the crew shot down. 'Under new management' describes the change from 'U' to 'M' or from 'U to Me' as it is worded.

21-year old Flying Officer Francis Archibald Randall RAAF skipper of Lancaster 'Q-Queenie' (W4988) on 460 Squadron RAAF which crashed at Larös north-west of Helsingborg in Sweden after being shot up by a night-fighter over Berlin on 31 August/1 September 1943. A month after being shot down Frank Randall was back on the squadron again, crewed up with a new crew and fully operational once more. Returning from Berlin on 16/17 December 1943 Randall radioed to say that the Lancaster had clipped a tree. Shortly afterwards the aircraft crashed into a wood ten miles south of the Binbrook airfield runway near Market Stainton, south-west of Louth and detonated an ammunition dump, killing everyone on the crew. Randall had learned just before the raid that he had been awarded the DFC. (*Christine Bubery nee Bell*)

F/Sgt 'Bill' Burgum RAAF's crew at Stanton Harcourt, Oxfordshire in April 1943. L-R: Sgt Arthur Cox, wireless operator; F/Sgt 'Bill' Burgum, pilot; F/Sgt Harley Harber, tail gunner and in front, the bomb aimer Sgt Don Hempstock. They were flying Halifax HR980 'E-Edward' on their third operation, on 23/24 August 1943 when they were shot down and killed by Oberleutnant Rudolf 'Rudi' Altendorf of 2./NJG4. All but two of the crew are still listed as missing.

Halifax II JN909 DY-B on 102 Squadron, which F/Sgt Edward Thomas Samuel Rowbottom flew from Pocklington on 31 August/1 September 1943 on the operation on Berlin but who was shot down near Münster and crashed near Sinningen with the loss of the pilot and four of his crew. One other crew member evaded and one was taken prisoner.

Lancaster JA916 OF-L on 97 Squadron piloted by Wing Commander Kenneth Holstead 'Bobby' Burns DFC, exploded over Berlin on 31 August 1943 and crashed in the target area. Burns lost a hand and he and four crew were taken prisoner. Two crew were killed. After he was repatriated in 1944 Wing Commander Burns DSO DFC* resumed his flying career. He later served on the PFF Headquarters' staff. (IWM)

Halifax crews on 78 Squadron at Breighton eat breakfast after returning from Berlin in the early hours of 1 September 1943. The raid was the second of three launched by Bomber Command against the 'Big City' between 23/24 August and 3/4 September but the results were disappointing and 78 Squadron lost seven aircraft on these two operations.

Lancaster III ED659 SR-T on 101 Squadron piloted by Warrant Officer Dennis Arthur Tucker which was shot down on Berlin on 3/4 September 1943. There were no survivors.

Lancaster W4364 'Billie' on 103 Squadron at Elsham Wolds which on 23/24 August 1943 became the first Lancaster to complete fifty successful trips. On the platform is the Station Commander Group Captain Dickens, rivet gun in hand, who has attached a dummy DFC to the aircraft nose. Back row. Ground crew. Front row, left to right: 'Eddie' Edwards, mid upper gunner, Norman Turrell, flight engineer; 'Mac' McDonald, wireless operator; Cliff Annis, pilot and captain; Jack Birbeck, bomb aimer; Johnny Oldershaw, rear gunner; Johnny Renwick RCAF, navigator. W4364 was lost on a raid to Nuremberg just four nights' later. Only Annis, who was badly injured, Birbeck and Turrell survived.

In January 1943 Squadron Leader 'Jim' Verran DFC began a second tour on 9 Squadron, flying Lancasters from Waddington. Returning from a raid on Berlin on 1/2 March 1943 he was seriously injured and three of his crew were killed in a collision with another Lancaster also attempting to land. On 26/27 August 1944 he was shot down, suffering third degree burns. A German doctor saved Verran's life, carrying out skin grafts without an anaesthetic due to the shortage of drugs and with only paper bandages. All five of his crew died. (Aase Olesen via Sue Shore nee Page).

Lancaster 'E2-Easy' (EE138) on 460 Squadron RAAF was one of two Lancasters claimed shot down on the return leg from Berlin on 3/4 September 1943 by Leutnant Karl Rechberger of 12./NJG 3 piloting a Ju 88C-6 night fighter. Squadron Leader Carl Kelaher and his crew were killed, the aircraft crashing at Vestager in Denmark. Carl left a widow, Phylis Kelaher; they had been married in London on 15 July 1940.

Warrant Officer 'Eddie' Wheeler, WOp/AG on Flt Lt Joseph Henry Jean Sauvage's crew on 97 Squadron.

Sgt Lawrence 'Laurie' Maurice Parker from Bundaberg, Queensland, the ground staff sergeant in charge of 'A-Apple', Flight Lieutenant Reginald Carmichael's Lancaster on 467 Squadron RAAF at Bottesford in June 1943. It was Carmichael, from Bourke, NSW who decided to record the crew's raids with a foaming beer mug for every operation flown. He and his crew were killed on the Berlin raid on 3/4 September 1943. Sgt Parker, aged 25, was killed on the night of 3/4 December 1943 when 'G-George' (JB140) lost two engines on take-off for Leipzig. The Lancaster swung off the runway, collided with JB138 on 61 Squadron and crashed into a party of ground crew watching the take-off killing Parker and injuring another airman. F/Sgt Cecil Rowland Frizzell on JB140 died of his injuries on 5 December. 'G-George' also had frothing beer mugs on the bomb log to record its operations. On 3/4 December Walter King of the *Sydney Morning Herald* flew on 'G-George' with Squadron Leader William A. Forbes RAAF and crew on the operation to Berlin and on return asked 'why the foaming mugs of beer' to which Parker, smiling, had replied, 'Trips to the "Land of Mugs" - big mugs'.

F/Sgt Robert Barr McPhan RAAF skipper of Lancaster EE132 on 460 Squadron RAAF which was shot down on the Berlin raid on 3/4 September 1943 killing McPhan and four members of his crew.

On 31 August/1 September 1943 the radio-listening world went by proxy to Berlin with Lancaster ED586 'F for Freddie' on 207 Squadron at Langar. The crew took Wynford Vaughan Thomas (right), a BBC Home Service commentator and engineer, Mr. Reginald Pidsley (left), with them.

Crews on 77 Squadron at Elvington January-February 1944 who had bombed Berlin three times in 1943-1944. Flt Lt 'Pete' Cadman's crew on extreme right are (L-R) Sgt W. 'Triv' Trivett, rear gunner; Sgt 'Smoky' Powell, WOp; Cadman; Sgt H. Clayton, bomb aimer; F/O G. McGlory, navigator; F/O 'Curly' Holliday, flight engineer; Sgt 'Scats' Batty, mid-upper gunner.

Part of a vertical photographic-reconnaissance aerial taken over Berlin, showing an area immediately south of the Tiergarten (bottom) and east of the Zoological Gardens. Lützow Platz is at left centre, surrounded by a considerable area of buildings gutted by incendiary fires resulting from repeated raids by Bomber Command aircraft.

# Chapter 6

# Blitzing the 'Big City'

*'I can remember my first operation quite clearly, because when we went to the squadron they said, "Oh, you're all right. At first they give you a couple of easy ones to do."*

*'When we went to the briefing room we'd no idea what the target was. But as a flight engineer l knew it was a long trip because I knew what the fuel load was. I also knew what the bomb load was, and I had worked out that we were going quite a distance. But when they revealed on the map the actual route to the target, it was Berlin, the "Big City".*

*'It was rather frightening at first, and then I thought, "Well, you start at the deep end; it can only get shallower."*

*'We went out across the North Sea going northwards. We crossed over northern Denmark and approached Berlin from the north. We were followed by an enemy aircraft for quite a while. The rear gunner was the first to spot the aircraft. At one point he closed in on us and we thought, "The attack's coming!" The rear gunner opened up followed quickly by the mid-upper turret, and the aircraft suddenly swerved over and dived and went down somewhere below us.*

*'It was my first operation and I had no idea what a target looked like. We could see in the distance the coloured markers that had been laid down by the Pathfinder Force. The enemy had laid above an avenue of huge lights, some gigantic form of flare. It felt as if you were flying down a fully lit avenue and you expected to be attacked at any moment. My skipper had a pact with the bomb aimer that when we got to the target he would fly as far as he could straight and level across the target so that the bomb aimer had every chance of releasing the bombs at the right time. The skipper always said, "But I won't go round again."*

163

*'You did nearly everything in as near as you could to total darkness. The navigator had to have lights on his navigation charts and he was enclosed by curtains, and the wireless operator the same. The gunners sat in total darkness just searching the sky. The bomb-aimer would be down below in his compartment. The skipper and I would be left in the cockpit. He would look out to the port side, and I would look out to starboard. We had an agreement amongst us that while we flew we wouldn't talk to each other, so it was a lonely flight. We didn't exchange any normal conversation. If somebody had something to say, it had to be important.*

*'The skipper and I arranged a mutual sign language where he would point to things in the cockpit and I would manipulate the various gadgets as he required them. That worked well unless I got it wrong. He was a big fellow and I would just feel his hand on the back of my head. You knew you hadn't done the right thing and then he would point again.'*

**Norman Berryman, Bomber Command flight engineer.**

With hands behind his head Sergeant William F. Trivett lay on his back staring up to the ceiling, listening to the fading pulsating roar of the low flying bomber aircraft that had awakened him. It was 0600 hours on Tuesday, 31st August. 'Triv' was the rear gunner on the 77 Squadron Halifax crew at Elvington skippered by 21-year-old Flight Lieutenant Peter M. Cadman. Trivett's immediate thoughts were of Monday night's events, when during a test run up of their aircraft's engines prior to take-off for the raid on the twin towns of Mönchengladbach and Rheydt, the port side which supplied energy to his rear turret had overheated far in excess of the acceptance level. Despite frantic and heroic efforts by the ground crew to get them airborne, they had missed their deadline of extended take off time and were ultimately 'scrubbed' from the night's flying operation. Cadman's crew, who presented themselves back at Flying Control in full flying kit were dejected and disappointed. So much effort had gone into the day's preparation by all trades for this operation and with the rest of the squadron airborne and on course for Germany, they felt like imposters. Trivett's aggrieved frustration showed to the extent that a veteran of two Bomber Command tours, now working in Flying Control, came over and placed his hand upon his shoulder. 'Take a tip from me,' he offered. 'Don't ever get upset over being scrubbed from a flying operation. Remember, that could have been the "op" you were supposed to go missing!'

The sound of the low flying aircraft's engines had died away and Trivett turned his head to look down the line of beds in this RAF aircrew Nissen hut. 'Three of the beds were empty. This was ominous and bode ill will for the crew that had apparently gone missing on last night's raid on Mönchengladbach. Their stay on the squadron hadn't been long - just two days - and they had gone missing on their first "op". It wasn't an uncommon happening either. It was recorded that your first five "ops" were to be your hardest, after which luck was needed in heavy doses. I tried hard to place the missing faces - but really, I hadn't time to get to know them. Soon their kit bags and belongings would be removed to the guardroom for safe keeping, to await the padre's attention and his helpers to sort any dubious correspondence, leaving only personal effects if needed to be sent home. Soon the next of kin would be receiving those dreaded telegrams; "The Air Ministry regret to inform you that..." giving cold comfort to shocked and tearful relatives. To the Air Ministry the missing crew would be just another statistic in the mounting numbers of aircrew who failed to reach that coveted tour of thirty flying operations. Tomorrow a new replacement crew will arrive from a Conversion Unit to fill their places yet, even more tragic, few people will have known of the missing crews' existence on the squadron.

'To be remembered on a squadron fell to a select band blessed with an abundance of luck that enabled them to stay alive long enough to complete their thirty operations. Distinction would be bestowed upon them when during a riotous night in the Mess the celebrating crew, by custom, would be allowed to write their names upon the ceiling. Sadly, this eventful and much looked to occasion wasn't shared by too many crews, for during 1943-44 when "Maximum Effort" was the byword of Bomber Command, statistically one in three aircrew survived to complete a tour. That was when a meticulously planned night flying operation deep into a defensively hostile Germany would return minus thirty or forty, maybe even fifty of Bomber Command's aircraft would have been shot down and of course later there was a loss of seventy-six on Leipzig and ninety-six on Nuremberg.

'No more time for daydreaming or reflections. It was 0700 hours. I was on my feet half dressed and on my way to the ablutions for a warm water wash before the masses got up and drained the heating system cold. The fresh air and damp, dewy grass, the invigorating early morning chill; oh, it was great to be alive.

'I returned to tidy my bed. Re-entering the Nissen hut was like walking into a foggy swamp. Stale breath, burning cigarettes and the accompanying blue hazy smoke, plus a few bods who it appeared had lost the knack of controlling their surplus wind culminated with a smell most foul. I gave an exaggerated consumptive like cough that bent me over and the effort rasped my throat and brought moisture to my eyes. A muffled voice from beneath a blanket part surfaced to say, "Cough up and die you bastard".

'In this NCO aircrew hut I was billeted with my bomb aimer Harry "Clay" Clayton from Wigan [who, like their navigator, Flying Officer Gerard "Mac" McClorry from Lancaster in Lancashire] was an ex-policeman; wireless operator Flight Sergeant Arthur "Smokey" Powell and mid-upper "Bill" Batty. [Trivett was a Londoner] Powell came from Leeds; as did Sergeant William J.W. "Scats" Batty, the mid-upper gunner. The rest of the crew being commissioned slept in the officer quarters.' Their skipper, born at Tientsin in Northern China, educated at Grenham House, Birchington and Charterhouse and having joined the RAFVR in 1941, had trained in Canada and received his commission the same year. He had been an instructor before joining 77 Squadron on his first tour 'What a character,' Trivett once described him, 'harum-scarum and full of fun on the ground - in the air calm and cool as a cucumber, a leader and a first-class pilot - you could go anywhere with him because he imbued you with a feeling of confidence in his and your own ability. Wild and fun-loving on the ground, but in the air a completely different person - cool, calm, competent and composed, to use a little alliteration. He wore a ceremonial cap on which the cloth covering the peak was worn, with the result that in a slight wind he had a flap flopping away above and below the cardboard; his battledress was also a little scruffy to put it mildly. He had a mascot, his childhood teddy given the title "Flight Sergeant Wakey-Wakey".'

Trivett continued, 'at 0745 hours it was off to the mess for breakfast before its closure at 0830 hours, but before leaving the hut I lingered long enough to glance back at those three empty beds and ask myself what was that profound prognosis that I found hard to accept last night? "Don't worry about a scrubbed operation; it could be the one on which I was supposed to go missing!" I readily accepted it now and silently counted my blessings.

'There was no queuing for breakfast (only at dinner time). Straight in for porridge and beans on toast with a splat of tomato sauce from a pressurised bottle that has just caught the edge of the plate and stayed on it.

'Breakfast tucked away inside of me I strolled to the 'Flight offices'. Here aircrew assembled in their respective sections, i.e. wireless, navigator, flight engineer and of course gunnery sections. I took notice of an information board laying out the procedure and programme for the day. From the gunners point of view it could be a film on safety and escape, aircraft recognition, dinghy drill, night vision techniques and observation, FFI, medical parade, sport, clay pigeon shooting, anti anything injection (nothing for anti war) and the odd lecture pushed in the programme. The working day would end at 1700 hours. More often than not many bods were skiving and you would be exceedingly lucky to find a full house after 1430 hours. Just half an hour into a lecture on aircraft recognition, a head popped around the door and informed the lecturers that all outside phone lines were dead. We were geared to know the significance of that. Eyes looked out of the window and there on the perimeter track a WAAF drove a tractor pulling a trolley load of bombs. A couple of armourers sat astride the load.

'I felt deflated and disappointed. "There goes my celebration drink tonight," I thought. My heart was set on catching the 1900 hours off duty bus into York and eventually "Betty's Bar", the Mecca of 4 Group aircrew squadrons. It was a safety valve from flying operations. Visits and acquaintances were made in almost every pub in this lovely city of York but "Betty's Bar" took pride of place. Many had been the greeting across the bar to somebody apparently back from the dead - or even mistaken identity. "Hello stranger, am I glad to see you. I heard you went for a 'Burton'." It would be passed off with a laugh and after a drink - well several - arrangements would be made to meet again the next free night; why not?

'But aircrew could only plan one day to the next. Although operating from different RAF stations both would be flying on the same mission. After returning, on your first free night you'd make for "Betty's Bar" to renew acquaintance with your long-lost pal. You stand by the door entrance. Even on a crowded evening you could see them all come in from here aided by an exceptionally long mirror on the wall. The mirror carried hundreds of aircrew signatures, but there was a suspicion that one signed your life away. While there was that fraction of doubt, my name never went upon that mirror. You waited for your friend because you knew he also wanted to make this meeting. But before the night and its drinking time had flown away someone would tell you what you already knew deep down in your gut, - your friend had "gone for a Burton". But grieving and sorrow was only for close relatives. It was an accepted fact that every night raid would suffer casualties. What a great comforter that inner built feeling that told oneself that it would always be the other crew who would go missing.

'Since being stationed near York I had secretly wished when my twenty-first birthday came around that I would love to celebrate in "Betty's Bar" with the companionship of my own crew and our faithful ground crew who serviced our "N-Nan" aircraft. I am sure it would be a riotous evening to remember in my future years. I hoped I would make it but there was always the uncertainty in war. The sadness of missing and killed young aircrew was seldom dwelt upon, there was too much living to do in maybe so short a time. Many of these lads could relate to terrible experiences i.e. near misses, the crashed landings, the lumps blown out of aircraft - but only in select company when blasphemy was fiercely injected that a life and death situation would appear by them to have been an hilarious experience.

'Our training day finished early at 1115 hours. We were dismissed from the Flights to carry out the usual pre-op inspection of your aircraft. The armourers had already seen to the turrets, but it was always good practice to let them see we cared. The perimeter track was busy with transport running aircrew out to various aircraft. I rode with "Bill" Batty my mid-upper gunner to our Halifax "N-Nan" ("Naughty Nan") on its dispersal pad. "Bill" and I had harmonised our respective guns and turrets for the raid on Mönchengladbach but that was scrubbed, so we got off lightly. Our ground crew had attended to last night's offending engine and after their test run ups stated that it would be OK for tonight. All around the perimeter track trailers of bombs were being delivered at different dispersals and petrol bowsers seemed to be in plentiful supply. Such was the lead up to the start of an operational day in Bomber Command and at 77 Squadron, Elvington, Yorkshire, in particular.

'A steady stream of aircrew was now making their way back to their Messes ready for lunch. Then it was back in the ante room of the Sergeants Mess. Many were smoking cigarettes. Some hiding behind newspapers; others played cards or told jokes. At the far end of the room a navigator played a tune on the piano, but for all the attention he was getting, he could have been in solitary confinement, but, amongst the remaining aircrew the usual guessing game started.

'It was in whispers first: "Where's the target then?"

'Nobody knows - nobody will know till briefing but in helping to pass the time - the guessing game went on.

'"It's full tanks, so I'm told."

'"Who told you that?"

'"Well I think it is!"

'"There you go again! Sounds like a long trip then!" A head popped around a paper to join in the conversation, "Where do you reckon then - the

Ruhr?" The commanding voice of a gunner, "You twit! Get back behind your paper and cartoons; that's only just past Southend!" Another bod picked it up and referred direct to the chap with the paper. "It's full tanks remember!" he mocked.

'Not to be belittled, the "paper man" came right back. "So what - I remember once before - we had full tanks - and when we got back there was plenty unused in the tanks." It went embarrassingly quiet for just a couple of seconds before a razor of wit sliced through the Mess. "Oh, cor blimey, surely ain't that what you'd expect if you abort when you see the enemy coast?" It was play acting and teasing at its best, for two or three crews in this room, it could be the last laugh they would have. An orderly entered the ante room and as of one accord aircrew rose from their chairs, the battle order was being pinned to the notice board, for those at the back necks grew as they stretched to read the crews detailed for tonight. I picked out the name of my skipper and read the six names directly below his and my eyes lingered a little on the last one, "Sergeant W.P. Trivett, rear gunner". Not that I didn't want to go, but my heart was set on having a good drink in "Betty's Bar" in York that night.

'At 1500 hours dinner was served in the Mess, which seemed a little quieter than usual. The Tannoy crackled and a WAAF's voice carried through the Mess. "Will all detailed pilots and navigators report for Briefing at 1430 hours." Short and to the point. A buzz of expectancy in the air. 1400 hours. Dinner was over. Crews sauntered back to the anteroom to await the call. It wasn't long in coming. "All detailed crews report for main briefing 1600 hours." If one has any uneasy feelings or any secret thoughts, then this was the time to shed them. Now you had spare time to write a letter (sometimes called a last letter), play cards, walk back to you billet, a quick wash and shave, press your uniform, or in aircrew parlance, have a tom tit!

'At 1545 hours crews were walking towards the briefing room. Outside its door three or four service policemen with Alsatian guard dogs patrolled the entrance. Who looked the more ferocious twixt police and dogs was debatable. Crews were assembling outside. On the grass forecourt an aircrew bod deep in thought picked his teeth with a matchstick; a few appeared loud of mouth and confident. Some gave a nervous laugh to any conversation, while those with more than a few ops to their credit, talked quietly in small groups occasionally looking around at the tell-tale reactions for they had been through these stages themselves.

'The doors of the briefing room had opened at 1600 hours and we filed in while being heavily scrutinised by the "doormen". Inside were the pilots and navigators who had been plotting the routes and times. There was a heavy feeling in the air accentuated by the mist of blue smoke from cigarettes. All curtains were drawn and the lighting that added more warmth to the bodies now crowding in caused its own problem. The long slatted wooden forms were soon hidden by the sitting aircrew. We awaited the arrival of the Station Commanding Officer. With the shuffling of feet and the knocking over of the odd form, 130 aircrew came to attention that heralded his presence. It needed only the customary wave of his hand in acknowledgement, a nod to the wing commander to uncover the target and the show was on.

'All eyes focused on the target area. A few stifled whistles - a few "Cor Blimeys", "Good God" and a single "Oh I do say old chap", released the tension of the day.

'So there it was, the "Big City" - BERLIN. There was the constant gum chewing and with a bit more flair, those who bit the end of a pencil and the virtuoso who could beat a tattoo with pencil between his teeth. A few hearts beat faster and I would suspect a few nearly stopped, but overriding it all a background buzz of excitement.

'The respective flight officers gave us a collective briefing i.e. what to look for and so much to be stored in the head. Times, routes, turning points, bomb loads, petrol quantities, heights, timed waves of aircraft, flare markers, expected temperatures during flight, speeds, flare codes, aiming point colours, not forgetting the number of aircraft detailed for this operation; the allotted time of take-off, what wave time one would go through the target. Oh, I almost forgot; of course, the weather upon which the whole operation depended. It seemed to go on ad infinitum. It all added up to much planning and so much painstaking detail.'

On the Battle Order on the night of 31st August/1st September were 622 bombers - 331 Lancasters, 176 Halifaxes, 106 Stirlings and nine Mosquitoes. Three Mosquitoes on 105 Squadron and six on 109 Squadron would mark for the heavies by dropping red TIs near Damvillers in north-east France and Green TIs near Luxembourg.

'The briefing ended with Wing Commander Carr the Officer Commanding telling us in a rather haughty voice of the significance of this operation. He offered his best wishes to one and all for success and returns and concluded with, "I wish I was coming with you". Well if ENSA visit the station, they need not look far for a stand-up comedian!'

At other bases that fine August morning reaction to the news was mixed. 'Our hearts dropped again when we saw that the target was Berlin again,' wrote Warrant Officer 'Eddie' Wheeler on 97 Squadron at Bourn. 'It seemed that the targets were becoming so much harder these days and I gained the impression that time was running out for me and the odds were increasing. I was becoming more nervous than ever before and was looking forward to finishing my tour of ops.' Four nights' earlier, on a trip to Nuremburg, his Lancaster was coned by searchlights and suddenly the heavy flak had stopped, which indicated fighter activity could be expected. Sure enough, a fighter attacked from the starboard quarter and his pilot corkscrewed as the gunners returned fire. Wheeler was sitting at his radio listening to the Group broadcast and as he looked up he saw that there was a clean hole through the crystal monitor about eighteen inches from above and to the right of his head. 'A cannon shell had pierced it and gone straight out through the front of the aircraft. I was rigid, not daring to move an inch. The contact was brief and the fighter sheered off, much to our relief.'

Others like J. Norman Ashton, the flight engineer on 'Reg' Bunten's crew on 103 Squadron, took the news of the impending trip to Berlin in their stride. Bunten had been trained in Florida on single-engined Harvards and subsequently, in England, on twin-engined Oxford and Whitley aircraft. Ashton, who had joined the RAF in 1940 as an engine fitter and volunteered for flying duty in 1942, thought 'Reg' would be cool, confident and capable and equal to any situation which might arise. 'Corky' Corcoran, the Canada-trained bomb aimer was deeply religious and a Yorkshireman, 'and proud of it'. 'Bill' Bailey, 'a typical Londoner - bright and breezy as a Cockney sparrow' - was the navigator. Recently married and very much in love, he too had trained in Canada. 'Reg' Boys the wireless operator was 'a solid type, dependable, methodical and had probably never heard of the word panic'. 'Eddie' Smith the mid-upper gunner was tall and had the bearing of a typical Canadian. Hailing from Sioux Lookout, he had worked for an airline company, had been a gold miner, trapper and a guide on hunting and fishing expeditions. 'Entirely fearless,' was Ashton's guess; 'and a man to have around when things got dicey. Woe betides the night-fighter pilot who was rash enough to get into "Eddie's" gunsight.' 'Doug' Wilkinson the rear gunner was of smaller and sturdier build and differed greatly in outlook. Yorkshire bred; he was often very quiet and busy with his own thoughts, but, on occasion, would leap into the conversation and talk for hours. 'He would,' thought Ashton, 'sit behind those four Brownings without a qualm and never would it occur to him that any "Jerry" could possibly catch him napping.'

'As the battering of the Ruhr continued throughout the early summer,' wrote Ashton, 'it became increasingly obvious that, with the approach of longer periods of darkness, Bomber Command would soon be seeking pastures new. There had been rumours and counter-rumours of long-range trips, eyes were wont to wander farther east on the target maps, there was the odd occasion when fuel tanks had actually been filled to capacity and there had been a few early scrubs. The tension, which had been building up for days, was broken when the CO informed us at briefing that the German capital was at last to feel the full weight of an attack in strength by Bomber Command. A spontaneous burst of cheering greeted this announcement. We had all wanted a "bash" at the "Big City" more than anything else in the world and this was it, for "William" and crew'.[1]

At Lissett, Sergeant 'Harry' Simister, the flight engineer on Pilot Officer Kenneth Ward's crew on Halifax II 'R-Roger' on 158 Squadron wrote: 'The briefing was not unusual and take-off was at 2100 hours.' Simister was just short of his twentieth birthday when he joined the RAF in April 1940. His thoughts now were more with his mother. She had just received a telegram from the Air Ministry telling her that his brother, a navigator on Beaufighters, serving in the Mediterranean area, was missing.

At Chedburgh, home to 620 Squadron's Stirlings in 3 Group, Pilot Officer John A. Martin DFC, a flight engineer who had flown about twenty-five bombing operations and was an old sweat by now, wrote: 'Everyone else had gone. Sergeant [William Dennis] "Big Taff" Whitfield [twenty-two, of Skewen, Glamorgan], the fellow who slept in the next bed to me, arrived. He was the flight engineer on another crew [captained by 20-year-old Pilot Officer Macquarie James Campbell RAAF of Port Macquarie, New South Wales]. They went to get briefed for their operation that night and when they came out we went in for ours. I asked "Taffy", "What do you think of the operation tonight?" He said to me, "With this crew, I have got no hope, no hope in this wide world getting through with this! They're hopeless".'

'Briefing over,' wrote 'Triv' Trivett, 'all pockets were emptied of letters, photographs, old bus tickets, landladies' addresses; in fact, anything that would give the enemy information. All this flotsam that was left was placed in your own numbered bag and collected on return. In the packed room, the heat of bodies, the cigarette smoke and the enforced security closure of windows was almost overbearing and suddenly daylight was seen through an opened door and cooler air drifted in and kissed ones face. Ecstasy.

'Now back in the mess for an operation tea of fried egg and chips, which in these days of rationing was considered a delicacy by many of our own people back home. I enjoyed my meal; I always did and I was

---

1 *Only Birds And Fools* by J. Norman Ashton DFC. (Airlife 2000).

determined to enjoy the other egg that I would receive on return despite the usual banter from other crews asking could they have my other egg if I went for a "Burton". This apparent callousness was commonly accepted by most crews, but behind it all was a cover up for a little nervousness. For a short while it made them one of the boys. There was one cocky sod who once asked me, if I thought I'd ever finish my tour! I replied, "I don't think you should be asking me that because you won't be here to see it." Unfortunately, it was a case of many a true word spoken in jest.

'Meal over it was back to the billets to put on extra woollies for night flying and then back to the Mess to get transport to the flights. Most aircrew took a casual walk, but I was a bit bulky with my extra clothing and there was no point in sweating unnecessarily, so it was a ride for me.

'At the flights I prepared to inspect my flying gear. Should I wear electrically heated suit or an Irvin sheepskin jacket? The electric suit was not so bulky. I plugged in the suit and made sure it all warmed up. (Had one suit I didn't pre-test and on the trip, the left had remained cold - so did the right leg and foot. The left foot was so hot I had to unbutton the connecting studs to take it out of circuit. Try that with three pairs of gloves on, silk, woollen, leather.) For a short while I could have taught St. Vitus a few hops, but the smell of burning was the cause of turning it off and then I nearly had frostbite. I made sure it didn't happen again.

'In spite of a pleasant day, the met forecast was very cold at 20,000 feet. In the crew locker room there was quietness as private thoughts came uppermost. Hands went in and out of pockets in search of any overlooked item that could give "Jerry" a lead on information. I was wearing two pairs of socks, vest, shirt, pants, long johns, trousers, pullover, battle dress, heavy white sea socks, flying boots, gloves and an electric flying suit - and that was just to get out to the aircraft. Before getting inside I would don a Mae West buoyancy jacket and over all this, a parachute harness to keep it all in place. The rear turret was a very cold and lonely place.

'At 1900 hours all crews were togged up and assembled outside of flight control awaiting transport to take them to their respective aircraft. (At this stage most were saying, "Please God, don't scrub it"). While waiting for transport I had time to look around and I saw Freddie Cox, a rear gunner. I'm sure he was doing his last op of his second tour? There was "Daffey" and his crew. "Freddie" Taylor my gunnery leader had no crew and picked the op as it came along. He had certainly picked a right one tonight. There was Warren's crew. We joined the squadron the same day as them. There was Robinson's crew and Mansoon's and not forgetting my own skipper Peter

Cadman. Hang about, who did I see talking to the Officer Commanding? Air Commodore "Gus" Walker, an ex-English Rugby international of course.[2]

'There were so many well educated people amongst this lot, at any other time and place in the world, with my council school education, I would have felt awkward and out of place, but as has been said before, war and death are great levellers. There were lads with gaudy scarves, another with a balaclava under his helmet, while two I saw had sheath knives strapped to their legs. I carried one inside of my sock and leg, worn with the thought that it may be vital in the event of being one of the unfortunates.

'At 1915 hours my Skipper jumped aboard the tailboard of a transport bus and called his crew to go with him. I made a spirited effort to follow but the bulkiness of clothing held me back. Somebody took my arse in his hands and gave me a push upwards - with every good intention and I was up on the wagon. We were driven halfway around the perimeter track and dropped off at the dispersal of "N-Nan". Inside of the aircraft testing oxygen and intercom to all stations and that the illuminated gunsight was OK.

'Engineer conversed with pilot and the engines were given a quick burst. Gun turrets were operated under power; gauges were checked up front, revs, vacuum and power, all engines switched off. The skipper accepted the aircraft and signed the Form 700. All outside for the odd joke with the ever-faithful ground crew. The last smoke for 8½ hours and then the ritual of watering the grass. In the rear turret 8½ hours sitting still can be a long time.

'The evening sun was low over the airfield; a lovely breeze and I could feel the first chill of the evening. All was quiet. It was the perfect setting to end the day, well almost, one hoped. The minutes ticked slowly by and the skipper glanced at his wristwatch and said, "OK chaps, time to pile in". As I crawled along the fuselage to reach the rear turret I realised how cumbersome it was to wear all my attire. It was a pleasant autumn evening and as I squirmed into my turret the exertion had made me sweat. I secured my parachute in the fuselage outside of the turret; there was no room for it inside with me. I knew after we took off my back would feel like an ice-cold

---

2 On the night of 8/9 December 1942, 133 bombers and Pathfinders, including 108 Lancasters, were ready to be dispatched. While bombing-up at Syerston incendiary bombs fell from the racks of a 61 Squadron Lancaster, exploded and set fire to the aircraft and the inhabitants of Newark and district were able to hear for themselves the explosion of a 4,000lb bomb. Group Captain Clive 'Gus' Walker, the Station Commander went out to the bomber on a fire tender and the Lancaster blew up killing two men and blew the Group Captain's arm off. 'Gus', who had played rugby for Yorkshire, Barbarians and England, returned and post war became AVM Sir Gus Walker CBE DFC AFC.

towel had been laid across me. This moment alone I would gladly have changed places with any "up front member" who could sit in battle dress and Mae West and have hot air from the engines piped down their necks.

'At 2000 hours a bright green flare fired from a Very pistol arced gracefully over the airfield. The silence was rudely shattered by the first aircraft to be off starting its engines, followed by another, and then it was our turn and the air filled with a cacophony of warlike intent. Engines were now revving and we were taxiing from the oil stained apron of our dispersal, making our way around the perimeter and as the aircraft rolled slowly by the faithful ground crew I noticed they were giving me in the rear turret a two fingered victory salute, - well I did have my doubts - for I've never seen a salute performed as energetic as that! One thing I could be sure of; if and when we got back, whatever the coldness, however inclement the weather, you could bet your last sixpence some of those lads would be on duty, directing "their" aircraft to the dispersal with torches cutting circles of light through the darkness.

'Having arrived at the end of the runway we turned into wind, waiting the off. Flying Control had an assembly of viewers waving away each aircraft: wives, girlfriends, some you could bet with watery eyes, seeing off their aircraft that was carrying someone special to them. They stood with their thoughts and maybe a short prayer. The engines vibrated, straining against the bomb load. Laboriously the aircraft trundled down the runway and agonisingly gathered speed. The tail became airborne, yet anxiously I watched the runway become longer and longer and suddenly the rumbling tyres disappeared and we were airborne. I took the safety catches off my guns and now I was in business. The pilot and bomb aimer, with engineer, were going through their cockpit drill. Over the intercom I heard, "wheels up, flaps up, revs 2,650". Having established alibis well, the navigator took his cue, "Skipper set course 065° now."

'"Wilco 065."

'At Elsham Wolds there was quite a crowd of onlookers at the end of the runway and as "Reg" Bunten swung "William" into position Norman Ashton gave a quick acknowledgment of their hand-waves and thumbs-up signs. Good old "Doc" Henderson was there as usual and certain of the crews who were not operating had come along to give us a cheer. A number of ground staff lads and WAAFs had also turned up and it felt comforting to know that we had their prayers and best wishes. In the same quick glance I noticed the fire-tender and the "blood-wagon" standing by and hoped that their services would not be required, either before or after the trip.

'"William" rocked slightly as "Reg" applied the brakes and the skipper and I re-checked every control and setting. The previous aircraft was just getting airborne when we got our "green" from the chequered caravan, and "Reg", dead cool as usual, murmured, "OK chaps, here we go!" The engine note increased to a roar and as the brakes were released "William" rolled slowly forward, gathering speed as the throttles were progressively opened. A quick check on the engine instruments and exhaust flames and then I pushed the throttle-levers through the "gate" and nipped-on the friction-nut. I smiled at "Reg" and reported: "All engines OK, full power on!" The aircraft tore down the runway like a thing possessed, with the four Merlins screaming out their war-song. "Reg" gave me "Wheels up!" as he eased "William" off the deck and pressing back the safety-catch with my wrist I whipped up the undercart-lever. After our gallant aircraft had tucked his legs into their nacelles, I reduced power and raised the flaps by degrees. Mother Earth began to slip away into the evening dusk and, as we entered the cloud-layer which was blanketing the setting sun, I felt that she would retire gracefully to light her lamps against our return.

'Climbing through cloud, we gained height over base, each one of us busy at his job. "Corky" was stuffing propaganda leaflets into the bomb compartment - they would be delivered, along with the bombs, on Jerry's doorstep. "Reg" and I were getting "William" settled into his stride for the long trip. "Bill" had drawn his black-out curtain across and was busy passing out times, courses and speeds - and searching for his spare pencils! "Reg" Boys, in his own little world of switches, knobs and dials, was already beginning to perspire and craftily turned down the heating-system at his side, knowing full well that "Corky" would soon be calling for more heat! "Eddie" and "Doug" were swinging the turrets and accustoming their eyes to the evening light, at the same time keeping a look-out for the presence of other aircraft - with their trigger-fingers ready to deal with any intruding night-fighters. "Joe" the mascot stood cool and confident; defying the powers-of-evil to do their worst.

'We broke cloud into the glory of a late summer evening. A few scattered tufts of medium cloud picked up the rays of the reluctantly-setting sun and tossed them to us in an assortment of reds and gold's and violets. The sky, blood-red where the sun blazed angrily on the devouring horizon, was mellowing from its familiar azure to a darker blue in which the first stars had already begun to twinkle. It was a beautiful and impressive sight and, as I gazed, I assured myself that if it was true - as aircrew alleged – that, "Only birds and fools fly - and birds don't fly at night!" then I was thrice-content to be a fool.

'And as I mused, I watched the other aircraft. They were all around us; above, below and on all sides; some, mere specks in the distance, others near enough for their squadron letters to be distinguished; their grim, black shapes relieved only by the red and green navigation lights and blue exhaust-flames and occasionally by a momentary flicker of light as the sun's rays caught the Perspex canopies. But pleasant as the scene outside my window was proving, there were sterner things to occupy my mind and time. After a check on the altimeter, I turned on the oxygen and warned the crew to connect their masks, check the supply and report back. On re-checking the operation of the fuel tank selector-cocks, I found to my surprise that the starboard cock had jammed. Fortunately, the snag was soon sorted out. I detached the panels from the inside of the fuselage wall to check the run of the chains and spotted a short strip of metal wedged between the sprocket and the chain. Somewhat relieved by the simple solution, I removed the culprit and made a mental note to have a few quiet words with the ground crew. My log-sheet was already recording the fact that "William" was in grand form and it was with a smile of satisfaction that I heard "Bill" tell "Reg" that we were over base at our briefed altitude and could now set course. "Reg" repeated the bearing and turned "William" into the darkening east - that east which held so much hatred and hostility but, for us, no terrors.

'We crossed the home-coast, over our rendezvous point, at 16,000 feet. "George", the automatic pilot, had taken over from "Reg" and was climbing "William" up to our operational height of 22,000 feet. I had changed the superchargers into "S" gear and, as the engines were behaving perfectly, I assisted the gunners by keeping a good look-out for other aircraft - friendly or otherwise. Although the sky in the west was not yet completely dark, the assassin's cloak was slowly being drawn over our shoulders. The luminous dials on the instrument panels were already coming to life, looking like little groups of glow-worms sitting round in circles. High in the heavens, our old friend the "Plough" was plainly visible. I was always happy to see it and automatically murmured my old catchphrase, "Port side, going out; starboard side, coming home".

'It was still possible to see some of the other Lancs; a few were foolishly burning their navigation lights, several high-flying types were leaving vapour trails behind them, exhaust-glow gave away the position of others and one was keeping very close company with us. Once or twice it had drifted across our roof in that curious, apparent, sideways motion and "Eddie" voiced his feelings on the matter in a few well-chosen words. A collision, just as we were getting settled down, would have been very annoying and, in any case, the North Sea was certain to be jolly cold at night.

'"Reg" made a crew check and, apart from the usual minor snags, everything was "bang on". "Bill" complained that his "Gee" set was not too good but he was "coping"; "Doug's" warning light had flashed on a few times and he had effected a temporary cure by covering the glass with a wad of chewing gum; "Eddie" had the usual moan about his attention being distracted by the insulator on "Reg" Boys' aerial; whilst our worthy bomb aimer was calling for more heat. It was good to hear their voices. We had a quiet crew but when they spoke over the intercom, I felt the warmth of their friendship. Battle orders would prove that there were several hundred aircraft proceeding towards Germany at that precise moment but, nevertheless, we seven were alone. Each man responsible for his own task and each prepared to sacrifice everything for the well-being of the crew as a whole.'

'Triv' Trivett on Flight Lieutenant Peter Cadman's Halifax recalled: 'the bomb aimer came in. "Navigator, we are crossing the coast NOW!" The message was acknowledged. The sky was still light, much too light for my liking. My thoughts ran riot. What if "Jerry" had sent out intruders - Ju 88s, he'd have a field day for I could see at random heights and distances an armada of aircraft beginning to link up at what would hopefully be a defined narrow aircraft stream. I looked down under the tailplane of the Halifax. I saw a wide expanse of the 300 mile North Sea crossing and I inwardly shuddered to think how cold and unfriendly it seemed down there. Some ships could be seen. I wondered, are they ours? How do they view us up here? Do they say, "Good Luck", or do they say, "Achtung"! The enemy sea-going wireless operator would by now be rhythmically tapping out his coded messages to German shore base as we made our way in. By the time we arrived those night-fighters could be airborne ready to get into the stream!

'On this particular raid there were 700 aircraft detailed carrying 4,900 aircrew. Perhaps they were too preoccupied in their respective jobs to ponder on the outcome. How strange it seemed that one never really saw the cards stacked against oneself. It has been said, there are no easy "ops"; some are just harder than others - but whatever the reasoning, one always found an excuse for a safe return.

'Our height was now 10,000 feet and we were now all breathing oxygen. With the aircraft climbing steadily and the sun having now gone down, I was left with my two constant companions, loneliness and coldness, but conscious of the growing darkness and grateful for the throb, throb, throbbing, of our Rolls-Royce Merlin engines, all was quiet in this aircraft.

There was no idle chatter, only orders and direct observation concerning safety of the aircraft and relevant information had precedence. I looked deep into the dark sky searching all around. The mid-upper gunner "Bill" Batty would be looking after his search area. There was little conversation between us except in emergency, yet for all our vigilance we were aware that the aircraft was very vulnerable from below. It was for this reason that the skipper was often asked to move the aircraft in order to have a good look below.

'A call from "Harry" Clayton jolted my senses. "Searchlights ahead navigator."

'I hated searchlights. We were once coned by many searchlights over Bochum in the Ruhr: it was not a pleasant feeling flying along in a cone of searchlights, blind to the outside world and everything being fired at you. But tonight we had been promised some cloud. Various four-engined aircraft were seen dimly flying in a steady stream intent on crossing the enemy coast dead on track; this being essential if our losses were to be minimised. I looked through my gunsight. Its red illuminating sight ring which seemed OK on take-off now stood out fierce against the darkened sky. I dimmed it down on its rheostat control. I felt happier now. That could have ruined my night vision. The familiar crack that accompanied the switch on of the intercom, stabbed at my ear drums as the bomb aimer informed the navigator "Mac" McClorry our pinpoint on the Dutch coast put us dead on track. However, the "nav" was anxious about the absence of a route marker. Working on ETA (Estimated time of arrival) we made a slight deviation of course and we were now starting a long run in across Germany and its defence. The bomb aimer warned us gunners of a fighter 'drome lit up to starboard. There was also another 'drome which had just lit up inside of the Dutch coast. They were certainly waiting for us tonight. Many night-fighters would be off the ground now climbing high, hoping to get into the bomber stream. Then the fireworks would start. They would be looking for the odd straggler or even those of a later wave. The thin stretch of cloud seemed to be widening and searchlights were gathering in concentration. We levelled off at 18,000 feet. As I looked down my heart was in my mouth at the result of the searchlights playing on the bottom of the thin cloud. It was like a fresh white sheet as I saw aircraft racing across it like birds disturbed in their nest.

'The "Jerries" were flooding the underneath of clouds with their searchlights and I suffered an uneasy naked feeling. Surely to a fighter patrolling 1,000 feet above in the inky blackness we must be easy prey silhouetted as we were above the illuminated clouds. My eyes were hanging out like organ stops as I scanned above and to the sides, praying that I wouldn't see the flicker of tracer fire that would reveal the position of an unseen "Jerry" fighter.'

'Reg' Bunten's Lancaster was at 20,000 feet when Norman Ashton first noticed the faint pencils of light prodding the dark sky many miles ahead. 'As we flew nearer, the faint lights sharpened into the cold, blue-white beams of searchlights - some playing a lone hand and others in criss-crossing groups. As if realising that there was fun to be had for the asking, the flak-ships and land-batteries bestirred themselves and soon the curving strings of "flaming onions" and the dull-red flashes of bursting heavy flak lent colour and interest to the proceedings. Then one searchlight fastened on to a tiny, glittering object and immediately, a score of beams hurried over to lend a hand. The dreaded "cone" was quickly formed and flak began to pump up its centre to the silvery target at the apex. The cone leaned over from side to side in an endeavour to hold its prey and, suddenly, the silver object changed into a golden ball of fire which slowly began to slide down the exultant beams. One of our aircraft was already missing and the gunners down below on Texel Island chalked up their first success of the night. The enemy's front gate had been kicked open but our entry would be hotly disputed.

'"Enemy coast coming up, navigator," said "Corky". A rather obvious remark to make, as far as we in the cockpit were concerned, but to "Bill", behind his black-out curtains, it provided a rough check on his navigation and time. I sensed a spirit of high adventure as I repeated "Corky's" words to myself, "Enemy coast coming up!" What man, with British blood in his veins, could resist the thrill of pride and sense of achievement I felt as we roared steadily towards the outer bastions of that forbidden territory into which - so boasted the swashbuckling Goering - no aircraft would ever penetrate. I could be forgiven for comparing our crew with the men of Agincourt, "... *We few, we happy few, we band of brothers ...."* and feel with them that, *"... gentlemen in England now abed Shall think themselves accursed they were not here and hold their manhoods cheap while any speaks That fought with us ..."*

'At 22,000 feet, we levelled out and, having evaded the inquisitive searchlights, settled down to a steady cruise to the next turning point. A Lanc on our starboard bow was doing a spot of weaving but we stooged along straight-and-level in "George", as was our usual practice. I looked back through the Perspex blister and saw the gun-turrets swinging; "Eddie" and "Doug" were still busy searching the sky. We could expect fighters at any time and it was not advisable to be beaten to the draw. Textbooks praised the rate-of-fire and bullet-pattern of the .303 turrets but there was no denying that a Lanc, at the receiving end of a burst of cannon-shell, was a very dead duck.

'Away to starboard, I could see a running battle taking place. Both aircraft were invisible but the streaks of tracer told their own story. The end came very quickly. A dull-red ball appeared in the sky and, growing bigger and brighter every second, slowly began to lose height. As it fell, sporadic bursts of tracer came from the rear of the flames, obviously the Lanc had lost the battle and the fighter would be hurrying away to find fresh customers. The raging inferno broke into two parts and, several thousand feet below, was temporarily hidden by a thickish layer of cloud. We were now leaving the falling aircraft behind, but I saw the glow reappear beneath the cloud and then a vicious glare, like the sudden opening of a furnace door, tore a ragged gash in the darkness. That, I well knew was the Lanc hitting the deck. The "chopper" was already beginning to swing.'

'A few miles astern of us below in the cloud,' wrote 'Triv' Trivett, 'a bright flash left a red patch of cloud to die off in a few seconds and it was gone as though it never happened. It could have been flak, collision or a fighter. One thing for sure; it was pretty instantaneous and "they" couldn't have known much about that.

'It was folly to look into the light for so long. We must be seen for miles. I asked the skipper to weave gently so as to make the night-fighter aim a little more difficult and for us gunners to have a quick look below the aircraft. This I was assured he was only too willing to do. We were past that searchlight belt - there would be others - I felt a little more secure, comparatively lost in the dark sky, but conscious of the cold air. Yet I knew we were visible because I could see the glowing red-hot exhaust engine stubs of other four engined aircraft as they passed our starboard. I called up my navigator to tell him of these aircraft's movements and he replied that in another ten seconds we would be turning. Casually he gave the skipper a new course - he also thanked me. Nice fellow. Snag is if he got lost, so did I. However, being able to cooperate with one another was the recipe for making a competent crew.

'Way out on the port quarter an aircraft had jettisoned its load. It sparkled on the ground like fairy lights around a grave in a cemetery. A sure sign of fighter activity and to confirm my thoughts a stream of coloured tracers cut across the sky until the far end of the tracers grow into a red ball of fire. First blood to the fighter. The intercom cracked: "Keep a sharp look out gunners".

'The skipper was giving us unnecessary orders. My eyes were attracted to that unfortunate aircraft and seven crew which were now racing down to basement level - its tail like a shooting star. It was too dark to see parachutes but I was looking. I suppose it could have been worse; there may be survivors, but there were not many from the North Sea.

'In the rear turret I was totally isolated with my thoughts. In my visual search for the enemy, I again took in the burning pyre of that stricken aircraft, scattered and burning like a candle in a field. What an impersonal thing this night fighting was. No sign of chivalry. Just hide and seek in the dark sky and we the bomber on account of our larger size and inferior armaments are outmanoeuvred, out gunned, out sped, and when battle was joined, often out classed. We were seeking darkness to hide and the fighter was just seeking. If I didn't see the fighter first, it could take only a few seconds, from the darkness a quick burst of fire and with a coffin load of explosives - oblivion - but that at worst must be better than a flyer's death - burning. I kicked myself for being a defeatist. The training called for positive thinking and be first!

'I was fidgety in my turret - the flak was getting thicker now as we penetrated deeper into Germany and as I changed my search to port, a vivid flash that brought daylight momentarily to the sky almost blinded me, but not before I was able to discern the disintegration of a four engined aircraft. A lucky shot or predicted flak? Surely a direct hit in the bomb bay. Darkness had closed around me. The intercom was switched on. Above the amplified engine roar I heard the skipper: "What was that flash rear gunner?"

"'A direct hit - a blow up skipper".

"'You OK?'"

"'Yes."

"'Good." End of conversation.

'There were times when I thought our aircraft was all alone in the sky, but for a brief moment of time when that flash rent the sky I could see aircraft all around us. Lucky wireless operators and navigators who could in a minor way cut themselves off from the outside world by just pulling their curtain closed in their little compartments. Thankfully there seemed to be a lull in ground to air activity. It must have been fifteen to twenty minutes that we had been flying in darkness, but experience warned me that "Jerry" had eased up the flak in order to give his fighters a free run around the sky. We could be lulled into false security. Vigilance was the watchword - always.

'The intercom came to life. The engineer said: "Blue searchlight on the starboard side gunners". I turned my head. The blue beam slanted 60° forward parallel to our track. Fighters orbited this beacon during a lull in their bomber contacts, the angle of the beam laying off the direction in which we were travelling. There was no let-up in this search of the night sky. It is what bombers thrived to do - be heard but not seen. The cold air came into the turret through the open clear view panel and I was thankful for the small warmth of my heated suit. We were getting nearer the target area now. The sky was taking on a strong violet/blue mantle, the effects of searchlight activity welcoming the PFF. The engines roared through the intercom.

'"Nav" to "Skip", target ten minutes."

'"Roger."

'The rumbling sound of exploding shells came through the clear view panel that was ever open to the outside coldness. Sometimes the Halifax trembled and occasionally even staggered as though it had received a punch in the belly and the smell of cordite and smoke that filtered through my oxygen mask. It was the difference between war films and reality.

'The reassuring voice of the skipper on the intercom broke the silence inside this aircraft.

'"Everyone back there OK?"

'We went through a set procedure. I took a deep gulp of oxygen before answering in case my voice sounded high pitched. "Rear gunner OK Skip."

'"Mid-upper OK?"

'And so down the line through the crew.'

'William' on 103 Squadron was steadily eating up the route to the target and everything was going fine. 'The engines were in magnificent form,' wrote Norman Ashton, 'and the entries of instrument readings on my log-sheet began to look monotonous. Thanks to "Bill", we were bang on track and dead on time. A few of the other aircraft were not quite so lucky; they had strayed away to starboard and had been given a hot reception by Osnabrück. The searchlight and flak people were really annoyed at the intrusion and were teaching the off-track types a sharp lesson. I did not actually see any aircraft shot down but the accuracy of the shooting, for height, pointed to the possibility of damaged wings and fuel tanks. There had also been a real firework display over on the port side which we found comfortably exciting - comfortable because we were miles away at the time and exciting because of the fantastic amount of light flak that was being pumped up. A "dummy" attack had been laid on Bremen and the defenders were banging away with everything that would fire. The whole area was brilliantly confused, with the orange trails of light flak tracer intricately weaving through the forest of searchlight beams - it seemed impossible for anything to penetrate, but the occasional dull-red flashes at deck-level proved that there was nothing "dummy" about the bombs which were being dropped. Nice work, boys! Probably have drawn some of the fighters away from the main attack.

'As we approached the last turning-point, a carpet of medium cloud began to roll slowly over the countryside and, one by one, the twinkling lights on the ground were hidden from view. The Met people had forecast the probability of a cloud-covered target and, rather resentfully, we realised that the attack would develop into a "Wanganui" sky-marking effort. There was a sense of frustration in the "blind" attacks and one always had the uncomfortable feeling that the bombs were hitting everything except the target. Still, it had its advantages - searchlights were comparatively ineffective and flak was not so great a menace and, providing the cloud tops were high enough, fighters could be avoided by utilising cloud-cover. Thus did an impartial Nature protect both friend and foe.

'South-east of Berlin, "Reg" swung "William" on to course for the run-in to the target and, after a quick crew-check, warned us to keep a good look-out for fighters or other aircraft. "Corky" was busy pushing out "Window" and making final adjustments to his bombsight and computer box; "Reg" had taken over from "George" so that the compressor could feed the bombing equipment; I made a thorough check of all control settings and switches and increased the oxygen supply, ready for the extra altitude we hoped to gain after bombing; "Bill" juggled with times and distances; "Reg" Boys left his sets, to search from the astrodome; and the ever-watchful "Doug" and "Eddie" continued to scour the night sky.

'The dark carpet beneath us began to change to a patchy white as searchlights were trained on to its underside; and bombers, hitherto unseen, came into view as their black shapes were sharply silhouetted against the light background. Bursts of heavy flak peppered the sky, obviously box-barrage stuff, OK for height but not as accurate as the predicted variety - "Window" was proving its worth once again. Away in the distance, the first flares went down and the familiar vivid red glare, with green stars dripping from the centre, told us that the Pathfinder boys had confirmed the Met forecast; the cloud was too thick for ground-markers to be seen. Without warning, a brilliant yellow-white glare lit up the sky on our port bow - then another, to starboard - one more to port, further ahead - another to starboard - and then, at intervals, right on to the target! We soon realised what the score was - the crafty Hun was laying illuminating flares right along our track, providing a brightly lit street down which his night-fighters could patrol, making contacts at leisure.

'Almost before the gunners had accustomed their eyes to the new conditions, "Jerry" began to reap dividends from his ingenuity. "Doug" Wilkinson, the rear gunner, reported an Me 109 moving in and "Reg" prepared to take evasive action. I looked back through my starboard blister and saw the enemy fighter, fairly high on our starboard quarter. There was a Lanc stooging off our starboard wing-tip and "Reg" pulled away slightly so that we could have more sky to play about in. Over the intercom, I could hear "Doug" inviting the swine to come in closer and threatening to blast him to hell. At that moment the fighter dived in to the attack and turned in towards the other Lanc with its cannons blazing. There was a blinding flash as the shells struck home and the bomber became a raging inferno, which, in its agony, coughed out a dazzling array of greens, reds and yellows. In an incredibly short time, an angry cloud of black smoke was the only visible reminder that another Lancaster, with its crew of seven, had flown its last mission.

'Away in front, the clouds gradually became saturated with red from the fires below, like the slow spreading of a stain on a white sheet. The sky-markers were still going down and the fighter flares still hung in the sky and the general effect was as though we were riding down Blackpool promenade during "Illuminations" week - although the occasion was not quite so peaceful. The illusion was quickly shattered when "Corky" Corcoran the bomb aimer quietly murmured; "Bomb doors open!" and we commenced our bombing run. Straight and level, we flew steadily on, more vulnerable than at any other period of the trip and with every second seeming like an hour. A Lanc drifted across our canopy and I could see its yawning bomb bay, not more than twenty feet above us - much too near for comfort. We ran up on the flares and at last "Corky" pressed the "tit" and our messengers of high explosives and incendiaries swept down to fulfil their destiny. I was too busy watching the kite overhead to notice the shudder as "William" disgorged his load and then, with a sigh of relief, I saw their bombs come showering down past our starboard wing-tip. We had been hit by a falling bomb on a previous trip - luckily without serious damage - and I just hated to think of the beastly things coming through the roof. "Corky" asked for the bomb doors to be closed, "Reg" held steady for the camera and then turned on to the course out of the target. It was all over. Our long-cherished hopes of blitzing Berlin were realised at last - but we all wished the weather conditions had been better.'

The enemy used 'fighter flares' to decoy the bombers away from the target and there was some cloud in the target area. This, together with difficulties with H$_2$S equipment and enemy action, all combined to cause the Pathfinder markers to be dropped well south of the centre of the target area and the Main Force bombing to be even further back and bombs fell up to thirty miles back along the line of approach. The intensely bright white flares dropped in clusters of a dozen or more from about 20,000 feet at the corners of the target area and a double strip apparently dropped by rapidly moving aircraft around the perimeter of the area and igniting at about 17,000 feet lasted for several minutes and served to illuminate the bomber stream.

On Peter Cadman's Halifax the bomb aimer had moved into his prone position and from now on it was all his. He held a short conversation with the skipper about grouping of the Target Indicators etc. Sitting in the rear turret 'Triv' Trivett had his back to this vista of searchlights but his turn would come when they were moving through the target area.

'The clouds were illuminated by the searchlights beneath them and we in Halifaxes, Stirlings and Lancasters were like black birds of prey moving across this light background. The sky seemed full of red darting lights, some bursting yellow - some orange. The lazy way tracer shells had of climbing to the heights then shooting past at incredible speed – it was all so uncanny. Sitting in my turret and scanning all around, it seemed as though I wanted to look in a dozen directions at one time. My eyes seemed to be on extended spring wires, rigid in concentration. The quiet voice of the flight engineer came through on the intercom as from somewhere afar.

'"Lanc coned in searchlights over there Skipper."

'"A laconic ........ his luck," ended that informative conversation.

'The bomb aimer was next on, his breathing laboured and come to think of it, I was not doing too bad myself. The flak was a bit heavy now and I heard the "whomp", "whomp", through the open turret window more often. Pathfinders had put down their Target Indicators - red flares dripping green; they were brilliant in colour. The mauve sky was now tinged with pink as the raging fires below reflected on the clouds. As I carried out my search I could see a Lancaster and Halifax emerging from sinister black shadows to having tail fins and wing edges tinged as though having been touched with an artist's brush and here and there a glint from a Perspex cover as a searchlight swept over it.

'The bomb aimer had taken over. A series of "Left - Left" - "Right a bit" - "Steady, steady": that agonising ten second run seemed like eternity. We were so vulnerable on this run. A Lancaster was high above us on the near port quarter, his bomb doors were open and I was looking up into a cavernous bay with a neatly laid out armoury. It worried me. SURELY he could see us down here? He couldn't be that stupid - could he? And suddenly like someone bringing back a plateful of peas the deadly cargo was spewing out and falling with the precision of lemmings going over a cliff. I didn't suppose I was the only one muttering, "Come on - sod the bombing picture – let's get out of here!" In the middle of my muttering I heard "Bombs Gone Skip". The time was 2342 hours.

'Ten minutes later we turned to port on our first leg home that would take us clear of this conflagration. As we turned I was sitting on top of the world with a grandstand seat apparently sailing through space in a glass bubble. As I surveyed the scene before me during the course of my search I was left speechless with awe. It was like a hornet's nest. The searchlights had almost been subdued, the part cloud cover kept the searchlights down. At times I felt I could have put out my hand and cast rude shadows in the beams, but other aircraft weren't so lucky. I saw a Halifax caught by a few searchlights who froze on it. The Halifax was doing a series of corkscrews; the pathetic aircraft surrounded by bursting flak and lay twisting and turning like a silver moth around a flame. He could elude his captors no longer and his end was a short matter of time as cannon shells from fighters set him ablaze. Parachutes were seen to emerge and descend into the target area, but during the aircraft's final dive tracer fire was still answering the challenge of the fighter from the gun turrets. But I don't suppose they could get out anyway. Not for them a decoration - or even survivors leave, but they were reconciled to their fate when they compared the reception that awaited the parachuted descent of their fellow comrades into that bombed and burning target area. The clouds were now awash with a crimson glow. From my position of looking out of my turret, I am confronted with a truly awesome sight of pure wanton destruction of a city with brilliant white incendiaries starting the fires, the tall spindly searchlight fingers groping here and there like a spider waiting for its prey to enter its net and seldom to release it, red and yellow shell bursts leaving the smoke blobs of black and grey of the spent shells. They disfigure the panorama yet are an essential part of it, mingling with the invisible hanging of the brilliant red and green target indicators and rising to meet all the drifts of smoke that can be smelt through the clear open view panel of my rear turret all helped to colour this moment. There in the middle of it all, Stirlings, Halifaxes and Lancasters, who so far have survived half the journey, scudding for the beckoning cover of darkness and home. We have seen an ugly head of war.

'We were through the target area now on our long leg return. The click of the intercom - the roar of the engines amplified in my ear galvanised one instantly.

'"Fighter below crossing to starboard gunners."

'I recognised the bomb aimer's voice. Looking out to starboard I see the single engined fighter. He had seen us and came up level, slightly behind the starboard beam. He flew parallel for a few seconds - enough time to give my skipper standard evasive procedure. Prepared to turn to starboard and then his wings flipped up giving a plan view. He was turning in and I concluded starboard: GO! The next second my stomach went into my boots as the Halifax went into a tight turn. I didn't see the going of him but coming back on course we never saw him again. However, the time taken to relate far exceeded the time of action. I don't think the enemy pilot worried too much in missing us - his pickings tonight were plentiful.

'We were in darkness again with the target fifty miles back. Suddenly we were bathed in a brilliant white light. I could see from above, possibly a mile either side of us, two rows of hanging white flares. It had turned night into day and they were cascading right along our track home.

'All around us four engined aircraft were zigzagging along. We had never experienced this tactic before. There were aircraft all around us in this almost daylight sky. I was standing up in my turret but leaning forward to get a view below. All eyes in those aircraft must have been hanging out. After what appeared a very long 15-20 seconds the flares burned themselves out and darkness descended once more. I was alone with my very private thoughts of that incident. God, there must have been some very frightened men in those bombers.

'We were now in and out of cloud and mighty thankful at times for the relief from constantly staring from darkness to light and back again to darkness. My eyes were beginning to feel like two balls of fire, searching the sky as I had for this last five hours and base was still almost four hours away. Looking directly astern, the glow of a red spot could be seen far into the distance. I thought it must have been sheer hell there in Berlin; 2,000 tons of HE and incendiaries in forty minutes by 700 aircraft. A few miles on the starboard searchlights had picked up an aircraft and it was absolutely surrounded by bursting shells and he was so selfish he was sharing it with nobody. The aircraft had strayed over a town. During the course of my searching, I glanced back at him every minute or so, but he was still there twisting and turning and suddenly he made the break. There was no aircraft but plenty of searchlights and they seemed so mad; they were waving in all directions. When that crew got home, the ground crew must surely have some kind of mess to clear out. Some minutes later all the searchlights in the distance had been extinguished and with the drumming of our own engines, all was quiet. Once more the safety of darkness closed in. In the loneliness and coldness of the rear turret I counted my blessings and thought how lucky we were to have a navigator and pilot who together kept us on track and away from much of the trouble of being outside of the stream of aircraft.'

'The journey back to the coast was uneventful,' wrote 'Triv' Trivett. 'The German fighters had had their fun; tomorrow we'd hear how successful they had been. On the intercom I could hear that the searchlights were active on the coast. "Jerry" would put up his usual coastal barrage hoping to catch the low flying damaged aircraft and those who had drifted off track. They need not worry about us; we were going home anyway.

'Our route tonight had been a long curving track across Germany, Belgium and France and we were now crossing the French coast to make our way to Beachy Head. The excitement of the night was now draining away and I felt shivery. We were slowly losing height, but this was not the time to lose concentration because many a crew thinking they were home had been shot down by an unexpected intruder. Over the intercom I heard, "English coast ahead". I waited impatiently for Beachy Head lighthouse to pass under the tailplane and as it did so I saw the water pounding the coast. It always seemed an unfriendly act but tonight it seemed to be doing a jig. Once again the engines were amplified through the microphone as the Skipper said: "Well done all", but we were not home yet, there was still a vigil to maintain and we had still to get down in one piece. Nevertheless, I was sitting here in a happier frame of mind. If I did have to bail out, at least I should land in my own country.'

'The "Reaper" was still busy on the run out to the coast,' wrote Norman Ashton, 'and we saw three more aircraft go down in flames. Then I jumped for joy when I saw a single-engined fighter hurtling down at terrific speed in a practically vertical descent, with grey-black smoke streaming behind like a comet's tail. It was good to know that the battle was not going all one way. We kept our height until we reached the enemy coast and then began to let-down for a fast run home. The engines were grand and we had bags of petrol, so we were not faced with a possible ditching or a landing at an emergency 'drome - unlike some of the poor devils who would be preparing to touch down on the watery runways of the North Sea. The Air-Sea Rescue boats would, at that very moment be speeding out to save the lives of "press-on" types who preferred the danger and hardship of a night-ditching to the somewhat safer course of bailing out and risking capture on land.

'At 8,000 feet I removed my oxygen mask with a feeling of relief and brought out the coffee flask. For seven hours I had been chewing gum and I was as dry as dust. I was to remain as dry as dust - my flask was broken and, to my disgust, I found that the coffee in the other flasks had gone sour.

'Soon, the welcoming searchlights on the home coast came into view and we knew that we were amongst friends again. Several frisky types were pooping-off "colours-of-the-day" cartridges and a few aircraft were burning navigation lights. The blackness of the night was slowly being pushed back by the rather hesitant dawn which peeped carefully over the eastern horizon. With the gradually increasing light, the red glow of the exhaust-stubs was dying away and black numerals and fingers superseded the glow-worms on the instrument panels. As we crossed the coast, dotted circles of light on the ground, with the attendant "Sandra" lights, indicated the positions of airfields and we knew that - true to her promise - Mother Earth had placed her lights in the window to guide and welcome our return.'

Geoffrey Willatt, on Pilot Officer 'Robbie' Robertson's crew recalls: 'Having released our bombs, we were told to come north out of the target towards Norway. We were climbing to a safe corridor above clouds which contained very severe icing - a very dangerous hazard. Many planes had been lost in such conditions when all controls sometimes became frozen solid. "Robbie", from time to time, called up each member of the crew on the intercom to find out whether all were fit and functioning properly. We wore oxygen masks throughout the entire trip, oxygen being switched on always at 10,000 feet. When there was no answer from the rear gunner, being the person least occupied at that time, I volunteered to go back to investigate. There were, apart from the main supply, small bottles of oxygen at various emergency points, which could be temporarily fixed to our masks. This supply would only last a few minutes, i.e. until the main supply could be reached for re-connection. I hooked up my mask with one of these bottles and stumbled back along the length of the plane to find the rear gunner lying unconscious over his guns with his mask off his face. Obviously, I had to drag him to connect up with the nearest connecting point. In trying to do this I tripped over something and accidentally ripped off my own mask and bottle. I remember standing there losing my senses and falling over backwards. Apparently, "Robbie" then sent the flight engineer back, who found us both lying side by side. "Robbie" then decided to dive down through the dangerous icy clouds to oxygen level, where masks were not needed. I regained consciousness to hear the alarming crackling of ice on the wings just before we came out of cloud over the North Sea. We arrived safely back at Syerston.'[3]

As 'N-Nan' passed London on the starboard side 'Triv' Trivett gave a thought to his family down there and thought of them asleep in their shelter. The time was 0345 hours. 'They could sleep sound tonight,' he wrote, 'for we had given Berlin a little bit of its own medicine with interest. They weren't too particular when they dropped bombs in our back yard during the London Blitz. We even had a land mine in our own street plus HE bombs; not to mention a few incendiaries. There were no military targets where I lived. While still carrying out my search from the turret I clearly recalled the consternation that land mine caused. Had it dropped another fifty feet it would have blown us all to kingdom come. Its parachute had caught up on the corner of a building and the mine hung below it resting against the wall. During our "after air raid inspection of the local area", my father and I had walked along the pavement right under that hang mine and we didn't know of its existence until some very young sailor came down a little later turfing us all out of our homes, after which they disarmed the mine and took it away to Hackney Marshes.

'Flying now up the country and so near to London had set off a train of thoughts and in retrospect I could see happenings clearly; like when the German bombers set fire to the City of London and Londoners saw clouds over their heads tinged with crimson and fires on the ground that turned night almost too day. Similar I would think to how we left Berlin tonight. It was in that very weekend when I came out of the Trocadero cinema at the Elephant and Castle and was confronted with blazing buildings all around me. With smoke in my nostrils, heat on my face, and fire engines gasping for more water, while fire hoses that criss-crossed, losing pressure where punctures created their own small founts. At seventeen years of age I selfishly shrugged off the attention of an elderly man in Bermondsey

---

3   Willatt was the only one on 'Robbie' Robertson's crew to survive when they were shot down on Mannheim on the night of 5/6 September by a night-fighter whose opening burst of fire hit the pilot in the head and mortally wounded Sergeant James Cunliffe, a last minute addition to the crew as a replacement for Moseley the English flight engineer. Group Captain 'Frank' Hodder the Syerston Station Commander also died. Willatt would spend the next two years in Stalag Luft III at Sagan. *Bombs And Barbed Wire: My War in the RAF and Stalag Luft III* by Geoffrey Willatt. (Parapress Ltd 1995). Geoffrey Willatt died aged 98 in 2009.

Street who wanted me to take him home in the opposite direction because he was afraid to walk alone. I wasn't to know he had just two minutes of his life left - to be killed by the very next bomb that screamed down. I had been tormented by that act many times. I asked myself, was that providence or the benevolent love of God that saved me?'

When at last 'Reg' Bunten sighted Elsham he took over from 'George' [the automatic pilot] and then called up Flying Control. 'Five crews had previously called up, but they must have got down pretty smartly for we were given "Prepare to land" as we stooged across the 'drome,' recalled Norman Ashton. 'We swung into the circuit and made our preparations. "Corky" came up from the nose and stood behind my position; "Bill" gathered his charts and maps and stuffed them into his bag, ready for a quick getaway after landing; "Reg" Boys passed the Aldis lamp forward so that I could use it whilst taxiing; and "Reg" and I checked all our control-settings and clipped on our masks. With wheels safely down and locked and flaps partially down, we turned into the "funnel" at 700 feet and made our approach. Nicely "in the green" and lined-up beautifully on the runway, with flaps fully down, I cut the throttles back as we wafted over the boundary and "William" sank on to the tarmac with scarcely a shudder. "Reg" had brought us in to his usual wizard landing. As we rolled along the runway, I opened my window and breathed a contented sigh as the good, clean air of England swept into my face.

'The ground crew signalled us into dispersal with their torches and, after testing the magnetos and clearing the engines, I snapped off the cut-off switches. The four Merlins slowed and gradually stopped - each having completed about one-and-a-quarter million revs during the trip. The boys bustled out of the aircraft with their piles of kit and before I followed, I paused for a moment to give "Joe" a thankful pat on the shoulder; the gallant little man had done the trick again. The ground crew welcomed us as we climbed out and asked about "William". I assured them that he was absolutely "bang on" and getting better every trip.

'How good it was to feel the ground under my feet once more. And how glorious that first puff of the priceless cigarette. The workaday world may count its treasures in precious metals and stones, but for honest worth, give me the sensation of terra firma and tobacco, after eight hours flying.

'A few minutes later, the crew-coach pulled alongside and we were whisked off to the locker room to change and then down to "Ops" for debriefing. As we walked along, aircraft were still droning around the circuit and I wondered if all our kites had made the grade.

'The Ops room was crowded when we arrived. Returned crews were laughing and discussing the trip in abnormally loud voices - loud because the sound of the engines would still be roaring in their ears. The crews looked dirty and tired but there was, about them all, an air of pride in a job well done. WAAFs were handing out cups of extra-sweet tea, well-laced with rum to chase away fatigue and to replace some of our lost energy; the padre handed out cigarettes and chatted with the boys; and the section leaders received reports and log-sheets from the various categories. From time to time, everyone glanced at the gen-board on which the names of crews were added as they reported back from the trip. The list was lengthening but there was some uneasiness about two or three of the "early" crews who ought to have been back - possibly they had been delayed by engine trouble or had been forced to land away from base. At intervals, crews left for debriefing and soon it was our turn. With infinite patience, the debriefing officer drew from us the story of our part in the night's attack. We all felt very tired and found it hard to concentrate. Recounting the incidents seemed an effort - like the hazy recalling of a half-forgotten film.

'After debriefing, we went over to the Mess for breakfast and, having done justice to a really good meal, finally made our way to the billet. The sky was quite light and the sun was already thrusting out its first rays; birds were arguing amongst themselves in the treetops; and early-rising farm folk were leisurely making their way to the fields. All was peaceful and normal. As I looked around, I found it hard to believe that only a few hours ago we had been over the "Big City".'

'London had long now slipped by us,' wrote 'Triv' Trivett, 'and looking out of the turret, I kept an eye open for our own 'drome at Elvington in Yorkshire. In all directions on the ground various airfields in the form of the familiar white circle of Drem lighting were lit up and many were receiving their own returning aircraft. There were so many airfields the country must be a floating aircraft carrier. "Bill" Batty had sighted the predetermined flashing letter and the Skipper joined the left-hand turning circuit around the airfield awaiting permission to land. Dead astern of us a distant white flash lingered a second and momentarily lit up a fair stretch of the sky. What an ironic turn of fate. Having survived the German defences then to crash in mid-air, or more than likely to land with a hung up live bomb in the bomb bay. I heard my Skipper acknowledge Flying Control's, "N-Nan" OK to land" with "Wilco, out". The trailing aerial was being wound in and with a slight bump and a bounce, we were home. The time was 0415 hours.

'We taxied to the dispersal guided by the airman with a torch in each hand and making mystic circles with his arms. It was a treat to leave the aircraft and stretch ones legs. Eight and a half hours was a long time to be cramped up in one position. Upon landing after an op, for a few minutes Cadman sometimes acted in a strange way, shouting and bawling at anything or anyone who displeased him. This didn't last long and was obviously the release of his pent-up feelings and who can blame him for that?

'We chatted to the ground crew. Theirs was a thankless task, hanging about in all weathers waiting for their aircraft to land. They were smiling tonight. Sometimes their aircraft and aircrew went missing. Next day a replacement aircraft would be delivered and the ground crew would have to get used to new names and different characters.

'The wagon was there to take us to de-briefing. In the smoke-filled room, the debriefing was underway and while awaiting our turn a tea, coffee and a cigarette were taken eagerly - but we didn't forget to make our way to the man issuing the rum ration. It was said that the rum helped the coffee to go down. Always at debriefing a WAAF dispensed coffee, whilst the padre doled out a tot of rum to each crew member, imbibing a tot or two himself in the process. Some of us didn't like rum so we passed our ration to one of the other lads who did and in their tired state they went to bed reasonably happy. And the padre? I have seen him tottering out of the room long before all the planes were back, too inebriated to continue and leaving the WAAF in full charge. I suppose he was living up to the title of "sky pilot"!

'You could notice the difference in the aircrew since beginning the operation. Some had grown a stubble of beard; some were showing a tensed face with fatigue. Maybe those advanced into their tour were just tired of the proceedings and wished that they could go straight to bed and get the sleep they craved for. A new crew just completed their first op were being briefed and were glad to be back and letting it be known they had been "over there" and successfully returned. With lots of luck and God's blessing, they would be able to go over there and back another twenty-nine times and they would then be entitled to write their names upon the mess ceiling on a future riotous night in the Sergeants Mess. It was now our crew's turn to be debriefed. A set pattern of questions was asked by the intelligence officer, i.e. "Anything special about; The fires, flares, searchlights, flak, fighters, explosions in the target area, smoke, position of aircraft going down (from navigator's log)? Any parachutes?" etc. Our debriefing didn't take long. It was while we were drinking our ration of rum and coffee that I quietly confided in my navigator that it hadn't been a bad trip for my twenty-first birthday; in fact it was a piece of cake. However, my navigator betrayed my trust in him by informing our CO, Wing Commander Lowe. It was suggested by him that now I am a man I should start drinking like one and I gulped at a handy size mug full of neat rum and with tired voices singing "Happy Birthday to you", I stepped outside to breathe the invigorating fresh country morning air. It tasted good; God, it felt great to be alive.

'The Flying Control building was just a short distance away. It was here inside the room that officers and WAAFs were logging the return of aircraft. At debriefing we heard there were still four more to come in (outstanding). I came from debriefing thinking time was running out for them, but there was always the hope that they had put down at another airfield through petrol shortage or damage and information was late in coming through. Tomorrow we'd count the cost. There seemed to have been a fair share of aircraft under attack in the target area and there was more than usual tracer fire during the run home. I wondered if the new flare dropping had anything to do with that.

'The early morning air was playing havoc with the rum inside of me. I had been expected to finish the double neat rum issue - and I did. My head was a little dizzy. Enjoying the luxury of a couple of stout supporting arms, I don't remember if my feet touched the ground as we left debriefing.'

'It was at the returning operational meal when one sat at the table and cast unobtrusive glances at the empty spaces,' wrote 'Triv' Trivett. 'Names of the missing were seldom spoken of. One tried to picture an aircrew person who you shared a joke with at early teatime, i.e. "Can I have your returning egg if you don't come back?" Although it was accepted standard of bad taste and bizarre joking it suddenly hit home when crews went missing and you wished you had bitten your tongue at the time. I always enjoyed my egg on return from ops, but the thought of a greasy egg on top of the rum was too much for me. I offered the egg to another gunner sitting opposite me. He hesitated before answering. "No! No! It wouldn't seem right - after all you've got back from your op!"

'I thought I saw his eyes brighten and not fancying it myself, I replied, "but I don't want it – it's yours!" His face was poker straight, yet I knew there was a punch line somewhere and it came.

'"Now if you had gone for a Burton, well, I would have enjoyed that egg, - but not now!"

'Touche.

'It was but a short walk from the Sergeants Mess to the billets. I was apprehensive when opening Nissen hut doors after ops. I hated those empty missing beds, but the hut had a full complement tonight. The missing were from elsewhere on the station.'[4]

Back at Elsham Wolds Norman Ashton wrote: 'How glorious to climb between the sheets! I never sat down on a trip and my legs had been taking the strain since the operational meal on the previous day. I felt so weary that I fell asleep as soon as I laid my head on the pillow. Early in the afternoon we were awakened and - feeling fully rested - pottered along to the Mess for a late lunch. As we entered the Ante Room the BBC announcer was saying, "Last night, aircraft of Bomber Command attacked Berlin in great strength. Forty-nine of our aircraft are missing".'[5]

---

4  'J-Jig' flown by Harold Evans Vivian Gawler and his eight crewmembers failed to return. Only one of the gunners survived. 'A-Apple' flown by Flight Sergeant Ralph Owen Chester and crew were lost with only the two gunners surviving. Flight Lieutenant John Leslie Wilson RAAF and crew were all killed on 'G-George'.

5  *Only Birds And Fools* by J. Norman Ashton DFC. (Airlife 2000). One Lancaster FTR to Elsham Wolds. 'E-Edward' and Flying Officer David Walter Alexander Philip's crew were all killed.

# Chapter 7

# The Morning After the Night Before

*'... The Stirling and the Halifax are now our major worries. They presage disaster unless solutions are found. I understand that the Stirling is to go in favour of the Lancaster as fast as the changeover can be achieved. The Stirling Group has now virtually collapsed. They make no worthwhile contribution to our war effort in return for their overheads. They are at half strength, and serviceability is such that in spite of the much-reduced operational rate and long periods of complete idleness due to weather I am lucky if I can raise thirty Stirlings from No.3 Group for one night's work after doing a week of nothing, or twenty the night after. There should be a wholesale sacking of the incompetents who have turned out approximately 50 per cent rogue aircraft from Short and Harland's, Belfast and Austin's, not forgetting the Supervisors responsible at the parent firm. Much the same applies to the Halifax issue, nothing ponderable is being done to make this deplorable product worthy for war or fit to meet those jeopardise, which confront our gallant crews....'*

**Letter from Sir Arthur Harris to the Secretary of State for Air, Sir Archibald Sinclair which summed up the despair felt at HQ Bomber Command and by Harris in particular at the thought of the continuing use of the Stirling.**

On most Sundays Wing Commander Edwin John Little DFC, a devoted and fervent Christian, would be found in church preaching or helping out, such was the character of the man who was, unlike many of his contemporaries, a prolific writer and was most happy when writing sermons and prayers. Known by family and friends in Elstree, Hertfordshire as 'Jack', he had joined the Royal Air Force in 1936. He looked older than his twenty-eight years due mainly to his receding hairline. A keen sportsman, he was a rather serious young man whose personal beliefs were at odds with the occupation he was in, yet he was an experienced pilot having completed a tour on 40 Squadron during 1941 where he was awarded the DFC and he had been awarded three Mention In Dispatches. On Wednesday, 18th August 1943 he had arrived at Downham Market in Norfolk to assume command of 623 Squadron. Flying Officer Peter Paddon recalled that, 'It was his intention to fly with each of the new crews; I seem to recall that he sang *Onward Christian soldiers* while on the bomb run.' On the 23rd/24th he had flown as second pilot on John Overton's Stirling when the actions of Sergeant 'Bert' Bennett had resulted in the award of the CGM. 'Harry' Baker, the bomb aimer on Overton's crew who remembered, 'the hairy trip to Berlin on the 23rd' recalled, 'Isn't it ironic that such faith and dedication to God failed to save him from getting the chop a week later, while the rest of us bad sods survived!' Wing Commander Little and the recently posted crew of 20-year-old Flight Sergeant Oliver James Tanner of Queensland, Australia, were among the Stirling casualties on 31st August/1st September when twenty Halifaxes, ten Lancasters and sixteen Stirlings had gone missing and eighty-six bombers had aborted. The loss of the Stirlings was a staggering sixteen per cent of the total dispatched.

Five Stirlings on 75 Squadron RNZAF, including 'O-Orange', which crash landed at RAF Coltishall, failed to return to Mepal. One of the missing was 'K-King' piloted by 21-year-old Flight Sergeant Keith Alexander McGregor RNZAF. Sergeant Geoff Bond RAFVR the engineer wrote: 'We reached Berlin about midnight, the city was burning fiercely and we had just dropped our bombs and were just on the outskirts of Berlin when two German night-fighters suddenly attacked us without the slightest warning from our two gunners who hadn't evidently spotted them. Cannon fire hit us from underneath and I was hit by the first burst. We immediately went into a dive which gave me the impression that the controls had been hit, or that Keith was also hit by the first burst too. I was blown from my position and when I came too, tried to use my intercom, but this was out of order. By this time the aircraft was burning and it was impossible for me to get to the front of the plane where Keith and four of the other boys were.' Geoff Bond got out after assisting Sergeant George F. Dummett RAFVR, the mid-upper gunner, who had been hit in the face by a burst of flak just below the eyes and was blinded for a week. Bond jumped clear of the burning aircraft and watched it going down and exploding shortly after. Dummett recalled, 'The cold air soon revived me. I pulled the chute handle and the first thing I thought was, "Blimey, ain't it noisy" and hoped that I was not going to land in the middle of the fires - at the same time thinking I would have rather been back in the comfort of the Stirling. I was a captive at about 0230 hours, rather the worst for wear and was taken to Potsdam Castle.' He and Geoff Bond were the only survivors.

Pilot Officer John Martin on 620 Squadron was in the astrodome of his Stirling when they got to Berlin and he had a very good view. 'There's one going down, there's another one going down, there's another one going down. They were just going down like flies. Berlin was like flying down Royal Avenue in Belfast. Once you started into Berlin, you never thought you were going to get to the other end of the city. It was so long. All the lights were on, everything was as clear as a bell. I was able to read the letters on the side of "P-Peter", "Taff's" Stirling, which was going over ahead of me when a fighter came up and right in front and shot it down [sic]. That was the end of "Big Taff" Whitfield and four others on the crew.[1] We were lucky and got back.' One of the two survivors on Campbell's crew who were captured was navigator Flying Officer H.G.F. Cox RNZAF. In a PoW report, Cox stated: 'At approximately 3am, as a result of damage caused by flak and enemy fighters, our aircraft was losing height rapidly and became out of control. At a height of less than 2000 feet, Campbell ordered bail out. I left from the forward hatch with Campbell still at the controls. On reaching the ground, I saw a fire about one mile to the north, which I assumed was our aircraft. The Germans said all were killed except me and Flight Sergeant A.H. Smith RNZAF the air bomber.'

About two-thirds of the forty-seven aircraft that were lost were shot down over Berlin by night-fighters. At Lissett 158 Squadron was particularly badly hit, losing four Halifaxes. 'R-Roger' piloted by 'Ken' Ward was one of these. Sergeant 'Harry' Simister recalled: 'The trip out was uneventful and we arrived over Berlin at 2330 hours, right on time. The old "Hallybag" lurched upwards as our bombs fell away. Then all of a sudden we came under attack from a German night-fighter. Our two port engines burst into flames.

'The pilot reported loss of controls and cried back to us "Bail out, bail out". We'd gone through practices like this, with the hangar floor only feet below. This time it was for real. The sky outside was lit up by the searchlights,

---

1  'P-Peter' finally crashed at Looberghe (Nord), 12kms SSW of Dunkirk. Campbell, Sergeant Sydney Edmund Birkett the 28-year-old WOp/AG; and Sergeant Thomas Harold Loke the 22-year-old rear gunner are buried in Dunkirk Town Cemetery. Sergeant Albert Edward Taylor the 20-year-old mid-upper gunner and Sergeant Whitfield were lost without trace and are remembered with honour on the Runnymede Memorial.

the fires and the tracer bullets. We were all calm as we lined up to jump out into the dark void. My parachute billowed out and pulled me roughly out of my free fall. Below me the bombs burst with deep "crumphs" and the fires seemed to cover the earth. As I glided down I noticed the smoke from the fires was drifting away from the fires. At least I wouldn't be roasted alive.'

Ward and Pilot Officer Alfred Percy Arnott the air bomber and Sergeant Thomas Lockerbie Craven the mid-upper gunner died on the aircraft. 'Seconds earlier and the whole crew would have perished - instead of only three,' wrote Sergeant Ronald Arthur Thurston the wireless operator. 'Bailing out of a blazing bomber over Berlin could possibly be described as "bailing out of Hell, into Hell". No evasive action can possibly be carried out on a bombing run. To bail out of a blazing bomber, still under attack, with two engines on fire and completely out of control, coned by the searchlights amongst over 600 bombers dropping bombs from various heights, night-fighters, flares and bursting shells from anti-aircraft guns gave more thoughts of the extreme danger when the parachute opened and gently drifted away from the nightmare of the target. Thoughts in the dark and dangerous sky of the fate of the rest of the crew. How many had been killed in this Hell? You look around in the darkness for parachutes - you see nothing. The searchlights sweep the sky as if looking for you - assisting the night-fighters in their attack. You watch with fascination the blazing target, the explosions of the bombs and the retaliation of the anti-aircraft guns, with little thought of the danger of the thousands of tons of flak in the air. You wonder if the tracer bullets you see are coming from an air gunner's turret or from an enemy fighter attacking another bomber. You watch with dismay a blazing bomber plunging to earth and wonder if anyone got out. Your parachute now seems to be going up instead of coming down and you feel slightly sick with the swaying. You begin to wonder what height you are when you see a night-fighter only a little way above you and how long and where will you hit the ground? Will you be shot when you are in the hands of the enemy or shown mercy as a PoW? All these thoughts as you slowly, alone and completely helpless, descend into the unknown. Your face feels wet with perspiration - or is it raining? You feel a little numb in this dark unreal world and wonder if you are dreaming. The crunch of an anti-aircraft shell nearby reminds you that you are not, as the bombing continues. You listen to the humming engines of the bombers. Some will be shot down on the way home - perhaps over the sea. All the way back to the English coast - and sometimes inland - they will be pursued by determined enemy night-fighters with their excellent radar and equally brave pilots eager to be credited with the destruction of another bomber. The bomber crews are alert to all this and do not relax for one moment. As you are mesmerised by the red glow in the sky from the fires; observing the flashes from the anti-aircraft guns and the shell bursts in the sky, you begin to think of your loved ones at home. In a few hours they will receive that dreaded telegram, which they have been expecting ever since you started operational flying - "Regret to inform you that your..." and you begin to wonder when and if you will ever see them again.'[2]

'Ron' Thurston, William Nicholas Avery the rear gunner and Norman John Stubbings the navigator were taken prisoner. Harry Simister managed to walk to the road to Potsdam, twenty miles from Berlin. On 3rd September he discovered a cycle leaning against the wall of an old farmhouse, so he stole it and then cycled hurriedly towards Brandenburg. For the next few days he pedalled northwards. By the sixth day he was exhausted and he happily fell into a ditch to sleep. By the ninth day he had reached Lübeck and there in the dock was a freighter flying the Swedish flag. After twice failing to take passage Simister cycled on to Rostock, covering the sixty-two miles in a day. By now he had been 'on-the-run' for ten days. Rostock was no good for him and he decided to return to Lübeck which offered the chance of a ship to Sweden or maybe to Spain. He was unsuccessful so he decided to head for Hamburg where he found help and pressed on for Osnabrück and then on to Rhine and a large railway terminus only twenty miles from the Dutch border. He finally made it to Holland cycling all the way. There the Dutch Resistance got him and Sergeant 'Reg' V. Wallace, who had bailed out over Holland the same night and had evaded from near Münster on their way to Belgium. Wallace was the flight engineer on 21-year-old Sergeant Edward Thomas Samuel Rowbottom's crew on Halifax II 'B-Bertie' on 102 Squadron at Pocklington. He and Sergeant John Kenneth Keele, his 19-year-old navigator and three others on the crew were killed. Flight Sergeant 'Russ' Lloyd Collins RCAF one of the air gunners was taken prisoner. After many adventures, 'Harry' Simister and 'Reg' Wallace finally reached Switzerland on 16th October.[3]

---

2   *Into The Silk* by Ian Mackersey.
3   In November 1944 Harry Simister was recommended for the Military Medal and this was gazetted on 19 February 1945. Simister's remarkable achievement was the one of the few morale boosts that Lissett was to receive, for 158 Squadron lost four crews on the raid, which brought their total to nine crews missing from two major attacks flown against the 'Big City' during August 1943. See *RAF Bomber Command Losses of the Second World War: 1943* by W.R. Chorley.

The three other Halifaxes on 158 Squadron that failed to return were piloted by Sergeant William Kidd, who skippered *Zombie's Zephyr*, Squadron Leader N.H. Elliott, who captained 'P-Peter' and Pilot Officer Ernest James the 30-year-old pilot on 'C-Charlie'. William Kidd and four other crew members were killed, the two others being taken into captivity. Elliott and four other crew members were taken prisoner, the two others being killed. There were no survivors on *Zombie's Zephyr* which was shot down by a night-fighter and crashed at Dürnberg.

'Although we had a satisfactory trip,' recalls Warrant Officer 'Eddie' Wheeler on 97 Squadron, 'we were upset to hear that Wing Commander Burns had been shot down.' Kenneth Holstead 'Bobby' Burns DFC* was an American from Oregon who was piloting 'L-London'. He was the victim of a head-on attack by an FW 190 a few minutes short of the target. Burns called to his crew: 'This is it. Out you go blokes.' Pilot Officer Earle George Dolby DFC the 23-year-old Canadian bomb aimer had asked if he should let the bombs go, but Burns had said, 'No - leave 'em be and I'll aim the kite where they'll do some good.' He trimmed the aircraft to head down for the already burning centre of Berlin ahead. Then he unclipped his seat harness and was just raising his hand to take off his helmet when there was a huge flash as the bombs exploded. Dolby and Warrant Officer Oliver Lambert DFM the rear gunner were killed. Burns and the three other members of his crew survived and they were taken into captivity. Burns woke up lying on soft ground under some pine trees on the outskirts of Berlin. His right hand and half the forearm were missing. Strangely, as the numbness wore off, the worst pain came from his right ankle and foot. He looked at his watch. It was still ticking and he saw by the luminous hands that it was 3.30 - he had been there three-and-a-half hours. A signalman found the American wing commander near his signal box beside the tracks of a Berlin suburban railway. Still unconscious Burns was taken to the sick quarters at Tempelhof where he was given an immediate blood transfusion. Then he was rushed to hospital in north-west Berlin where doctors cleaned up the stump of his arm and drained one of his lungs which had been collapsed by the explosion and had filled with blood. Some weeks later when he had been moved to prison camp, it was found that Burns had yet another injury; his back was broken. In 1944 Burns was repatriated to England via Sweden. He recovered and after being fitted with a false hand, resumed his flying career.[4]

---

4   *Into The Silk* by Ian Mackersey (Robert Hale 1956). Four other members of his crew survived and they were taken into captivity. Pilot Officer Earle George Dolby DFC RCAF and Warrant Officer Oliver Lambert DFM the rear gunner were killed.

# THE MORNING AFTER THE NIGHT BEFORE

Of two Lancasters on 106 Squadron there was no sign. One, piloted by Flight Sergeant John Lawrence Hendry had crashed in the vicinity of Bramsche. Hendry, a New Zealander born in 1915 and three of his crew were killed. The three survivors were taken into captivity. Flying Officer 'Harry' Douglas Ham meanwhile, had taken 'L-London' off from Syerston at 2010 hours. The outward trip had gone well, with no opposition until the target approach leg. Then flak came up in a terrifying hail of shells and tracers, exploding all around the wallowing bomber. For nearly ten minutes the Lancaster was buffeted and bounced around the sky, but it released its bomb load over the target and then swung out of the flak zone in a fast climbing curve, heading for safer air. Sergeant N.D. Higman the eighteen-year-old rear gunner was, 'paralysed with fear and feeling distinctly sick in the guts'. Nothing in his training had prepared him mentally for such an ordeal, while the sight of another Lancaster exploding in mid-air in a huge gout of flame merely added to his terror. Fighting against an almost overwhelming desire to faint, the gunner remembered his skipper's last words before take-off; 'It may become a bit rough over there, but for Christ's sake keep watching for fighters, Higman. I'll take care of anything else'.

The Lancaster survived the holocaust of flak and was drumming steadily homewards when Higman saw a shadow in the port quarter behind. It was a fighter! Yelling a warning into his microphone, Higman let loose with all four Brownings as the silhouette grew larger, with strings of tracer leaping directly at the rear turret, then rushing past Higman on each side. The ensuing few minutes were a kaleidoscope of lights, wheeling clouds and moon, cordite stink and rattling; with Higman valiantly trying to keep his seat and still bring his guns to bear. Unbeknown to him cannon shells had ripped out most of the pilot's instrument panel, smashed the wireless set, wounded the navigator and knocked him unconscious and slashed chunks out of the forward length of fuselage. The port inner engine had been put out of action. Ham eventually evaded any further fighter onslaught and then took stock. He had no way to obtain a position fix, his navigator was in no state to help and the Lancaster was sloppy on the controls. The port inner engine began pluming smoke ominously - he could expect a fire any second. A rough check on the time told him he should be somewhere near the coast, but where? The intercom was obviously 'out' and to add to his problems he was heading into a sky of dense black cloud which eliminated any hope of guidance from the stars.

Determined to try for home, Ham set a guessed course north-westwards and struggled with reluctant controls for as long as he could. The skipper was hit in the leg and arm. The bomber was extensively damaged, having a hole in it eight feet long through which Sergeant Norman Leslie Ernest Gale the 24-year-old flight engineer who came from Sway in Hampshire nearly fell as he went about tending his wounded comrades and seeing to the engines. Gale was the seventh son of the seventh son in a family of twelve - eight sons and four daughters. 'Harry' Ham bravely stuck to his controls, but at times Norman Gale had to take over them when the pilot was overcome with faintness owing to loss of blood. Then, on the point of physical exhaustion, Ham realized that the fuel state was almost zero. A fuel tank had been punctured by flak and petrol was leaking from it all the way on the 600 mile journey home, the tank being practically dry when the bomber reached England. The port outer engine grunted to a stop, starved of fuel and then the starboard inner began to slow. Yelling to James Walter Weight the bomb aimer to tell the others, Ham gave the order to bail out. Each man made his way to the escape hatch. Sergeant Pitman the navigator, now conscious though still dazed, was helped into his chute and through the hatch by the wireless operator. Sergeant T. Waller the mid-upper gunner climbed down from his turret, made his way back to Higman's rear turret and banged on the doors, and certain his knocking had been acknowledged, he went forward and bailed out. Higman stayed in his seat, still searching for fighters and he only relaxed when they were well out of Luftwaffe range. Receiving nothing on intercom, he flipped open his rear doors and looked down the fuselage. To his horror he realized he was on his own. Panic set in. Closing the door, he rotated the turret to the beam, having grabbed his parachute pack from its stowed position and then back-flipped out of the turret.

Coming to earth at the edge of a small copse, Higman made for cover and got rid of his chute and harness and buried them as best he could. Then, in inky darkness, he set off. For the next eighteen hours he lay low, avoiding all paths and roads and snatching sleep in a thick patch of gorse. As darkness approached again he set out in a vaguely northern direction. Near-exhausted, hungry and dying for a drink of water he came out of a small clump of trees - and nearly tripped over an RAF corporal making love to a blonde WAAF! The astonishment was mutual ... Higman then learned that for eighteen hours he had successfully 'evaded capture' within two miles of a tiny RAF signals unit near the coastline of Kent!

Ham made a forced landing and pancaked in a field at 0300 hours on the Romney Marshes in Kent but unhappily the crippled Lancaster struck some obstacles and burst into flames and Ham was badly injured. Norman Gale struggled miraculously unhurt from the wreckage, but despite his dazed and shaken condition he three times fought his way into the burning bomber and twice came out dragging injured airmen with him. He was awarded the DFM. 'Harry' Ham and James Weight, who were severely wounded, unfortunately died of their injuries on 1st and 2nd September, respectively. The pilot was awarded a posthumous Mention in Despatches. Norman Gale was one of four men on Flight Lieutenant John Alec Bulcraig DFM's crew on 57 Squadron who were killed on 18th July during the raid on Revigny.

A Lancaster on 61 Squadron at Syerston piloted by 30-year-old Squadron Leader Dennis Crosby Wellburn from Vancouver in British Columbia crashed near Bleasby, Notts, after a collision with a Lancaster on 1654 Heavy Conversion Unit at Wigsley, Nottinghamshire. The latter was being flown in a southerly direction by 30-year-old Pilot Officer Joseph Widger Murphy MacDonald of Radnorshire, Wales, on a cross-country training exercise. The other Lancaster was being flown in a northerly direction. Neither crew saw the others navigation lights and collided head-on at 0326 hours. There were no survivors. All eight crew members on Wellburn's aircraft died. Sergeant Alan Paterson the 25-year-old rear gunner left a widow, Margaret Smart Paterson of Montrose in Scotland. 'Joe' MacDonald and his six crew members were killed, their aircraft crashing near Southwell six miles west of Newark-on-Trent. MacDonald left a widow, Phyllis MacDonald of Knighton, Radnorshire. His flight engineer, Sergeant George Robert Joyce, was only nineteen years of age. Flying Officer Walter 'Steve' Jobling DFC, the 34-year-old navigator and Sergeant John Henry Hutchinson, the 38-year-old mid-upper gunner, also left bereaved wives in Lincoln and Liverpool.[5]

Halifax 'P-Peter' on 419 'Moose' Squadron at Middleton St. George, flown by 22-year-old Flying Officer William Donald Leslie Cameron RCAF, was also involved in a collision, with a night-fighter. Cameron, a broad, silent man, from Sarnia, Ontario, was on his nineteenth operation. William was a graduate of Sarnia Collegiate. Prior to enlisting, he was employed with the Sarnia Imperial Refinery where his father worked in the pumping department. His all-sergeant crew were on their sixteenth operation. Flight Sergeant Victor Joseph August 'Windy' Wintzer RCAF, the 24-year-old bomb aimer of Toronto, Ontario, had just released the bombs and Cameron was preparing to turn for home when it happened. The outer tip of the port wing had been sliced away and the port outer engine caught fire, which Sergeant John Thomas 'Paddy' Mullany, the 26-year-old Australian flight

---

5   See *Aircrew Remembered.*

engineer from Chekenham, Victoria, extinguished, but the propeller refused to feather. Finally, with the Halifax vibrating badly and sections falling off and the aircraft down to 5,000 feet, Cameron gave the order to evacuate the aircraft. He and fellow Ontarian, George Ernest Percy 'Ernie' Birtch, the diminutive navigator, 23-years old, died in the aircraft. So too did 'Windy' Wintzer and 'Paddy' Mullany. Beverly W. Scharf the six foot tall mid-upper gunner who was also from Sarnia and is believed to have added a year to his age before being accepted into the RCAF, bailed out safely. 'Bert' Boos the rear-gunner from Calgary, ten years older than the others, whose favourite pastime was making passionate love during the day to his girlfriend in Harrogate's public gardens, also went out through the open rear escape hatch. 'Les' Duggan the WOp/AG, a former roundsman for the Co-op who had turned twenty-one on the night of the Peenemünde raid, who was dropping 'Window' when the collision occurred, also made it out. He not only lost over five of his thirteen stones in Stalag Luft VI Heydekrug; his nerves too were shot to pieces. Returning home after the war he had trouble eating and for a time occasionally frightened his family by dancing on his bed brandishing a German bayonet.[6]

Two other Halifaxes on the 'Moose' Squadron also failed to return. The crew on 'N-Nuts' skippered by 22-year-old Canadian Flying Officer Robert Stewart were on their eleventh operation. 'Bob' Stewart was from Chester-le-Street, County Durham, Nova Scotia and he had recently got married. On Leverkusen during the night of 22nd/23rd August with wireless communications out of action they had returned to Middleton St. George early. On Berlin on 23rd/24th August heavy icing built up on the wings at the higher altitudes. The additional drag on the airflow brought them dangerously late over the target, almost five minutes after the last wave had left the target area, which left them the only target of any flak batteries or searchlights. Now, on the night of 31st August/1st September the Halifax was jumped just before 'bombs away' by a Ju 88 night-fighter. Sergeant Douglas Haig Armour Garland the 24-year-old rear gunner from Carlton Place, Ontario, fired a burst at the attacking aircraft before the fighter put three of the four engines out of action and wounded Garland on the right side of the head. Sergeant Albert Embley the WOp/AG moved through the damaged aircraft and managed to get Garland out of the rear turret, but the rear gunner's parachute was found to have been burnt, shot up and of

---

6   See *Bomber Boys* by Mel Rolfe (Grub Street 2004, Bounty Books 2007).

no use. Embley had Garland wrap his arms around him, between his back and the inside of Embley's parachute and then to wrap his legs around the waist and they would jump together in this way. At some point in the parachute descent Garland started to slip away from Embley's grasp and by the 2,000 foot mark he completely slipped away into the night and into the Black Forest below.

Sergeant Harold R. Tenny the RAF flight engineer, Pilot Officer S.E. James, navigator and Sergeant Leonard Northcliffe, air gunner, bailed out safely and were taken prisoner. Tenny had said to 'Bob' Stewart that they should bail out since the aircraft was on fire and they still had their bombs on board, but his skipper and Flight Sergeant Vincent Alton Francis Cleveland the 22-year-old bomb aimer from Toronto, Ontario died on the aircraft.

'K-King', piloted by Flight Lieutenant D.J. Corcoran RCAF, was the other 419 Squadron Halifax lost. It was over Hanover when fighter flares fell on both sides of the aircraft. Both gunners reported sighting another Halifax directly underneath their own aircraft. A few minutes later 'Monica' began to indicate an aircraft approaching from the rear. The gunners could not find the attacker indicated by the 'Monica' signal. A fighter then came from below and the Halifax was hit from the nose section along the bottom right to the tail section where a shell crashed through the side of the rear turret but did not injure Flying Officer D.E. Larlee manning the guns. Indications are that the night-fighter pilot screened his aircraft behind the lower Halifax and continued up beneath 'King' and then opened fire. Larlee, whose guns were still working, noticed that the port wing and engines were now on fire. With the Halifax in flames a second attack came from the port quarter below. Larlee fired in the direction that the enemy muzzle flashes came from, still not able to see the fighter itself. Corcoran called for a bail out using the call light while holding the aircraft as straight as possible using all his strength. From that point on he only remembered undoing his Sutton harness getting ready to bail out. He blacked out at this point and it was as he drifted down that he regained consciousness. Then there was an explosion. Corcoran found that his parachute ring had not been pulled, so it must have been opened by some other method of force. His earphone section of his flying helmet was ripped off the helmet and he also had bruises around the head and shoulders, but he was alive. When Larlee made his exit from his rear turret the air stream pulled him out while entangling his left foot in part of the turret structure. He was now being dragged down by being partly trapped in the falling aircraft. He finally managed to free his foot about 2,000 feet from the ground. His landing had attracted the attention of firearms wielding farmers who could easily see the white parachute. With a badly sprained knee and torn ligaments in his leg he could not outrun them and he was captured. He joined Corcoran, Sergeant W.E. Greensides the mid-upper gunner and navigator, Warrant Officer A.G. McKenzie DFM in captivity. Warrant Officer2 Hans H. D'Aperng the 22-year-old WOp/AG from Odessa, Ontario; Sergeant Dennis William Sweet the 22-year-old RAF flight engineer from Bedford and Flight Sergeant Albert Charles Harris the 34-year-old RAF bomb aimer from West Dulwich, London were killed. Sweet and Greensides were on their first operation.

At Elvington 'Triv' Trivett lay back on the top of his bed with arms behind his head staring up to the ceiling, listening to an increasing drone of an aircraft with a miss beat labouring engine. The inside of the Nissen hut was noticeable; brighter with the airfield, Drem lighting having been switched back on. 'My head was feeling heavy. I remembered I should be thanking someone for allowing me to come home safely home on this, my special day. Whether I finished offering my thanks I'll never know, for the latent power of the rum - while fully clothed and lying on top of my bed, just obliterated everything from my mind for the next six hours. I needed that rest. There might be another "Maximum Effort" tonight!'[7]

---

7  On 10 April 1944, while on a refresher course before resuming instructing duties, Flight Lieutenant Pete Cadman DFC, only son of Mrs. G.E. Cadman, of Oakworth, London Road, Canterbury and Flying Officer H.H.V. Roots were killed flying single-engined landings in an Oxford when the other engine failed on the approach.

# Chapter 8

# Panic in the Heart of the Reich

*Wearily I go to bed*
*Bombs still falling round my head*
*O flak, now let thy watchful eyes*
*Guard us till the sun doth rise*
*O Father God, avert Thy gaze*
*From the havoc that the Tommies raise*
*With Thy help we'll not despair*
*And soon the damage will repair*
*Friends and neighbours, each must roam*
*Parted from his blazing home*
*Great and small must share the woe*
*Of ruins and no place to go*
*Shut little mouth, sink little head*
*Pray for final Victory instead*

**'Prayer' offered to German children to recite at night.
In Berlin the great loss of life in the Siemensstadt and
Mariendorf districts and also to Lichterfelde now forced
Goebbels, who had persuaded one million of its four and
a half million inhabitants to leave Berlin before Bomber
Command's main attacks began, to order the evacuation
of all children and all adults not engaged in war work to
country areas or to towns in Eastern Germany where air
raids were not anticipated. By 1944 1.2 million people,
790,000 of them women and children, about a quarter of
Berlin's population, had been evacuated to rural areas.
An effort was made to evacuate all children from Berlin,
but this was resisted by parents and many evacuees
soon made their way back to the city.**

On 3rd September Hans Georg von Studnitz got out his diary and wrote that, 'life was becoming ever-increasingly dominated by the war in the air. Everybody was certain that there would be a raid. Hans Flotow[1] gave a small dinner-party. We talked about nothing but the air raids. The whole thing reminded me of a meeting of persecuted Christians in the Roman catacombs! The behaviour of the Berliners has, on the whole, been marvellous. We get plenty of practice in dealing with incendiary bombs and the correct use of sandbags and stirrup-pumps. An incendiary which pierced the rafters of our house gave us some trouble because the bomb had stuck in an inaccessible place in the woodwork between the two storeys. The enemy aircraft have an unpleasant habit of dropping explosive bombs on areas already set on fire by incendiaries. Every evening the main topic of conversation is always: "Will they come tonight?"'

In England, Friday, 3rd September was a rather dull day. All was quiet in the Breckland village of Kenninghall a few miles east of East Harling. Deep in rural Norfolk little had changed for centuries. Land in the parish has been held by the King since before the Norman invasion. Before the war the village numbered less than 2,000 souls, but after the outbreak of hostilities and the German raids on London in 1940 all that was to change. Construction of an airfield was begun at Fersfield nearby, while the old-fashioned village school, which still had open fires, became so overcrowded because of an influx of evacuees from Wembley that the classroom had to be divided into three by curtains. Some, like the mother of 8-year-old Dawn Catten, decided that she would rather face Hitler and his bombs than Dawn's great aunt, who was extremely house proud and so, after six weeks, they returned to their home on the outskirts of London, leaving the rest of the villagers to get on with their lives. That is, until a little before midday on 3rd September when 14-year-old Brian Womack noticed a four-engined bomber circling around over St. Mary's, the village church. As he got closer he could see that the bomber was on fire.

NFTs (Night Flying Test) had taken place in the morning and there were some cross-countries while for others it was an opportunity for an air firing exercise. On 156 Squadron in 8 Group PFF, former Spitfire pilot, Flying Officer Clifford Foderingham DFC RCAF had lifted Lancaster 'U-Uncle' off from Warboys in Huntingdonshire and headed towards south Norfolk. The 22-year-old pilot, born in Toronto, and his crew had flown on nine ops in

---

1 Hans Ludwig Carl Theodor von Flotow, a German diplomat.

the past six weeks. Foderingham's father was from Georgetown, British Guyana and his mother was from Hartlepool. While on 101 Squadron at Stradishall he had ditched his Wellington III in the North Sea returning from the raid on Osnabrück on 17th/18th August 1942 and he was awarded the DFC in November. Flying Officer Angus Stewart DFM, the wireless operator, who was from Ontario, received his award for helping two of the injured in the ditching. Navigator, Flying Officer William Gordon DFC, suffered a leg injury in the ditching but he returned to action in January 1943. Before joining the RAF in 1938 Flight Lieutenant Kenneth Watkins, the 28-year-old rear gunner from Westcliff-on-Sea, had a varied peacetime career as a salesman and an actor. The 30-year-old bomb aimer Flight Sergeant Horace Ross was from Saskatchewan. Flying Officer Robert Hood DFM, the 23-year-old Australian flight engineer from Sydney, had been commissioned in December 1942. In April 1943 he had been awarded the DFC after completing twenty-seven ops.

To Brian Womack it seemed that 'U-Uncle' was trying to miss the village. It was on fire and when it crashed at Green Farm nearby there was 'just a big bang'. Young Brian wanted to see what was 'up' but his father would not let him. Young Jim Gooderham, who lived at the family home at Dairy Farm, North Lopham, was doing some work for his father in the barn when he heard the explosion. He rushed out and saw a thick pall of smoke. His father was not there at the time so Jim hopped on his bicycle and set off towards the smoke. At the crash scene the devastated aircraft was spread over two fields; it was so unrecognizable that for many years he thought that it was a Blenheim. 'There was nothing we could do for the crew,' he recalled. They had carried no parachutes aboard the aircraft for the exercise.

This isolated incident in rural Breckland served to prove that the war civilians normally only ever read about in their newspapers and listened to on their wireless sets was never far away. Relatively immune from the bombing endured in the cities, fresh food too was plentiful. On the RAF bases food was not always as good but the tradition was that crews always got two eggs on their plate when there was an op 'on'. 'We were eating high off the hog again, bacon and "real" egg (as we called it),' wrote Sergeant 'Philip 'Griff' Griffiths a Canadian wireless operator who flew twenty-six operations, including eight on Berlin on Flying Officer 'Russ' Ewens' DFC RCAF crew on 49 Squadron. 'The thought occurred to me, what happened to all the eggs in WWII - also, and another thought - were we like lambs being fattened for the slaughter?

'Somewhat later, as the crews gathered in the briefing room loaded down with our respective equipment (the "navs" were the heaviest carriers), these unbelievably high spirited young men were laughing and joking almost like they were going on a picnic, then as the group captain walked in we rose and were quiet. The covering was then removed from the large map of Europe and on this day the tape revealed we were going to Berlin again. There was a huge concerted groan from the crews as the "Big City" always gave us a warm welcome. It was acknowledged at the briefing that crossing the Dutch coast was not much fun anymore as it was now heavily fortified with batteries of AA and nearby fighter fields, so the "bright" idea was to circle and gain height over our own fields and then head east. We did go along with this and circled in controlled orbits and designated rates of climb over our own fields in 7/10 cloud!

'Can you now imagine perhaps 250 Lancs doing this, considering the close proximity of the 5 Group fields? We carried out this procedure with hearts in our mouths as our kite was almost continuously rocked and buffeted by the slipstream of adjacent aircraft. This fun piece of the trip was, I am sure, responsible for the grey hair of 5 Group aircrew. (I don't believe this was done again, primarily due to our opinions rudely and positively expressed at the de-briefing).' 49 Squadron lost one crew that night, that of Pilot Officer G.L. Ratcliffe. They were on their first mission and were all killed.

The loss of seventy aircraft in one night was hard to swallow and for a while our morale was on the low side. Perhaps we bounced back a little with the thought that such a nightmare couldn't happen again - we were very wrong. Along came Nuremberg!'[2]

Because of the high casualty rates among Halifax and Stirling aircraft in recent raids on the 'Big City', the raid on 3rd/4th September consisted entirely of Lancasters, 316 of them with the Pathfinder Force putting up fifty-five 'markers' and twenty-six 'supporters'. The latter were an unenviable breed. 'Supporters' would fly over the target area to draw flak, while the markers dropped their flares and then they would re-cross the target to drop bombs. Second Lieutenant John Edmund 'Jack' Russell's crew on 97 Squadron were detailed as one of the supporters. It was their first operation since joining the Pathfinders from 57 Squadron at Scampton, Russell was the son of Stanley Alexander Scott Russell of Kingston, Jamaica, in the West Indies and Susanna Maria Sauer of Staten Island, New York. They raised their family in Kings County, Brooklyn, where 'Jack' was born on 30th January 1920. As a youngster he worked as a newspaper delivery boy on the streets

---

2 *A Typically Hot Visit To the Big City* by 'Griff' Griffiths which appeared in the 49 Squadron newsletter.

of New York before finally enlisting in the RCAF in Montreal in July 1941. Russell took Lancaster EE193 off from Bourn at 2030 hours. 'The raids on Berlin were becoming monotonous when we found ourselves in flight again on 3rd September against the "Big City",' wrote Warrant Officer 'Eddie' Wheeler on 97 Squadron.[3]

At Syerston Pilot Officer 'Tony' Bird on 61 Squadron was on that night's Battle Order with his own crew. It would be his fourth operation since joining the squadron. A groan went up from the assembled aircrew at operational briefing with the announcement that the raid that night was... Berlin. The reaction was the same on 106 Squadron which shared the base with 61 Squadron. The crew skippered by 25-year-old Squadron Leader David William Southam Howroyd, who was from Kelvedon in Essex, was on the Battle Order. Flight Sergeant 'Tony' Sargeant the 19-year-old flight engineer remembered him as, 'a keen and very experienced flyer, strict on discipline.' Sargeant went down to 'C-Charlie's' dispersal to gossip with the ground crew as usual about the night's loads. He could estimate where the target might be from the fuel load. It was 1,700 gallons, from which it could be deduced that the target must be east of the Ruhr. The crew had heard on that morning's news bulletin that the army had landed in Italy which made them think they might be going to give them a hand.

Howroyd and his crew went to briefing thinking that it was not Berlin which Sargeant found comforting. At the engineers' briefing it was established that the fuel load had been increased to 2,000 gallons, thus wiping out any chance of the 'Big City'. Or so he thought. Alas, it was established that a special long-distance route was being taken, to Berlin. 'Boy, where we shaken when we got to main briefing,' wrote Sargeant. 'Berlin it was.'

'Blimey!' everyone said. 'Now we're for it.'

'Main briefing went off as usual with all the necessary gen from the met man about altitudes, wing company and so on.

'Our next stop was the mess at 1800 hours for a tea which was to last us until about 0500 the following morning, or so we thought. It was the usual eggs and bacon. We also filled our flasks with tea, which we usually drank after crossing the English coast on the way home because, after wearing oxygen masks for long hours, our mouths became parched and dry.

'We had very little time left as take-off was 1950 hours and the skipper always liked us down at the flights at least an hour before.

---

3  *Just To Get A Bed* by Edwin Wheeler DFC.

'"Jock" Kelly our mid-upper gunner and I rushed up to the billet to do our last-minute odd jobs in case we might not return, although we never thought that we wouldn't. He had been separated from his old crew because of a wound received while returning low over the Baltic from Stettin one night. Hit three times in the leg he was off flying for about six months. We palled up together right from the start and got to be like brothers. We shared the same room and rarely went out unless together and I must say we had some grand times which I shall never forget. "Jock" was from Newton Mearns, a small place just outside Glasgow. He left sooner than I, having so much extra clothing to put on when he got to his locker. I just put on my boots and another sweater and ambled down at about 1900 hours.

'"Les" ["Mac"] McKenzie in the rear turret was from Cambridge, a real old timer with eight years' service compared with us sprogs. He was well above the average age for aircrew, but he looked much older, with such a huge old-fashioned moustache he had cultivated on his top lip. "Mac" was a good type, quiet and reserved, but he enjoyed coming out with "Jock" and myself in the evenings.

'Doug Chappell the wireless operator was also a good type and very interested in his job, keen in all respects. "Chap" was from Kent; a policeman before joining up. He was also above the average age for aircrew. He got on quite well with "Tom" Saxby our air bomber, a flying officer. "Sax" was another ex-policeman.

'Pilot Officer "Tom" ["Dave"] Davies the navigator, another old fellow at thirty-four, was a quiet Londoner, a good friend of "Mac".

'Everything was peaceful and quiet around the flight offices and locker room except for sudden outbursts of: "Where's my bloody so-and-so?"

'We stood around outside the flight offices waiting our turn for the transport to take us out to our kite as other crews kept leaving. Now and again, from somewhere around the dispersals, came the sudden outburst of engines as the first wave was running up their machines before take-off.

'With the roaring of engines all around us, it was our turn to get into the transport and go to "Bar Charlie". As we climbed aboard the bus the wing commander and others wished us luck and shouted, as usual: "See you in the morning."

'There were no apparent signs of nervousness in any of the crews. If there was, they did not show it, they were just one big joking crowd.

'We got out to the aircraft and lay about chatting to the ground crew. We had plenty of time before take-off, so while the rest of the crew did the chatting the skipper and I walked around "Bar Charlie" doing certain checks and having a general look over to see that she was all right.

'The time came for us to climb aboard and get the engines started for the ground testing. They started a treat and all tests were satisfactory, so we gave thumbs up to the ground crew and taxied "Bar Charlie" out to follow the other kites around the perimeter track to the take-off point.

'While we were lined up waiting our turn I looked around and there, as usual, were people watching from a nearby farmhouse and, at the head of the runway, a crowd of WAAFs, ground crew and aircrew waving at each aircraft as it left, roaring down the runway.

'Then it was our turn. The skipper and I made sure everything was all right as far as we were concerned to get the huge aircraft airborne.

'Take-off is rather a tense moment because, as you might imagine, any engine trouble at such a time can be serious, especially with bombs aboard. Luckily everything was perfect and as soon as we were airborne everyone relaxed and settled down for the long trip into darkness. From now on we were just a team of seven men who seemed cut off from the rest of the world, with one job to do before we could return to earth. We circled around with many more aircraft for company, gaining height, until it was time to set course for Germany.'[4]

An hour after take-off 'Bar Charlie' was flying at about 12,000 feet, their course almost direct to Berlin. By this time the sky had turned dull and the night darker, so they set course, climbing steadily all the way. There was thick cloud now and it was almost pitch black.

At Warboys, twenty crews on 156 Squadron on the Battle Order began taxiing out. The Lancaster skippered by 30-year-old Flying Officer Michael O'Meara Shanahan RAAF began taxiing at 1948 hours. Shanahan came from Sefton, New South Wales and was married to Patricia Ellen. Four of his crew were Australians. Flight Lieutenant Hume Melville Stafford the 32-year-old navigator was from Nathalia, Victoria. He too had a wife, Eileen Grace. Flight Sergeant Neil Howard Denyer the 22-year-old bomb aimer was from Tumbarumba, NSW. The 25-year-old wireless operator, Warrant Officer John Cyril Collins, a champion surfer, was from Claremont, Western Australia. The 23-year-old flight engineer, Sergeant Tom Hoyle was from Catford, London, where his wife Henrietta lived. The 29-year-old mid-upper gunner, Sergeant George Wilson, was from Newtonards in

---

4  *Just Another Night Out* by John Sargeant, quoted in *Bomber Boys* by Mel Rolfe (Grub Street, 2004).

County Down, Northern Ireland, where his wife Annie was living. Warrant Officer David Laing Dodds the 23-year-old rear gunner was from Concord West, NSW. No word was heard from Shanahan's Lancaster after take-off. He and his crew were lost without trace.

'As with every operation,' wrote 'Tony' Bird, 'the most nerve-wracking period was the need to fly the aircraft "straight and level", not only during the run up to the target but also for a period of time after release of the bombs. This was to ensure that our individual "target photograph", which was taken automatically, took a clear picture, with the camera pointing directly at the impact point of the bombs. There was great rivalry amongst the crews to come back with the best target photograph.

'It was during this time, after dropping our bombs, when it was not possible to weave or alter course in any way, that suddenly an almost invisible master ultra-violet searchlight caught us in its beam. This master beam controlled a number of normal searchlights and within a second or two we were fully illuminated in a dazzling searchlight "cone" and although I was now able to twist and turn, the lights were easily able to keep us in view. At the 20,000 feet at which we were flying, the searchlight cone was perhaps a hundred yards across and now the flak was bursting perilously close to us. Suddenly, the flak stopped, but this was not a good sign - it was a signal for the fighters to attack.

'Our gunners were still completely blinded by the searchlights and they were quite unable to even see the enemy fighters, let alone fire back at them.

'We were soon hit in the port outer engine despite my intense weaving and flames quickly appeared from it. Although I was unaware of it at the time, this was a standard method of attack on the part of the German fighters for they had been briefed that this particular engine controlled the Lancaster's hydraulics, which in turn operated the gun turrets and the landing gear. Even had our gunners been able to see their targets, with their gun turrets now virtually immobilised, we were literally "sitting ducks".

'It was now obvious that my weaving was quite ineffective and I pushed the control column forward into a near vertical dive and opened the throttles to their maximum extent.

'In an effort to keep us in view, the searchlight beams were now pointing almost horizontally, but suddenly they gave up as we had passed the limit of their area of responsibility.

'"Ken" Kendrick, my flight engineer, had already turned off the fuel supply to the stricken engine and this action, plus the violent dive, quickly caused the fire to extinguish, although the engine was now useless.

'We had lost about 5,000 feet in the dive and as we would have wasted precious fuel in attempting to climb back to our normal operational height of 20,000 feet, we had little choice but to remain at our present height.

'Fortunately, the fighters had made no attempt to follow us down and I was later to realise that they rarely did so. The single engine fighter held only sufficient fuel for about one and a half or two hours flying and much of that was used up in just climbing up to the operational height of the bomber stream. Had they followed us down, it is probable that they would have had insufficient fuel left to climb back up to attack further bombers.

'Our navigator, "Ginger" Lucas, quickly worked out a revised flight plan for the return journey as we were now completely separated from the main bomber stream. Had we encountered any more enemy fighters, we could do nothing to defend ourselves from attack, but our luck was in - all the fighters were probably engaged in attacking the returning main bomber stream at 20,000 feet.'

Three crews on 97 Squadron were intercepted, two over the target and one on the homeward journey. There was so much fighter activity on the return route that Flight Lieutenant D.I. Jones had the whole crew except the navigator on alert looking for anything that moved. As the rear gunner, Flight Sergeant J.R. Burke, swung his turret searching, he saw a Ju 88 on the starboard quarter ready to attack. 'Corkscrew, corkscrew, starboard.' Jones obeyed the order instantly; a quick reflex action which probably saved the Lancaster for, judging by the tracer, the Junkers' fire just missed the bomber. Both gunners replied with long bursts and saw their tracer enter the fighter which turned over and dived through the cloud. They claimed it as 'damaged probably destroyed'.

'As we approached the target,' wrote Sergeant Bernard H. 'Jack' Lazenby, the flight engineer on 'Jack' Russell's crew on 97 Squadron, 'we had to fly through an avenue of fighter flares [dropped by four Mosquitoes well away from the route to Berlin to decoy night-fighters away from the bomber stream] that seemed to be stationary in the air and it was quite light. I was standing by the pilot looking ahead as we approached our aiming point when a stream of cannon fire came from ahead and across our starboard wing. An Me 110 then passed on our port side. It was unusual to be attacked from head-on. German fighters usually attacked from the rear or underneath.'

As he swung his Lancaster on course for base 'Jack' Russell saw the twin-engined aircraft on the starboard bow. He told the mid-upper, Sergeant 'Wally' Bark, to look out for it but got the reply, 'Sorry skipper, I have one in my sights on the port quarter and another behind him queuing up.

He's coming in skipper; dive to port, go, go, go.' Bark's fire was more accurate than the enemy's and he saw his tracer enter the nose of the fighter, which broke away and was not seen again. Seconds later the sky seemed to light up as Flight Sergeant Ronnie Marston, the rear gunner, shouted, 'Corkscrew, corkscrew'. A second fighter was attacking from the port quarter and fifty to sixty searchlights were trying to help it. Marston opened up at 500 yards, but the fighter pilot pressed home the attack and scored hits on the Lancaster. However, he too had no stomach for a second encounter.[5] 'The two gunners saw quite a few fighters that night but there were no more attacks,' added 'Jack' Lazenby. 'After bombing it was a relief to leave the city and get into the darkness.'

'The blind marking in particular seemed quite remarkable to me,' wrote 'Punch' Thompson on 83 Squadron. 'As our own yellow target indicators exploded in a pyrotechnic shower far below I saw four other sets of yellows burst and fall within an interval of three seconds. How could five aircraft take off from England, fly in complete darkness and radio silence for three hours or more without seeing each other and independently of each other, drop their flares in a space of three seconds? And the dropping had to be independent because the flares fell for longer than three seconds before they exploded. This may have been a fluke, but if it was, some rather remarkable navigation was required to produce such a fluke... The route home this time was north across the Baltic to the southern tip of Sweden, thence on a track north-west up the Kattegat and south-west down the Skagerrak. Before reaching the latitude of 57° north the aurora borealis had turned night into day, with nature's flashing green, white and mauve searchlights illuminating the northern half of the sky. I had never before seen the northern lights so beautiful, or if fighters were about, so dangerous.'[6]

The radio-listening world went by proxy to Berlin that night with 'F for Freddie' on 207 Squadron at Langar when Flight Lieutenant Kenneth Henry Francis 'Ken' Letford and crew took Wynford Vaughan Thomas, a BBC Home Service commentator and his sound engineer, Mr Reginald Pidsley (who as a civilian was made an Acting Sergeant (unpaid) with them to record the commentator's impressions on a one-sided wax '78' disc four miles high over Berlin: 'Now and again, as we watch, we see a burst of flak, a bright light winking among the concentrated beams. They have got every single searchlight you could imagine out there to catch us. We are coming

---

5 *Pathfinder Force - A History of 8 Group* by Gordon Musgrove.
6 *Lancaster To Berlin* by Walter Thompson DFC and Bar.

up to them all the time, waiting for it. In a moment it will be our turn to pass through them.

'A dark shape is going out ahead of us, another Lancaster, to lead in. There goes the flak again, a winking burst up among the searchlights. They must be having a go at us all right. Away to port another constellation is coming up. They work in great groups, trying to stop and grapple you as you come in over the coast. All the time, they are moving in. It is disconcerting to see that welcome waiting for us.

'I am counting the time, watching the hand on my watch creeping round. I know that it will be our turn in exactly three minutes' time. [Pause] In the cone of searchlights, they caught one of our aircraft... Up goes the flak around him, bursting in vivid flashes. Now there are winks from the ground below us. They may be after us because the searchlights are starting to move away. They have left that other bomber and they are moving now slowly towards us, feeling for us all the time. They are pumping up the flak in a steady stream.

'You suddenly see a white flash on the ground and then just seconds later, there is a vivid burst among the searchlight cones. There goes the flak, bursting in that cone of searchlights, darting from vivid white pinpoints, moving all the time, trying to follow that bomber. Again they come bending, the whole lot of them. They seem to bend towards us, following a master beam. We are moving away to starboard and it looks as if, this time, we've slipped through.

'It is pretty obvious now, as we are coming in through the searchlight cones. It is going to be hell over the city itself. There is one comfort. It is going to be soundless because the roar of our engines is drowning every other sound. We are running straight into the most gigantic display of soundless fireworks in the world. We are due over our target in two minutes' time. "Bill" our bomb aimer is forward, he is lying prone over the bombsight and the searchlights are coming nearer all the time. There is one cone, split again and then it comes together. They seem to splay out, like the tentacles of an octopus waiting to catch you. Then suddenly they come together.

'"Half a minute to go. OK, boys," said the skipper in a deadpan tone.

'"Left ... left," said the bomb aimer, or bombardier as he was called on this aircraft.

'"Hello, bombardier, ready when you are, bomb doors open."

'"Steady ... steady ... bit longer yet. Steady ... level a bit. Steady, bombs going. One, two, three, bombs still going."'

'F-Freddie' was attacked by a night-fighter but Letford's gunners, Warrant Officer Fieldhouse and Sergeant Devenish, shot it down.

Needless to say, Vaughan Thomas and the others were relieved to see England again: 'There it goes; our first sight of England, just a little light from a beacon, flashing at us from the darkness below. After the giant glare of lights we left behind in Berlin, it seems small and frail. But everyone on board "F for Freddie" is mighty glad to see it. "Con", our navigator, has got out the goodies that we were not able to tackle during the hectic hours over Germany. We are cracking open our fruit juice. Someone has got his mouthful of chocolate and Scottie the engineer, who is just ahead of me, is pouring out from his thermos a cup of hot tea. We have got our oxygen masks off. There is a sense of freedom throughout the whole of "F-Freddie". "Ken" our skipper has just said over the intercom: "Boys, we won't be the first home, but we're damned glad to be home at all." (Skipper continues after pause) "Hello, bombardier, English coast should be coming up now. Will you tell me when you cross it?"'

'OK, I'll let you know ... I can see it coming up ahead.'

'Thank you.'

'Nav' lights on, skipper.'

'OK, navigator, "nav" lights on.'

Bomb aimer: 'We should be over it in a few seconds. There it is. Good to see old England again.'

Skipper: 'Yes, after that trip, boy, that's a sight for sore eyes, that is.'

Navigator: 'ETA at base: fifteen minutes.'

'OK navigator, thanks very much ... Hello, engineer, skipper here. How's the petrol going? Are we doing all right?' 'Oh yes.'

'Everything running OK?'

'Just lovely.'

'Good show, boy.'

The wax disc made of the operation was rushed to London and broadcast on the ten o'clock news. In all it was broadcast nine times in English and on numerous European and foreign programmes as well as the American network. It was described as 'the outstanding broadcast of the war'.

The language was naturally more restrained than usual, but 'Ken' Letchford failed to repress his feelings when his gunners destroyed the night-fighter. That slip of the tongue became quite famous, for on many occasions when civilians were asked if they had heard the broadcast they answered enthusiastically, 'Rather! Wasn't that the one in which the pilot said, 'Bloody good show?' Shortly after the trip Letford was presented with a recording by the BBC. Wynford Vaughan Thomas explained that his voice sounded strange because there was a problem with his oxygen supply.

'O-Oboe' on 57 Squadron, which was piloted by Sergeant James Thompson Carruthers, was shot down at about half past midnight, from an altitude of 15,000 feet and twenty-five miles from the target by an FW 190 night-fighter of Stab/JG 300 flown by Unteroffizier Fritz Brinkmann and crashed into Wunsdorfer See near Zossen south of Berlin. The crew of seven - four British, two Australian and a Canadian - all lost their lives. Ten-year-old Günter Bethke, who saw the British bombers coming from the south and heading for Berlin recalled that, 'two German night-fighters attacked the British. A four-engined bomber swerved from the fight and curved in a burning loop over the lake. With a deafening crash the plane exploded. My father found two bodies and buried them on the morning after the crash near the lido. The English had the dead transferred later. Two more dead, still strapped in their seats in the fuselage were recovered by the Soviets at the end of the war. One crew member may have survived the crash but appears to have been shot by the lake's edge in the reeds immediately after the crash.'[7]

'S for Sugar' on 97 Squadron, piloted by Flying Officer (later Squadron Leader) Charles Peter Crauford de Wesselow, returned to Bourn without making an attack. A surgeon's son of White Russian origins who had re-mustered from the Brigade of Guards; de Wesselow spoke several languages fluently. In November 1942 he and his crew had force-landed in Portugal in a Blenheim and were interned until January 1943. The precise, immaculate de Wesselow collected antique glass and could call on a rower's physique for throwing a Lancaster around the sky. As he jettisoned its bombs a Target Indicator exploded causing severe structural damage that resulted in 'Sugar' being declared beyond repair. de Wesselow cursed his luck but at least no one was injured.

Flying Officer 'Russ' Ewens' crew on 49 Squadron, which had proceeded on to Berlin, found it to be 'a city in flames, with constant eruptions below as their bombs dropped. 'The sky was bright as day with dazzling white parachute flares, AA bursts, crossing paths of tracer and searchlights waving back and forth,' wrote 'Griff' Griffiths. 'Prior to the run in we saw about 150 yards on our starboard beam a Lancaster corkscrewing like mad and firing on an Me 110 which was about to start his deadly "curve in pursuit". We opened fire from our mid and rear turrets, which, along with the subject Lanc's guns, were twelve streams of tracer heading towards the fighter.

---

7   The wreckage of Lancaster B.III JA914/O is on display at the German Technical Museum in Berlin.

He obviously didn't like the odds as he banked away smartly, off to find a less wary target.

'We were straight and level on our bomb run, our most vulnerable time, and had just dropped our "big ones" when we were attacked by a fighter and raked by his 20mm cannon and machine-gun fire. We were lucky however as we continued to fly. We assessed the damage as best we could, which consisted mainly of one of our starboard wing tanks holed and leaking, the incendiaries still held up in the bomb bay and hydraulic damage so that our bomb doors were still open, we were to find out later that our brakes were also u/s. A jagged portion of the skin of the port mainplane was loose and flapping away in the slipstream (increasing our drag), the mainplane near the WOp's and the rear gunner's positions was badly holed and we could see lots of holes all around the fuselage. We found, a little later, that two of our superchargers had been damaged. "Spike" Triton our flight engineer sprang into action immediately. He switched the fuel system so that we were feeding the engines from the damaged tank in order that we could use all the gas remaining and then revert to normal usage when we had sucked it almost dry. It was "Spike's" great sleight of hand and super efficiency that saved our bacon, otherwise, as it turned out, we would never have made it home.

'We headed for home with our bomb doors still open and "things" flapping in the breeze, which gave us lots of drag and a worry of having enough gas to make it to a friendly shore. With eyes constantly on the fuel gauges, with a nose down attitude and judicious use of engine controls we made England. We were lucky we were not attacked by fighters or lit up by searchlights as all we could do was fly straight and level - just!

'We crept home and were of course way behind everyone else and Lincolnshire was dark beneath us, no welcoming runway lights, just darkness. We were by this time on "fumes" and were a little desperate so we sent out a distress call for lights and lo and behold runway lights came on just ahead of us and down we went immediately with the starboard outer coughing for fuel. Russ put her down beautifully, but we then found out that due to the hydraulic damage we had no brakes. Fortunately, it was a grass runway which slowed us a little and at the end of the runway we turned rapidly on to the taxiway at such a speed we were fearful of a ground loop - somehow we made it. Our engines cut out as we hit the runway and we had to exit the plane there on the taxi strip. I should mention that we got out in double fast time with the thought of the incendiaries hanging up in the still open bomb bay!

'Well, what a welcome we received, we found out that we had landed at a Polish training airfield and they were wonderful to us, they escorted us to the Sergeants Mess which was opened up for us, it was 3 am and we were offered, for a start, a glass of their homemade vodka (made legally of course), which they proudly acclaimed to be double distilled. Before long Polish aircrew, staff and cooks got up and joined us, they opened the kitchen and we were treated to some hefty and well-seasoned sausages, homemade bread, an apple strudel and more of their excellent "jungle juice". It was an unforgettable party as it turned out, for at the end no one was feeling any pain!

'We all had a well-earned hangover and pleasant memories. Their hospitality was tremendous and I will always remember their efforts on our behalf.

'The next day our crew chief came over to look the aircraft over and decided to drain the tanks for a start and behold there wasn't enough to fill his Ronson lighter (we all carried one of these in those days). He also found that the incendiary containers were torn and riddled with shot and shell.

'The Navy had a satirical saying for a mission like we had, it was, "If you can't take a joke you shouldn't have joined".'[8]

Norman Ashton, on 'Reg' Bunten's crew on 103 Squadron wrote: 'Our first operation to Berlin had been a ten/tenths cloud effort but this all-Lanc attack had the supreme satisfaction of blitzing the city in perfect weather conditions. The Met people [had] forecast ten/tenths cloud on the outward route and clear over the target at zero hour. They scored a resounding success. We confirmed the first part of the forecast as we flew deeper into Germany but began to doubt the second part as we approached the target - the cloud seemed to cover the entire continent. Then, when we had almost resigned ourselves to another "blind" attack, the cloud finished abruptly, like the unsuspected edge of a precipice and there was Berlin - unmasked, at our feet and at out mercy. After the attack the cloud drifted back over the city. The defences were terrific, but the target was well and truly pranged. The route home caught "Jerry" napping and, by the time he realised what the score was, we were beyond the reach of his fighters. After bombing, we swept north in the direction of Sweden and then turned west for Denmark and the North Sea. The brightly lit cities on the Swedish coast gave us quite a thrill, after the blacked-out towns to which we had become accustomed. Some of the lads must have strayed off track to have a closer look, because

---

8  *A Typically Hot Visit To the Big City* by 'Griff' Griffiths which appeared in the 49 Squadron newsletter.

the Swedes took rather a dim view and demonstrated their neutral anger by throwing up a fair amount of light flak. From every point of view, the trip was a great success and I had more than a little satisfaction in again entering "BERLIN" in my logbook.'[9]

The defences of Berlin were still strong and the loss of twenty-two Lancasters was nearly seven per cent of the force. A total of 141 crew members were killed, fifteen were taken prisoner and three were interned in Sweden. Two Australian squadrons were particularly hard hit: 467 Squadron RAAF, which had lost one commanding officer at Milan and his temporary relief three nights later at Peenemünde, now lost newly-appointed flight commander, 25-year-old Flight Lieutenant Reginald Carmichael and crew on 'A-Apple' on what was the aircraft's forty-fourth trip. When Carmichael's crew had taken over this Lancaster they refused to fly the aircraft until the mascot on the forward fuselage was painted out, Carmichael decided to record the crew's raids with a beer mug for every operation flown. Born at Bourke, New South Wales on 17th April 1918, Carmichael left a widow, Mavis Gloria Carmichael, living in Kings Cross, a suburb of Sydney. RAF Flying Officer Ronald Vincent Turner's crew and Canadian mid-upper gunner on DV237 were shot down and the Lancaster crashed at Döberitz with no survivors. The aircraft had flown just thirteen hours.

At Binbrook three Lancasters on 460 Squadron RAAF were missing. A new crew on 'E2-Easy' skippered by 22-year-old Flying Officer Sidney Milton Forrester from Adelaide, South Australia were flying their first operation since being transferred in at the end of August. 'Easy's usual crew, skippered by Flying Officer J. Oakeshott had been stood down for the Berlin trip. Thirty-year-old Squadron Leader Carl Richard Kelaher who was Forrester's flight commander, decided to accompany him. As Forrester's rear gunner was unavailable, Kelaher brought in 39-year-old Sergeant Arthur Rolfe from his own crew as the replacement. Rolfe came from Yeadon near Leeds and was married to Mary and they had a young daughter. Kelaher too was married. He and Phyllis Kelaher had wed in London on 15th July 1940. There were two other Australians on the crew, Warrant Officers' Ewin Garth Carthew, the 21-year-old navigator of Rendelsham, South Australia, and Cyril Augustine Walsh, the 30-year-old bomb aimer born in Cobden, Victoria and had been a schoolteacher. The rest of the crew

---

9 *Only Birds And Fools* by J. Norman Ashton DFC. (Airlife 2000). Norman Ashton flew twenty-nine bombing operations on 103 Squadron before starting a second tour of 25 operations on 156 Path Finder Squadron.

were Sergeant Herbert Freeman Jowett, the 20-year-old flight engineer of Burnley, Lancashire, who had lied about his age when he volunteered for service; Sergeant John Cresswell Coombes, the 23-year-old wireless operator from Bosham near Chichester, and Sergeant Ernest Albert Cecil Thirkettle the 22-year-old mid-upper gunner from West Dulwich, London who had married wife Jessie on 15th November 1942. Forrester had taken off from Binbrook at 1958 hours on the evening of 3rd September. They were never seen again. On the return flight from Berlin over Jutland, 'Easy' was one of two Lancasters claimed shot down by Leutnant Karl Rechberger of 12./NJG 3 piloting a Ju 88C-6 night-fighter. Everyone on the aircraft was killed, the aircraft crashing at Vestager in Denmark, which meant that wives of the three married men on the crew were now widows.

EE132, skippered by 30-year-old Flight Sergeant Robert Barr McPhan RAAF, who was from Wyong, NSW, was shot down with a full bomb load and crashed about 1000 metres behind a farm at Zwijnenburg near Benschop in Holland. McPhan and four members on his crew, who were on their eleventh operation, were killed. The two gunners managed to parachute to safety before the aircraft exploded and they were taken into captivity. 'Q-Queenie', skippered by 21-year-old Flying Officer Francis Archibald Randall RAAF, a science student at the University of Sydney, was caught by several searchlights over Berlin and attacked by German night-fighters. The port outer engine caught fire, but Randall managed to put out the flames and make his escape on three engines. Shortly after, 'Queenie' was caught in the light of flares dropped by the enemy fighters and once again attacked. This time the starboard outer engine caught fire and a fire started in the fuselage just aft of the mid-upper turret. The burning engine was stopped and the fire died. During the combat the bomb aimer, Pilot Officer Lindsay Grafton Greenaway RAAF had parachuted out over Berlin. With only two good engines Randall asked navigator Flight Sergeant Norman James Conway RAAF for a course to take them across Denmark on the return flight. He then changed his mind and asked for a course for Sweden. When they sighted the east coast of Sjælland and could see the lights in Sweden, the fire in the starboard engine started again and Randall ordered the crew to bail out while they were over Denmark. The first to leave the Lancaster was the flight engineer Sergeant Arthur Hilton Johns and wireless operator Sergeant Allen John O'Brian RAAF and the rear gunner, Flight Sergeant 'Harry' Knight Ward RCAF. Then Norman Conway left. He is believed to have landed in the sea off Sjælland and to have drowned. He has no known grave and is commemorated on the Runnymede Memorial.

The mid-upper gunner, Sergeant Herbert Bell's parachute had been lying in the fuselage and had been damaged by bullets from the night-fighter. Randall told him to unpack it to see that it was not too badly damaged. Bell then jumped with the unpacked parachute folded in front of his chest. When the parachute unfolded the lines tangled round his neck and injured him. Randall was the last to leave the doomed aircraft. A month after being shot down Randall, who was trained in the RCAF facilities in Winnipeg, Edmonton and Calgary, was back on the squadron again, crewed up with a new crew and fully operational once more.[10] Several other aircraft were badly damaged, Flying Officer Gardner continuing his journey to bomb Berlin, although his Lancaster had been badly damaged in a collision with another aircraft.

At Ludford Magna, three Lancasters on 101 Squadron were missing. ED410 skippered by 21-year-old Flying Officer David James Carpenter of Mitcham Common, East Surrey, was shot down by Hauptmann Herbert Lütje of 8./NJG6, the aircraft crashing at Suttrup, fourteen kilometres south-east of Lingen. Carpenter and five of his crew, including Sergeant Hugh McQuade, the 19-year-old rear gunner from Middlesbrough were killed. Only Flight Sergeant J.D.M. Flett the flight engineer survived to be taken into captivity. All seven men on Warrant Officer Dennis Arthur Tucker's crew on 'T-Tommy' were killed. JB149 flown by Flight Sergeant F.J. Hammond was claimed by Oberleutnant Lenz Finster of 2./NJG 1 flying a Bf 110G-4 from Gilze-Rijen airfield, the only survivors being the skipper and Flight Sergeant R.J. Singer, his Australian air bomber. On 44 and 100 Squadrons two Lancasters were lost on each with no survivors. 'S-Sugar' on 44 'Rhodesia' Squadron which was piloted by Squadron Leader Robert Grant Watson, himself a Rhodesian, was shot down by Hauptmann August Geiger of 7./NJG 1 flying a Bf 110 G-4 from Twente airfield. Watson, who had been educated at Plumtree School, and had entered the RAF College, Cranwell in 1931. 'Y-Yorker' on 100 Squadron, piloted by Flying Officer William Austin Gardiner, was claimed by Oberleutnant Werner Husemann of Stab/NJG 1 flying a Bf 110 G-4 from Deelen airfield and is believed to have exploded over Berlin. Six of the crew have no known graves.

---

10  Returning from Berlin on 16/17 December 1943 Randall radioed to say that his Lancaster had clipped a tree. Shortly afterwards the aircraft crashed into a wood ten miles south of the Binbrook airfield runway near Market Stainton and detonated an ammunition dump, killing everyone on the crew. Randall had learned just before the raid that he had been awarded the DFC.

# PANIC IN THE HEART OF THE REICH

Flying Officer Harold Kenneth Coates and crew on 49 Squadron had taken 'S-Sugar' off from Fiskerton at 1953 hours on their eleventh operation. Ten seconds after having completed the bombing run they were hit by flak, sustaining damage to both wings and the petrol tanks and the petrol cock. Crossing the North Sea on the way home, Coates realised that he would be unable to make land and prepared to ditch. He flew on for some time, but owing to mist overhanging the sea, he had considerable difficulty in judging distance. At 0335 hours a signal was received that placed 'S-Sugar' seventy-five miles off the coast of Northumberland. Coates managed to keep flying until 0407 hours when all contact was lost and an Air-Sea Rescue launch was sent out. Fifteen miles from Blyth, off Tynemouth, an attempt to ditch was made but the Lancaster started to rise again. Almost immediately afterwards it is thought that two engines quit and the aircraft hit the sea heavily. Such were the sea conditions that the aircraft broke up on impact and fire broke out on the water from the petrol and oil which spread from the damaged tanks. Coates was strapped in his seat and was submerged in the ditching. He was unable to help himself in any way and the surviving members of the crew were unable to release him. It is thought that the 25-year-old pilot was at least unconscious from the blow caused by the heavy landing. The six crew got out, but Sergeant John George Sacre the flight engineer, presumably floated away and was not seen again. The other five members of the crew were recovered from the sea by an Air-Sea Rescue launch, but on being taken on board, Sergeants George Stanley Pawson the 19-year-old rear gunner; Clarence Depledge Kendrew, the 20-year-old wireless operator of Wakefield, Yorkshire and Henry Jack, navigator of Tealing, Scotland, were found to have already died of exposure. Only three months earlier Clarence Kendrew and his fiancée Ethel had married at the same church where he is now buried. Sergeant L.R. Underwood the bomb aimer and the 22-year-old air gunner, Sergeant Raymond Stuart Nelson RAAF, were both taken to hospital with slight injuries and shock. (Nelson was killed on 26th November while flying on 83 Squadron on the raid to Berlin and is buried in Dürnbach War Cemetery in Bavaria.) Of the remaining squadron aircraft, six landed at Middleton St. George, one at Croft, one at Wyton and three at base.

Warrant Officer 'Eddie' Wheeler on 97 Squadron wrote: 'The 7½ hour return trip was carried out without too much trouble. There was no moon, no cloud and good visibility, our bombs were released from 19,000 feet and were seen to burst in a built-up area. The flak as usual was intense and accurate but we escaped damage. From the frequency of raids on the capital city, it was only too evident that the "Battle of Berlin" had started in earnest and we were repaying ten-fold the attacks on London in 1940/41. All our crews returned from this operation, one having to return early after two hours when Sergeant Miller's mid-upper gunner, Sergeant Williams was rendered unconscious at 20,000 feet after his electrically heated suit and oxygen supply failed.'[11]

Syerston suffered the loss of three Lancasters. ED385 on 106 Squadron, flown by 26-year-old Flying Officer Leslie Walter Roper RAAF from Bentleigh, Victoria, was lost with all seven crew. It is believed that the Lancaster was hit by flak and crashed in a forest between Burgdorf and Uetze, twenty kilometres east of Hanover. On 61 Squadron 'Tony' Bird had been given up for lost. 'Limping along on three engines at a reduced airspeed of 115 mph, we were an hour late in reaching base, but our faithful ground crew had stayed up to welcome us back. "We thought we would stay up in case you made it," said one of them laconically, but the joy and relief on their faces needed no words. We had made it back.'

But there was no word from Squadron Leader Howroyd and crew on 'Bar Charlie'. Before leaving Syerston the crew had seen aircraft all around with lights from each wing tip, but over the North Sea it had seemed that they were on their own. Those comforting lights had gone after leaving the English coast, but they all knew aircraft were still around. They flew on for about three hours, all quiet and undisturbed, except for a few searchlights which tried to pierce the thick cloud below. 'The flak over the coastline was also clearly seen, but nothing to put us off, the sort of welcome we always got on reaching the enemy coast. Not until about half-an-hour's flying time from Berlin did we see much sign of life from below. The dense cloud and darkness which had covered and comforted us suddenly ended. We were now flying in a clear sky lit by searchlights, fighter flares and explosions of all kinds above the suburbs of Berlin. Looking out everything seemed almost as clear as day.'

Not until about half an hour's flying time from Berlin did they see much sign of life from below. When they were due south of the city they went in on their briefed compass heading of 180 degrees. From the calculations made by the navigator, they were eight to ten minutes behind the correct bombing time. 'Knowing this was not very comforting,' wrote John Sargeant. 'The Main Force would have bombed and be well away by the time we arrived, and all the defences would be able to concentrate on us few stragglers.

'We arrived on our heading after avoiding a few searchlights and near misses from flask bursts that seemed pretty close on the starboard side.

---

11  *Just To Get A Bed* by Edwin Wheeler DFC.

When we turned on I saw quite plainly two or three aircraft each coned by twenty to thirty searchlights on our starboard side, having hell knocked out of them by flak. It was the same on the port side where half-a-dozen searchlights were doing their best to pick us up in their beams... As usual, combats with fighters could be seen going on all around by the lights of tracers from each aircraft.'[12]

Now it was 'Bar Charlie's turn for the run up to the target. As the crew got to their positions the skipper's voice came over the intercom: 'Everyone okay? Turning on.' Then the voice of the bomb aimer came over the intercom: 'Bomb doors open, Skip.' And 'Sax' Saxby dropped the whole bomb load without a moment's notice.

Suddenly the whole aircraft shuddered and a shout came from the rear gunner, 'Mac' McKenzie: 'They've got me Skip; I can't get out - the doors are jammed.'

Then the voice of the wireless operator, 'Chap' Chappell was heard. 'Okay "Mac"; going down.'

'We were still doing violent evasive action when the fighter attacked again,' wrote John Sargeant, 'this time from below, raking the aircraft from stem to stern. I was on the floor, having seen the fighter attacking the first time from the rear starboard quarter with his tracers entering the rear of the fuselage. I stayed on the floor, after being thrown there by the sudden evasive manoeuvre. Unable to do anything to help I waited for my "packet" if it was coming, while watching my panel of engine and fuel gauges for any trouble that may suddenly break forth. Luckily, they were okay.

'As I lay there during the second attack, an explosive shell burst immediately below my position and shrapnel whirled through the floor and out through the roof. A few pieces of shrapnel ripped into the back of my left knee. The lower part of my leg immediately went numb and I thought I had lost it, but I managed to stand up on my right leg. My other leg was intact, but I was unable to stand on it.

'I later discovered that "Sax" had been seriously hurt in the same attack. By now the intercom had become unserviceable. Whether "Sax" said anything I don't know. I saw him climb out of his compartment and fall in front of me. I thought he had done it on purpose at first, but as we were again attacked, without any serious damage being inflicted, he did not move

---

12   See *Just Another Night Out* by John Sargeant which is quoted in *Bomber Boys* by Mel
Rolfe (Grub Street, 2004) and *Aircrew Remembered*.

from his position on the floor. I went to examine him and found he was unconscious. His body was still warm and his pulse quite strong.'

With the bomb doors still open a Bf 110 had attacked without warning from directly astern. There was one definite hit by a cannon shell and Holroyd had heard 'Mac' McKenzie the gunner report that he was severely wounded. Although Howroyd carried out the appropriate combat manoeuvres during this and subsequent attacks, three further shell hits were experienced. All of the turrets were damaged and the fuselage was hit at the fore end. 'Mac' and 'Jock' Kelly, the mid-upper gunner, continued to reply effectively to the attacks and a claim to have destroyed the fighter was corroborated by the wireless operator in the astro hatch. As the intercom was severed during the combat David Howroyd was only aware that the attacks had suddenly ceased.

'I had my course already set on the DR compass,' said Howroyd, 'and flew it for some way, but I did not realize that it was out of action. We were then at about 10,000 feet so I started to climb and tried to find out the state of my crew. The bomb aimer was either dead or dying. The mid-upper gunner had passed out, owing to damaged oxygen supply and I was under the impression that he was dead. I knew that the rear gunner was badly injured. There was no intercom, or call lights and as we were by that time flying at over 20,000 feet it was difficult to make contact by word of mouth. We presently made landfall on the south-east coast of Sweden. At the time we did not recognize it and subsequently mistook Lake Vattern for the Kattegat. We were by then up to 27,000 feet, having no means of defence other than height. We obtained a fix seventy miles west of Denmark and changed course. We then knew we had to ditch but hoped to get within eighty miles of the English coast. All this time the wireless operator was trying to get fixes. "Tony" Sargeant was acting as my runner and helping the navigator with the wounded. "Tony" had previously said that he was all right, but we found out later that he too was wounded. My straps had been shot away and he managed to fix me up some makeshift ones from oxygen extension tubes. At 0450 hours he went aft, after I had given him three minutes warning of ditching. That was five hours after leaving Berlin.'

'We seemed to have lost our fighter [shot down in a fierce exchange of fire with Jock Kelly],' wrote John Sargeant, 'so I reported everything okay as far as I was concerned. The skipper shouted for power so I opened up and we left the area pretty quick, climbing hard. While "Dave" tried to find our correct position and get a course for home the skipper pulled the kite up hard on a course due north and I tried to clear up a little and check for any trouble we might not have noticed. "Chap" had by this time, helped by

"Dave", got "Mac" to a more comfortable position against the rear spar. "Jock" was okay and trying to do two gunner's jobs.

'"Dave" was taking astro shots, doing his best to pinpoint our position as the sky was clear above and below. We crossed the north German Baltic coast to Sweden and followed the west coast up to what we thought was Copenhagen.

'Whatever town it was it had quite a few flak batteries firing up in our direction, but the shells did not come very near, making us think we were not alone, even at 27,000 feet. From there we turned due west, knowing we would reach Britain somewhere along the east coast. We crossed Denmark without any trouble and set out across the North Sea.

'About eighty miles from the west Danish coast, "Dave" managed to get a "Gee" fix and immediately worked out our course and distance to base. I checked on the fuel situation and found we only had enough for three hours' flying. It was impossible for us to make base. The skipper had to decide whether to turn back, bail out over Sweden or carry on and ditch. Because of "Mac's" serious injuries, making it unable for him to bail out, the skipper decided to carry on and ditch. The actual thought of ditching and the dangerous consequences it might incur did not seem to worry anyone. I had total confidence in the skipper and thought nothing of it, no more than I had in landing.

'From then on we all got prepared. I got the pigeon, wireless and other equipment, which might be of use. "Dave" got an approximate ditching position and "Chap" bashed out the position on the W/T right to the end. We closed down the engines and undertook a steady controlled descent.

'I looked at "Sax" carefully, found him completely helpless and stone cold and reported his condition to the skipper. I went to the rear of the fuselage and warned "Mac" and "Jock" what to prepare for, after trying to cheer "Mac" up a little.

'I immediately got to work throwing out all unnecessary heavy equipment, such as the pyrotechnics and ammunition, as the rear turret magazines were completely full. While I was doing this all four engines cut due to lack of fuel. Everyone immediately prepared for the worst and began rushing about. By everyone I mean "Dave", "Chap", "Jock" and myself. The aircraft lost height quickly and rather uncomfortably fast in that half minute. I ran from my position in the rear to the fuel cocks on my panel up in the cockpit and luckily, just in time, managed to change the cock and the engines immediately responded. We were only twenty feet off the water when the engines restarted and the skipper pulled up the nose. After that shaky do I made a rough check on the fuel situation and told the skipper we could go on for about another half-hour.

'As time was so short the skipper told me to warn the others to get in ditching positions and prepare for the worst. They went aft and I got organized up front. What with the skipper's harness and hatches to release and check, I did not have much time to myself.

'I told the skipper when I was ready and we waited for the big splash. He gave me three minutes to get settled in the back and I went to my ditching position behind the main spar. It was 0450 hours.

'I shouted the position and time to the rest of the crew and we waited. I had just got crouched up in the comer when the skipper waggled his wings as a last warning and the engines gave their usual cough when he throttled back for the glide in. The last half-minute seemed a lifetime.'

'Ditching the aircraft presented no troubles,' wrote David Howroyd, 'although only ten degrees of flap could be obtained.'

John Sargeant felt two violent bumps come as they hit the water. 'I felt very little but "Dave" was not quite ready for it and he was thrown around violently. Fortunately, he only had his watch knocked from his wrist. (The body of "Tom" Saxby is thought to have been thrown into the sea by the impact.) Immediately water rushed in everywhere, through the damaged fuselage at the rear, and a huge spout rose from the flare chute. In a matter of seconds the fuselage was half full and both "Chap" and I leaped for the hatch together. I, being the smaller, wriggled out on to the starboard mainplane to the dinghy, only to find it already out and half inflated with "Jock" waiting to get in.

'We were all out on the starboard mainplane within thirty seconds, gathering ourselves together and ready in case "Bar Charlie" made her last plunge. But she remained afloat, so the skipper suggested we went back for the packs, also to inquire about "Mac's" condition. No one seemed to know exactly, so three of us went back to drag him out. He was conscious but in a pretty helpless state. We got him in the dinghy, also one pack, a pigeon and the radio. As soon as possible we started to paddle away from "Charlie" in case it sank suddenly and took us under too. We soon drifted away but "Charlie" remained afloat and we drifted with it, more slowly than if we were on our own.

'We arranged ourselves as comfortable as possible, especially "Mac", who had lost his boots. We had brought a parachute with us and wrapped his feet in it. He looked terribly ill but was quite conscious at the time. At around 0530 he went into a coma and died soon afterwards. He had lost a lot of blood and the shock must have been too much for him. We covered "Mac" up with the parachute having decided to bring him back with us, not knowing if we would see old England again.

'As soon as it was light and a rather large predatory looking bird had left the area, I launched the pigeon. At about 0900 hours I was keeping watch while the crew were asleep and saw two specks on the horizon, which came straight towards us at about 500 feet. They resolved into Hudsons, dropped smoke-floats and circled us. Emergency rations were dropped and at about 1100 hours an airborne lifeboat was dropped. At 1600 hours two naval motor launches appeared and we were taken aboard.'[13]

None of the crew knew that John Sargeant had been injured until they were taken aboard the launch. At 0700 the survivors were disembarked at Immingham docks. Sargeant was carried ashore on a stretcher and taken to the local hospital where he was treated like a hero when they knew his story. After a few days he was transferred to RAF Hospital Rauceby, Lincolnshire. While there he learned that the remainder of his old crew had received fourteen days' survivors' leave before getting three new crew members and going straight back on operations. John Sargeant was replaced by 19-year-old Flight Sergeant Alan Williams, and 21-year-old Flying Officer Alan James Horobin took the place of 'Mac' McKenzie, and Saxby's place as air bomber was taken by 21-year-old Flying Officer L.D. Cromb RCAF. On 9th October the crew took off from Syerston at 2251 hours to attack Hanover. The Lancaster was shot down by a night-fighter possibly flown by Unteroffizier Otto Kutzner of 5./NJG3 for his first claim of the war. All except Cromb were killed. Squadron Leader Howroyd left a bereaved wife, Barbara Arm Lester Howroyd and a young child.[14]

Although the smallest in numbers, this third attack on Berlin on 3rd/4th September was in some ways the most effective. Four Mosquitoes dropped 'spoof' flares well away from the route to the city to decoy night-fighters away from the bomber stream, which approached from the north-east and the usual diversionary attacks against towns and airfields were also mounted. Undershooting by the blind markers, the backers-up and the main force was a problem and there was a creep-back in these attacks so that most of the bombing by over 300 Lancasters fell short. Part of the bombing which did reach the capital's built-up area fell in residential parts of Charlottenburg

---

13 *Bomber Command Quarterly Review*, No.6.
14 See *Just Another Night Out* by John Sargeant which is quoted in *Bomber Boys* by Mel Rolfe (Grub Street, 2004) and *Aircrew Remembered*.

and Moabit killing 422 people and a further 170 civilians were listed as 'missing'. In the industrial area of Siemensstadt several factories were hit and suffered serious loss of production. The major water and electricity works and one of Berlin's largest breweries were destroyed.

On Saturday night 'Missie' Vassiltchikov dined with Nagy of the Hungarian Embassy and Victor de Kowa, a German stage and film actor. 'The latter is terribly jumpy,' she wrote. 'With tears in his eyes he announces that he cannot take it anymore, his entire neighbourhood (he lives not far from Tempelhof airport) was wiped out last night. Yesterday's raid was very bad. Even out in Potsdam we assembled downstairs.'[15]

'The attack,' wrote fellow diarist Hans Georg von Studnitz, 'caused its greatest havoc in Siemensstadt, along the northern circuit of the S-Bahn railway system, in the Müllerstrasse in north Berlin, in the Hohenzollernplatz and in the Fehlbellinerplatz. Pieces of a shot-down bomber fell on the Komödie Theatre in the Kurfürstendamm and on the roof of the Strempels' house. Bolko and Viktoria Richthofen's house in Schmargendorf was hit for the third time during the war and burnt to the ground this time... The Russians are advancing swiftly all along the eastern front. We are now forced to retreat across the Dnieper. Where it will all end no one dares to prophesy.'

Air Marshal Harris had no such doubts. He considered that the recent successes in the Battles of the Ruhr and Hamburg had confirmed his views that the time was now ripe for the 'Final Battle', the destruction of the capital of the Third Reich. It seems most of his crews were right behind him, as Norman Ashton revealed: 'One day, we were honoured by a visit from the Commander-in-Chief, Bomber Command. Air Chief Marshal Sir Arthur Harris was given a terrific cheer as he walked onto the platform in the station cinema. "Butch" - as we called him - wasted no time on formalities and said that he had come to listen to what we had to say. He invited suggestions, criticisms and opinions - nothing barred - on anything which we considered might improve the aircraft, squadron or command. As question after question was fired across the room, I studied the man who had earned the title of "The Hammer of the Reich". He looked older and kinder than I had imagined, but there was no doubt that he had a cool, calculating brain, and his whole bearing suggested that he would be utterly ruthless when occasion demanded. It was obvious that he was proud of

---

15  *The Berlin Diaries 1940-45* by Marie (Illarionovna) 'Missie' Vassiltchikov (Chatto & Windus, 1985).

234

his men and aircraft, and he promised us an extremely busy time in the coming months. The man-to-man talking revealed the fact that he was no mere figurehead, content to sit at HQ and pull strings, but that he knew most of the answers and could slug it out with the boys in a manner which proved he valued an honest opinion, be it expressed by Group Captain or Sergeant. I felt that his one ambition was to batter the enemy into an early submission and that he believed Bomber Command, given a free hand, was powerful enough to do it.'

With the aid of $H_2S$ Berlin was easily identifiable from the air at night and the long winter nights made the deep penetration flights to the 'Big City' possible. When the weather forecast predicted not only favourable conditions over the target but acceptable landing conditions for the returning bomber fleet, which usually numbered between four and seven hundred aircraft, Bomber Command would go to war. Then the vibration from two thousand Merlin engines running at climbing power (2,850 revs and +9lb boost) would make the glasses dance on the bars of Lincolnshire's pubs, much to the wonder of those whose wartime role was possibly more permanent than that of the aircrew who rode the sky above them. Harris made plans to raid Berlin again on the night of 4th/5th September, but it was all for naught. He then made plans to raid the 'Big City' on the night of 8/9 September, but again poor weather forced him to cancel the operation. At Bourn, Jack Lazenby on 2nd Lieutenant 'Jack' Russell's crew recalled: 'We were "on" again to attack the "Big City" and we were not feeling too happy, but we had just finished our operational meal when two warrant officers rushed in to say that operations were "scrubbed". What a relief. The attack by the fighter on our aircraft on the last operation on Berlin had riddled the starboard wing tip and we did not know about it until the following afternoon. It was not serious and the wing tip was soon changed. Transport was then organized and a crowd of us went into Cambridge and had a jolly good night, much of it in the "Criterion" pub.'[16]

The following night, 9th/10th September, saw little improvement and then the new moon period prevented any long-range operations for almost a fortnight. Still, the prevailing loss rate was high and a total of 178 victories were credited to German night-fighters in September and 149 more during October. Even so, on 11th October, Mr Winston Churchill sent Harris a

---

16　Two months' later, on 10 November, 'Jack' Russell now assigned to the 482nd Bomb Group, an American PFF unit at RAF Alconbury was killed trying to land a B-17 at Eye (Brome) airfield, an 8th Air Force Liberator base in Suffolk.

Message of Congratulation in which he said, 'Your command, with day-bomber formations of the Eighth Air Force fighting alongside it, is playing a foremost part in the converging attack on Germany now being conducted by the forces of the United Nations on a prodigious scale. Your officers and men will, I know, continue their efforts in spite of the intense resistance offered, until they are rewarded by the final downfall of the enemy. These growing successes have only been achieved by the devotion, endurance and courage for which Bomber Command is renowned. Airmen and airwomen of Britain, the Dominions and our allies have worked wholeheartedly together to perfect the mighty offensive weapon which you wield in a battle watched by the world.'

During November and December 1943 seven big raids were made on the German capital. The night of 18th/19th November marked the start of four and a half months in which RAF Bomber Command would make thirty-two major raids on Germany, sixteen on Berlin and sixteen on other large cities in the heart of the Reich. By 24th/25th March 1944 the 'Big City' would be subjected to sixteen major raids, which have gone into history as the 'Battle of Berlin'.

# Index

# INDEX

# INDEX

# INDEX

# INDEX